Speaking Out

Also by Judith Baxter

POSITIONING GENDER IN DISCOURSE: A Feminist Methodology

Speaking Out

The Female Voice in Public Contexts

Edited by

Judith Baxter

University of Reading

First published 2006 by
PALGRAVE MACMILLAN
Houndmills, Basingstoke, Hampshire RG21 6XS and
175 Fifth Avenue, New York, N.Y. 10010
Companies and representatives throughout the world

PALGRAVE MACMILLAN is the global academic imprint of the Palgrave
Macmillan division of St. Martin's Press, LLC and of Palgrave Macmillan Ltd.
Macmillan® is a registered trademark in the United States, United Kingdom
and other countries. Palgrave is a registered trademark in the European
Union and other countries.

ISBN-13: 978–1–4039–9407–3 hardback
ISBN-10: 1–4039–9407–2 hardback
ISBN-13: 978–1–4039–9408–0 paperback
ISBN-10: 1–4039–9408–0 paperback

This book is printed on paper suitable for recycling and made from fully
managed and sustained forest sources.

A catalogue record for this book is available from the British Library.

Library of Congress Cataloging-in-Publication Data
Speaking out : the female voice in public contexts / edited by Judith Baxter.
    p.   cm.
    Includes bibliographical references and index.
    ISBN 1–4039–9407–2 (cloth) — ISBN 1–4039–9408–0 (paper)
    1. Language and languages—Sex differences.   2. Language and
sex.   3. Discourse analysis.   4. Women—Communication.   I. Baxter,
Judith, 1955–
    P120.S48S565 2005
    306.44—dc22   2005054618

10   9   8   7   6   5   4   3   2   1
15   14   13   12   11   10   09   08   07   06

Printed and bound in Great Britain by
Antony Rowe Ltd, Chippenham and Eastbourne

To Dr Puleng Hanong, a brilliant contributor to this book, who died on June 8th 2005.

Contents

Acknowledgements

I would like to thank all the contributors to this book for their patience, dedication and hard work in dealing with my endless demands to revise drafts, make cuts, and provide further information. In particular, thanks are due to Deborah Cameron who gave guidance at different stages, read the final typescript through, and commented so helpfully on my Introduction; and also to Allyson Jule for her friendship and support. Finally, I would like to thank Jill Lake of Palgrave for making this project possible.

Notes on the Contributors

Judith Baxter is Lecturer in Applied Linguistics at the University of Reading. She has published in three areas: language and gender in the classroom; the language of management meetings; and (feminist) post-structuralist discourse analysis (FPDA). Her research monograph, *Positioning Gender in Discourse: A Feminist Methodology*, was published in 2003. She is currently engaged in research for a book entitled *The Language of Female Leadership*, to be published in 2006.

Deborah Cameron's publications on language and gender include *Feminism and Linguistic Theory* (1992), *The Feminist Critique of Language* (1998), and *Language and Sexuality* (2003, with Don Kulick). Her collection *On Language and Sexual Politics* will be published in 2006. She has taught at the Universities of Roehampton, Strathclyde, and London, and is currently Professor of Language and Communication at the University of Oxford.

Susan Ehrlich is Professor in the Department of Languages, Literatures and Linguistics at York University in Toronto. She has published in the areas of language and gender, discourse analysis, second language acquisition and linguistic approaches to literature in journals such as *Language in Society*, *Discourse & Society*, *Studies in Second Language Acquisition*, and *Journal of Pragmatics*. Her most recent book is *Representing Rape: Language and Sexual Consent* (2001).

Puleng Hanong (previously published under the surname Thetela) was a Senior Lecturer in the Department of Linguistics at the University of the Witwatersrand in South Africa where she taught courses in Sociolinguistics and Discourse Analysis. She held Master's degrees from the University of Edinburgh and the University of Liverpool, and PhD (Applied Linguistics) from the University of Liverpool (UK). She has published several articles in South African journals such as *Southern African Linguistics and Applied Language Studies*, and international journals such as *English for Specific Purposes*, *Discourse & Society* and *AILA Review*; and she has also contributed several chapters to books. Her research interests, theoretically and methodologically underpinned by Critical Discourse Analysis, included legal discourse, discourse and gender, media discourse, and discourse and culture.

Janet Holmes is Director of the Language in the Workplace Project and holds a personal Chair in Linguistics at Victoria University of Wellington where she teaches a variety of sociolinguistics courses. She has published on a wide range of topics including New Zealand English, language and gender, sexist language, pragmatic particles, compliments and apologies, and on aspects of workplace discourse. Her most recent books are the Blackwell *Handbook of Language and Gender*, co-edited with Miriam Meyerhoff, and *Power and Politeness in the Workplace* co-authored with Maria Stubbe.

Allyson Jule is a Senior Lecturer in Education at the University of Glamorgan, Wales. She is the author of *Gender, Participation and Silence in the Language Classroom: Sh-Shushing the Girls* (2004) and the volume editor of *Gender and the Language of Religion* (2005). Her research interests are gender in education, the use of linguistic space during various classroom discourses, and the role of religion in influencing language patterns.

Shari Kendall is Assistant Professor of Linguistics and Discourse Studies in the Department of English at Texas A & M University. Research interests are the discursive construction of gendered, professional, and parental identities in work and family discourse; relations among gender, discourse, and sexuality in legal contexts, the media, and everyday talk; and the theoretical frameworks of framing, positioning, and interactional sociolinguistics. Recent publications include 'Framing Authority: Gender, Face, and Mitigation at a Radio Network' in *Discourse and Society*, and 'Father as Breadwinner/Mother as Worker: Discursively Positioning Parental and Professional Identities', forthcoming in *Family Discourse*.

Lia Litosseliti is Lecturer in Linguistics at City University, London. Her research interests and publications are in the areas of critical/feminist linguistics, discourse analysis and gender identities, argumentation, and research methodologies. She is the author of the books *Using Focus Groups in Research* (2003), *Gender and Language: Theory and Practice* (2006), and co-editor/co-author of *Discourse Analysis and Gender Identity* (2002).

Meredith Marra is Research Officer for Victoria University's Language in the Workplace Project and a Lecturer in the School of Linguistics and Applied Language Studies. Meredith's primary research interest is the language of meetings (including her PhD research which investigated the language of decision-making in business meetings), but she has also published in the areas of humour and gender in workplace interactions.

Judith Mattson Bean is an Associate Professor of English and Assistant Vice President for Academic Affairs at Texas Woman's University. Her essays on twentieth-century sociolinguistics and discourse appear in *Discourse Processes, Language in Society, SECOL Review, Southwestern American Literature,* and *Language and Woman's Place: Text and Commentaries.* Her essays on nineteenth-century women speakers and writers appear in several books and periodicals.

Sara Mills is Research Professor in Linguistics at Sheffield Hallam University. She has published in two separate areas: feminist post-colonial theory and feminist linguistics. Her most recent publications are *Gender and Politeness* (2003) and *Gender and Colonial Space* (2005).

Stephanie Schnurr is engaged in research towards a PhD in the School of Linguistics and Applied Language Studies at Victoria University of Wellington. Her main focus is the sociolinguistic and discursive performance of leadership and gender at work, and in particular the multiple functions and strategic uses of humour in workplace discourse.

Sylvia Shaw is a Senior Lecturer in Communication and English Language Studies at Middlesex University, London. Her research interests include language and gender in public and political contexts, discourse analysis, sociolinguistics, and lexicography.

Denise Troutman has a PhD in Linguistics from Michigan State University and has a joint appointment in Linguistics and Writing, Rhetoric, and American Cultures. She is winner of the 2003–2004 American Fellowship from the American Association of University Women and the 2001–2002 Fulbright Award. Her teaching and research interests include language and society, discourse analysis, women and language, African American women's discourse patterns, and African American English.

Clare Walsh is Senior Lecturer in English at De Montfort University, Bedford. Her book *Gender and Discourse: Language and Power in Politics, the Church and Organisations* (2001) investigates how women in a range of public sphere contexts construct identities for themselves, primarily through the language they use, as well as how they are represented by the media. She is currently engaged in research for a book entitled *Language and Power.*

Introduction

Judith Baxter

'Woe betide any woman who speaks out in a public place.'

Anon

It is April 1999 in Detroit, USA, and the scene is set for a very public humiliation. I am in a vast, grey, windowless auditorium which recedes into the distance. I am standing on a raised platform with an overhead projector beside me to the left, and a university colleague sitting to my right. I feel exhausted as I have not had a decent night's sleep since I flew from London a few days before. Before me is a conference – full of people looking expectant. It is my first public lecture on a large scale, and my sleeplessness is the result of nerves and indecisiveness. Should I speak as spontaneously as I can from a few bullet-pointed index cards? I am going to be speaking to teachers, not academics, who are used to a more informal lecturing style. Or should I play it safe and read from a formally prepared paper? After a frantic, late-night rewrite, I opt for neither. I write a script which tries to *sound* like the natural flow of free thought.

Normally, when I give a paper at an academic conference, I may begin somewhat tentatively but I rapidly build in confidence. This time, the opposite happens. As I stumble through my constructed conversational patter, I quickly realise that the prepared script is not working. It is just not releasing me into that spontaneous ability to hold forth, nor is it offering me enough scholarly substance to hold the audience's interest. As I notice the attention of my audience drift, I begin to experience, in Sara Mills' words (Chapter 4), 'performance anxiety'. My mouth goes dry, my body temperature begins to soar, my face starts to burn. In that moment of panic, I start to forget what I want to say. I become increasingly aware of my audience's reactions, and less and less connected to my script. As I falter, I turn desperately to my colleague.

He rises from his seat, and although he is only there to change the overhead templates he takes over. Within minutes, he has the audience back on side. His easy, unforced manner, his effortless ability to crack the odd joke, and his evident knowledge of the field save the day. He soon has the audience smiling, relaxed, and involved. Not only am I grateful to him, of course, but I also feel annoyed with myself and aggrieved. At the end of the lecture, *he* is the one they all want to speak to.

At the time, I put it all down to my less-than-extrovert personality and a lack of practice. Today, I am altogether less sure that my case of stage fright was a consequence of a deficient personality or inexperience. I could not blame my colleague for taking all the praise for my talk, but equally I could not help wondering why he was so much more at ease with the situation than I was. As Mills (Chapter 4) suggests, performance anxiety is something that women are more likely to experience than men when speaking in public: the discursive rules operating in such settings are simply more in line with stereotypically male forms of speech. It was after my own unnerving experience that I developed a scholarly obsession with the subject of female speech in public contexts, which has ultimately led to the production of this book.

This is possibly the first collection of research work that exclusively focuses on the subject of the female public voice, which has always been a significant discursive strand within language and gender research literature. Historically, females have struggled to gain access to the public arena, and once there, gain recognition and respect for their abilities as speakers, as both Deborah Cameron (Chapter 1) and Judith Bean (Chapter 2) theorise in depth. Despite at least 30 years of equal opportunities and educational reforms, more notably in the western world, women still struggle for acceptance within institutional settings such as government, politics, law, education, the church, the media, and the business world. Indeed, it is easy to forget that there are cultures around the world where women are not permitted to speak *at all* in public spaces. Even in cultures where women *are* authorised to speak, females continue to experience difficulties with the way their talk is received and evaluated. Given that women are now making a greater impact in public life internationally, it seems timely to consider the opportunities and barriers facing women as speakers in public, formal, and institutional settings.

The book will contain a mix of two types of chapters. The *first* type will be critical discussion and reviews which reflect upon the subject from different theoretical standpoints. Deborah Cameron (Chapter 1) contextualises the subject and introduces subsequent chapters by examining some key historical and theoretical debates on the relationship of gender to 'public' uses of language. Judith Bean

(Chapter 2) presents a historical overview of the 'success story' of
how women speakers gained a public voice in nineteenth-century
North America. And Lia Litosseliti (Chapter 3) draws upon 'critical
discursive feminist inquiry' to explore dichotomised gendered
discourses about rationality/emotion and public/private and indi-
vidual/collective experience within current affairs debates in Britain.
The *second* type of chapters, forming the larger part of the book, will
present new research studies on the theme, or revisitings from this
angle to well-known research. These studies embrace such settings as
the academic community (Sara Mills, Chapter 4); parliament (Sylvia
Shaw, Chapter 5); theological colleges (Allyson Jule, Chapter 6); the
media (Clare Walsh, Chapter 7); courtrooms (Susan Ehrlich, Chapter
8); education (Judith Baxter, Chapter 9); indigenous South African
communities (Puleng Hanong, Chapter 11); comedy entertainment
(Denise Troutman, Chapter 12); and finally, the business world
(Shari Kendall, Chapter 10; and Meredith Marra, Stephanie Schnurr
and Janet Holmes, Chapter 13).

This collection of chapters coheres both from a thematic and to a
certain extent from a theoretical or paradigmatic perspective. For
example, almost all the studies in this book allude to notions of 'voice'
and 'silence'. As Hanong (Chapter 11) explores, there is both a literal
and a metaphorical connotation to these notions. Feminist linguists
over the last 30 years have used the terms as metaphors 'to figure out all
the ways in which women are denied the right or the opportunity to
express themselves freely' (Cameron, 1990: p. 3). The term is used
metaphorically to indicate that women's speech is often relegated to
non-prestigious genres (such as chatter or gossip) mostly associated
with the private sphere, while in the public sphere and especially the
'domain of official culture...the genres associated with women have
little currency' (Cameron, 1990: p. 3).

While clearly there are a range of differing and, indeed, competing
perspectives on the extent to which the female voice is universally
marginalised or 'silenced' in public contexts, there is greater commonality
among the authors in their use of a 'third wave' feminist (or feminist
post-structuralist) view of language and gender. There has generally
been a move away from the wholesale, deterministic positioning of the
'deficit', 'difference' and 'dominance' theories whereby women's language
was perceived to be lacking, different or powerless, towards a critical
examination of language as social practice (Litosseliti, Chapter 3). As
this perspective structures the ways in which the majority of the

chapters in this book are argued and expressed, I now attempt to summarise some of its key, underlying principles. There is thus a focus upon:

• The performative rather than the essentialist or possessive nature of gender (Butler, 1990; 1991): gender is something people *enact* or *do*, not something they *are* or characterise. Gender is seen less as a pre-existing quality and more as worked out or oriented to during conversation. Gender is not coterminous with sex but a type of 'coding' of styles and social practices (see Hanong, Chapter 11; Mills, Chapter 4).

• Linked to this, the importance of co-construction: the process by which gender identities are negotiated and constructed through social interactions and practices (Marra, Schnurr and Holmes, Chapter 13).

• The role of discourses, or 'practices that systematically form the object of which they speak' (Foucault, 1972: p. 49), which make sense of the world by shaping power relations, and therefore meaning, in all forms of social and linguistic interaction.

• Localised, context-specific gender issues rather than sweeping generalisations about the way that all women speak in public: gender identities are discursively constructed through specific 'communities of practice' (CofPs) (Baxter, 2003; Eckert and McConnell-Ginet, 2003; Holmes and Meyerhoff, 2003).

• Speakers' identities as fluid, multiple, multi-layered, shifting and often contradictory. People are powerful in some situations, less powerful in others (Baxter, Chapter 9). There is an emphasis upon female agency and resistance to localised, masculinist discourses, rather than the universal subordination of women to patriarchy (Ehrlich, Chapter 8).

• An eye to the global: feminist linguists still recognise that females are systematically marginalised or excluded from dominant linguistic practices (Shaw, Chapter 5; Walsh, Chapter 7). On occasions, there is a need to look more globally (Cameron, Chapter 1) for patterns of linguistic interaction. For example, a prevailing pattern around the world is for men to dominate highly valued public speech genres.

Powerful speech has long been associated with masculinity and powerless speech with femininity. The emphasis in this book's scholarship is upon *which* discourses within *which* contexts sustain such notions, and how these discourses can be challenged and, within the fullness of time, subverted. Looking ahead to the chapters in this book, almost all the contributors demonstrate in their work that dominant androcentric assumptions shape and define the social and discursive practices operating in public, institutional life. However, the contributors vary considerably in their belief about the possibility of change. As Litosseliti (Chapter 3: pp. 55–6) argues, this belief that change *is* possible seems to depend upon the way three factors are interwoven, namely the nature of the different and localised settings and communities of practice, the interactional goals of participants within a particular type of public discourse, and the 'subtle and complex links between discourses and women's and men's social positions' (p. 56). By reviewing just a selection of the chapters in this book, I will exemplify the range of evaluative positions authors adopt.

Several writers are openly *sceptical* about the scope for reform within the context of the community of practice they have studied. In post-apartheid South Africa, Hanong (Chapter 11) is concerned about the way women are afraid to speak out publicly about sexual violence and abuse because of the shame it brings to their own families, and the institution of the family. Despite a serious government commitment to challenging gender hegemonies by instigating social programmes, these messages do not reach the public, especially African indigenous society 'where patriarchal ideologies and cultural practices are entrenched' (p. 212). Hanong argues that the South African government needs to 'change attitudes' by carrying through social and educational programmes which actually reach local communities. In Canada, Jule (Chapter 6) also finds that institutional discourses have a powerful constraining effect upon the facility of women to speak out in a public forum. In her study of the dominant practice of lecturing in a theological college, she surmises that 'a masculine style of seeking public influence and participation as a way to be moral' (p. 21) produces males as the principal speakers and holders of power, and produces females as silent, dutiful listeners. Jule concludes that there is no space within this gendered discourse for women to speak on equal terms with men.

Other writers identify the continuing institutional constraints upon women's facility to speak out in public, but also note the potential for subversion and change. For example, Shaw (Chapter 5) in her study of the British Parliament feels it is 'difficult to see how women MPs can undertake a critical difference approach and challenge their perceived status as interlopers' but she does recognise the power and success of groups of female politicians committed to collective action. For example, she cites the Northern Ireland Women's Coalition (NIWC) who have successfully worked 'to promote an alternative set of linguistic norms for political debates through an organised campaign focused upon increasing the presence of women in the National Assembly'.

In other communities of practice, women have found ways to negotiate and implement alternative discursive practices which have allowed them to adopt powerful positions as speakers within public contexts. In New Zealand, Marra, Schnurr and Holmes (Chapter 13: p. 256) anatomise how women 'do' leadership in large corporations by 'achieving a balance between getting the work done and keeping people happy'. She celebrates the ways in which certain female leaders have successfully managed to negotiate the gendered imperative of 'doing leadership' and 'doing gender' while avoiding negative evaluations, such as not appearing authoritative enough, or coming across as too masculine. In the US, Troutman (Chapter 12) describes another success story. She demonstrates through the actions of female comediennes that the public sphere can be subversively challenged and is not a 'man's world only'. Through the use of 'bawdy language' the comediennes in her study display positive attributes: confidence, lack of inhibition, verbal expressiveness in public, and a different code of feminine politeness. Bawdy language serves as one vehicle for establishing and maintaining a strong social and personal identity, while simultaneously subverting masculinist speech norms.

Whether women should be appropriating the genres of masculine public discourse or exploring new, alternative ways of making the public domain their own is the concern at the very heart of this book.

References

Baxter, J. (2003) *Positioning Gender in Discourse: A Feminist Methodology*. Basingstoke: Palgrave.

Butler, J. (1990) *Gender Trouble: Feminism and the Subversion of Identity*. London: Routledge.

Butler, J. (1991) *Gender Trouble: Feminism and the Subversion of Identity*. New York: Routledge.

Cameron, D. (1990) 'Introduction: Why is Language a Feminist Issue?' in *The Feminist Critique of Language*, pp. 1–30, London: Routledge.

Eckert, P. and McConnell-Ginet, S. (2003) *Language and Gender*. Cambridge: Cambridge University Press.

Foucault, M. (1972) *The Archeology of Knowledge and the Discourse on Language*. New York: Pantheon.

Holmes, J. and Meyerhoff, M. (2003) *The Handbook of Language and Gender*. Oxford: Blackwell.

Part I

Theorising the Female Voice in Public Contexts

Theorising the Female Voice in Public Contexts

1
Theorising the Female Voice in Public Contexts

Deborah Cameron
University of Oxford, UK

Introduction

This chapter considers the female voice in public contexts as a theoretical issue: it asks whether and how women's relationship to public discourse may be accounted for in general terms. That question might seem to go against the grain of recent, 'third wave' language and gender scholarship with its emphasis on 'looking locally' (see Editor's Introduction). Researchers have become wary of generalizing about the linguistic position of women, and sceptical about the universalizing 'grand narratives' produced by some of their predecessors. The following discussion will reflect that scepticism, in that generalizations about gender will be examined critically, and attention will be given to the 'local' conditions affecting women's public utterance in different times, places and social groups. Yet at the same time, for both empirical and political reasons, I do not want to discount *a priori* the possibility of 'thinking globally' about the status of the female voice in public contexts.

Women's exclusion or marginalization from those linguistic practices and contexts to which a society accords particular value appears to be empirically very widely attested both historically and cross-culturally. While both Sherzer (1987), surveying the anthropological literature, and Kennedy (1998), in his comparative and historical examination of rhetorical traditions worldwide, cite evidence from various cultures and times of female participation in important speech genres and of individual women being recognized as skilled orators, both suggest that the more common pattern is for men to dominate highly valued forms of public speech. Discussing the relatively egalitarian Kuna Indians of Panama, for example, Sherzer says that despite being available in principle

3

to women, the 'ritual and traditional forms of discourse [that] constitute the essence of...Kuna leadership roles...are in practical actuality restricted to men' (1987: 102). In 21st century English-speaking societies, similarly, leadership roles and the associated linguistic practices are in theory available to both sexes, but there remains both prejudice and internalized anxiety about the female voice in public contexts. Doubtless the issue is complex, resisting the unidimensional explanations that have some-times been offered. But we may do women a disservice if in our eagerness not to (over) generalize or stereotype we deny that it is an issue. Rather we need an appropriately sophisticated way of understanding the issue and—in keeping with the contemporary emphasis on 'looking locally' in language and gender research—how its nature may vary in different social and historical conditions.

Mapping the terrain: Public/private and male/female

Although the problematic status of women's public speech is not exclu-sively a modern or western phenomenon, the phrase 'the female voice in public contexts' has a specific meaning in the context of western modernity,[1] where the binary oppositions 'male/female' and 'public/private' are both salient principles of social organization. They are also historically related: 'public' and 'private' were constituted as distinct spheres of activity and influence in part by their identification with masculinity and femininity respectively. Conversely, once these were established as 'separate spheres', men and women were differentiated as social subjects in part by their respective roles in the public and the private domains. It has been argued that this gendered notion of 'separate spheres' became established as the bourgeois class began to gain ascendancy in early modern Europe. Drawing on the evidence of conduct literature—texts written to instruct people in the attitudes and behaviour appropriate to their position in society—Armstrong and Tennenhouse (1987: 12) observe that by the 17th century, authors 'rather singlemindedly represented the social world as one divided into public and private, economic and domestic, labor and leisure, according to a principle of gender that placed the household and sexual relations under female authority'. It followed that other 'public' spheres of activity, such as law, politics and commerce, were placed under male authority. As one (anonymous) English writer observed in 1632:

> Women have no voyse in Parliament. They make no Lawes, they
> consent to none, they abrogate none. All of them are understood

married or to bee married, and their desires or [are] subject to their
husband...
(The Lawes Resolution of Womens Rights, 1632: 6)

Writers of early modern conduct literature made an explicit and
normative connection between femininity and public reticence or
silence. As an example, Armstrong and Tennenhouse quote Dod and
Cleaver's 1614 text *A Godly Forme of Householde Gouernment*, which laid
out the duties of a (bourgeois) husband and wife in two columns:

Husband	*Wife*
Deal with many men	Talk with few
Be 'entertaining'	Be solitary and withdrawn
Be skillfull in talk	Boast of silence

(Armstrong and Tennenhouse, 1987: 8)

Jones (1987) points out that this injunction to women to be silent
marked a shift in mainstream ideals of gender, championed first by
middle-class puritans in opposition to what they regarded as the deca-
dence of the aristocracy. Though the norm of silence was often justified
by appealing to ancient scriptural authority, it was not consistently
observed in the dominant public culture of the time. At the European
royal courts, for instance, courtiers of both sexes were expected to
engage in public displays of verbal skill, often in mixed company and
not infrequently on subjects that were sexually and politically charged.
'The court lady', Jones observes, 'was required to speak; [but] the bourgeois
wife was enjoined to silence' (1987: 40). In time, the conduct prescribed
to bourgeois wives would become the standard for properly feminine
behaviour in all social classes.

That is not, of course, to suggest that the behaviour of women in all
classes—or that of all women in any class—actually conformed to the
prescribed model. It is important to distinguish between the ideological
representations of gender found in texts like conduct books and the actual
practice of real historical gendered subjects. The historical sociolinguists
Nevalainen and Raumolin-Brunberg (2003) cite various studies which
have shown women's position in early modern England to be more
variable than contemporary ideological representations suggest. They
note for instance evidence suggesting that about a fifth of households
in Tudor and Stuart England were headed by women, either widows or
spinsters; that some women inherited land and property in spite of their
theoretical status as a legally dispropertied class; and that significant

numbers of women worked for wages in the cloth and service industries. Such women clearly were not confined to the domestic space of their own households and totally 'subject to their husband': even if they were the exception and not the rule, their numbers were not negligible.

Claims about women's exclusion from public language presuppose certain definitions of what is 'public' and what is 'private': Nevalainen and Raumolin-Brunberg note that these may incorporate a covert gender bias. They argue, for instance, that in the case of early modern England, 'the "separate spheres" model...ignores those public spheres where women's presence was prominent: in the street, in taverns, at the market, at church, and—in the case of noblewomen—at Court' (2003: 114). They go on to question the logic whereby gossip is excluded from the category of public speech, noting that it circulated outside the private household and had consequences for the public standing of its targets; women's gossip, they say (2003: 115), was 'a powerful means of social control...feared by men in a society where a man's reputation crucially depended on the opinion of others'. These comments raise the question whether some historical generalizations about the female voice in public contexts have less to do with the androcentrism of the public sphere itself, and more to do with the androcentric assumptions made by scholars when drawing its boundaries.

Anthropologists have posed analogous questions about the definition of 'public' speech in traditional non-western societies. Though the concept of separate public and private spheres is usually, strictly speaking, inapplicable in these cases, some influential feminist scholars in the 1970s focused on the relationship of women to ritual, ceremonial and other high-prestige linguistic genres, often concluding that women's role in these was very restricted and that their main communicative sphere was, indeed, private or domestic (Rosaldo and Lamphere 1974). Yet this line of argument has been criticized more recently for the same reasons Nevalainen and Raumolin-Brunberg criticize historians of the early modern west, that is, for downplaying the significance of contexts in which women's speech is prominent and socially consequential. Kulick (1993) reports that in the New Guinea village of Gapun women are excluded from decision-making assemblies that take place in the men's house, and do not master the highly indirect, consensus-seeking style of speech which is used in these male gatherings. It is, however, women who dominate—to the virtual exclusion of men—another speech-genre known in Tok Pisin as the *kros* (= 'cross', angry), in which a villager who deems herself to have been offended by another embarks on a lengthy monologue loudly abusing the person in question, the point being to ventilate the grievance publicly. As Kulick says, it seems curious to count the discourse of the men's house as 'public' speech while denying that status to female performances designed to be heard by the whole community.

But while the critical points made by these scholars are well taken, it could be argued that there is a non-trivial difference between participating in discourse in public *settings* and participating in the discourse of the public *sphere* as classically defined (e.g. political and legal debate). Here it is apposite to quote from a later historical document, the *Declaration of Sentiments and Resolutions* written mainly by Elizabeth Cady Stanton (1815–1902) and adopted by participants at the Seneca Falls Convention on Women's Rights, a landmark event in the history of American first-wave feminism which took place in 1848.

> *Resolved*: That the accusation of indelicacy and impropriety, which is so often brought against woman when she addresses an audience, comes with a very ill-grace from those who encourage, by their attendance, her appearance on the stage, in the concert, or in feats of the circus.
>
> (...)
>
> *Resolved, therefore*, That, being invested by the Creator with the same capabilities, and the same consciousness of responsibility for their exercise, it is demonstrably the right and duty of woman, equally with man, to promote every righteous cause by every righteous means; and especially in regard to the great subjects of morals and religion, it is self-evidently her right to participate with her brother in teaching them, both in private and in public, by writing and by speaking, by any instrumentalities proper to be used and in any assemblies proper to be held...
>
> (reproduced in Gurko 1974: 310–11)

It is striking how frequently the Declaration adverts to the question of women's right to speak publicly before mixed audiences, and to write for publication, on moral, religious and political subjects. Evidently these first-wave feminists ranked their exclusion from certain kinds of speech and writing alongside such injustices as the denial of the franchise to women and the legal subjection of wives to husbands. Securing access to public discourse for respectable bourgeois women was among their key objectives (Bean, Chapter 3, gives a more detailed account of the 19th-century American context). Yet it is clear that what feminists sought was more than just the right to speak outside domestic settings. The first Resolution quoted above pointedly distinguishes between women's involvement in public performance as actors, singers and circus artistes and their participation in serious discussions of public affairs, questioning why it is acceptable for female voices to be heard in the context of public entertainment, but 'improper' for them to be a source of authority and instruction. This example illustrates that what is problematic for women is not necessarily their relationship to any and every kind of public (in the sense of 'non-domestic') utterance, but more specifically their relationship to those settings, genres and ways of using language that carry the greatest weight of cultural authority for the community as a whole. Female voices are most obviously unwelcome in contexts where the community's most cherished values are ritually and solemnly affirmed, using a formal or elevated register of language to discuss 'the great subjects' in a quasi-'sacred' institutional space—the Parliamentary chamber, the courtroom, the church, the lecture hall, the men's house. It is less threatening for the female voice to be heard in public if the setting, subject matter and form of speech is 'profane'— considered by the community to be trivial, or vulgar, or in conflict with its 'real' values.

Since the mid-19th century women in many or most societies have achieved the first-wave feminist objective of being admitted to the public sphere, but they have not found it easy to participate in its discourse on equal terms. 'Exclusion' does not have to depend on absolute prohibition, but may be accomplished more subtly through a gendered division of linguistic labour *within* public sphere institutions. In the early days of radio broadcasting, for instance (I choose the example because the broadcast media are a relatively recent addition to what we think of as the public sphere), women's voices were deemed by the BBC to be unsuitable for 'serious or symbolic occasion[s]', though acceptable in more 'frivolous' contexts (the terms come from a statement made in 1937 (quoted in Kramarae 1981: 98) explaining why women would not be heard in BBC coverage of an impending royal visit). The BBC also prohibited women from reading the news for many years. Broadcasting as such was never off-limits to women, but the female voice was not permitted to profane what was initially conceived as its most 'sacred' function, the authoritative relation of public events. (Walsh, chapter 7, discusses the present-day analogue of this restriction).

So while women's exclusion from public discourse has never in practice been absolute, and women in many societies past and present have found ways to make their voices heard, there does seem to be a relatively widespread and long-lived pattern whereby the public contexts that have most symbolic value are also the most resistant to the equal participation of women. This pattern has provided the starting point for most theoretical accounts—in other words it has generally been the exclusion, prohibition or marginalization of the female voice in public contexts that scholars have felt the need to theorize. This 'negative' emphasis could itself be questioned. Some feminists have been more interested in the 'positive' side of the coin: in explaining how women have succeeded in carving out public discursive space for themselves (Troutman, Chapter 12), or in documenting the varied discourse strategies employed by women in public contexts (Marra, Schnurr and Holmes, Chapter 13), and making the 'critical difference' argument that women bring something distinctive and valuable to those contexts. Even in these approaches, though, there is usually a sense that women's position is still precarious and that the legitimacy or value of their contribution still needs to be asserted—it cannot be simply taken for granted. In the following survey, therefore, I will concentrate on the efforts made by feminist scholars to account for the 'marked' and problematic status of the female voice in public contexts.

Theoretical approaches: Economic and symbolic

For the purposes of this discussion it may be helpful to begin by distinguishing between two main types of feminist approach. One type could be called 'economic' or 'material', in that it foregrounds issues to do with the availability and social distribution of linguistic *resources* or, in the term made familiar by Bourdieu (1991), 'capital'. In seeking to understand why and to what extent particular groups of women in particular times and places did or did not participate in particular kinds of public discourse, this approach directs attention to the question of what opportunities they had to develop the linguistic skills that public contexts demanded—for instance, schooled literacy, proficiency in superordinate learned languages, familiarity with formal registers and standard language varieties, rhetorical training and so on. The other type of approach, while it does not deny the significance of these 'economic' questions, places more emphasis on 'symbolic' or 'ideological' factors—the cultural attitudes, representations and practices that underpin women's exclusion or marginalization as speakers and writers in public contexts. In this approach, the unequal gendered distribution of linguistic resources is not simply a free-standing fact explaining women's relationship to public discourse, but itself the practical consequence or expression of a 'deeper' cultural resistance to the female voice: the effects of that resistance can be observed, it is argued, even among women who (like the 19th-century suffragists, most of them educated middle-class white women) patently have not been deprived of the linguistic resources needed to participate effectively in the discourse of the public sphere.

The two approaches I have just distinguished should not be thought of as absolutely separate or mutually exclusive. As with all distinctions of this kind, mine entails some degree of idealization, the justification for which is that by imposing structure on a complex set of ideas it makes them easier to lay out in a relatively brief survey like this one. It is my own view that a satisfactory account of the female voice in public contexts must pay attention simultaneously to both 'economic' and 'symbolic' questions. But in the interests of clarity I will structure the following discussion by considering each approach in turn.

Gender and the distribution of linguistic resources

It is not surprising that feminists should have focused on access to linguistic resources as a key issue. The kinds of language which are most relevant here—those genres, styles and varieties which carry a particular weight of cultural authority and prestige—are generally not acquired in the course of everyday interaction, but mastered through specific instructional practices, ranging from the kind of apprenticeship described by Sherzer (1987) among the Araucanian Indians (whose young men refine their oratorical skills by speaking to 'audiences' of animals and plants) to the formal education and training provided in academic and religious institutions. In most societies for most of recorded history, women have had less access than men to these forms of instruction.

One kind of linguistic competence or capital whose gendered distribution has been studied quite extensively is the schooled ability to read and write. In literate societies, illiterate individuals are excluded not only from those forms of public language whose actual medium is writing, but also from those that demand a formal register of speech, or the use of a standard variety, because of the dependence of formal and standard speech on educated written models. While this is largely an issue of wealth and social rank, it has historically had a gender dimension, and in some places still does. Until the late 17th century in England, for example, female illiteracy was common even in the higher ranks of society. Studies examining the so-called signature literacy, the ability to sign one's name rather than making one's mark on official documents, suggest that in 1500 only about 1 per cent of English women were literate, while the corresponding figure for men was 10 per cent.[2]

As vernacular literacy became widespread, a more salient difference between English women and men of the higher social classes concerned their access to education in the classical languages. To the extent that public discourse norms required familiarity with classical rhetorical models, women were disadvantaged by the fact that most did not learn Latin and Greek. It has been argued, however, that in certain respects this exclusion from classical learning might actually have benefited women and girls. The anonymous author of a 1696 *Essay in Defence of the Female Sex* remarked that boys who were forced to spend their youth learning Latin lagged several years behind their sisters in terms of vernacular proficiency: while girls improved their 'command both of Words and Sense' by reading books in their native language, boys wasted time memorizing a largely useless foreign vocabulary, and 'at Seventeen or Eighteen...are but where the Girles were at Nine or Ten'. Donovan (1980) has suggested that the then emerging literary genre of the novel owed its distinctive linguistic character to the vernacular proficiency of women (and lower-ranking men such as Samuel Richardson (1689–1761), who did not have a classical education either). For Donovan (as for Virginia Woolf some decades earlier (see Woolf (1998 [1929])), it is not coincidental that the novel, by contrast with either poetry or serious non-fiction (e.g. essay-writing and criticism), has been a discourse genre in which many women excelled (even if some were forced to adopt male pseudonyms to avoid Victorian strictures on 'indelicacy').

Though the classical languages retained their symbolic value for centuries (particularly as a qualification for higher education), today in Britain knowing no language but English[3] does not impede access to educational, professional or other public arenas. In many societies, however, access to public discourse does require proficiency in a learned superordinate language (e.g. Spanish as opposed to the indigenous languages of Latin America, or, in diglossic situations like those which exist in the Arabic-speaking world, a 'high' variety that is not natively acquired). If girls in these societies receive less schooling than their brothers, one result may be to deprive them of the linguistic capital which is needed to access public discourse. Today it is rare for girls to be denied an education simply on the grounds that they are female (though this did happen as recently as the 1990s in Afghanistan under the Taliban), but it is still not uncommon for their opportunities to be restricted by comparison with those of boys, if families with limited resources prioritize the education of their sons, or if daughters' extensive domestic responsibilities discourage regular attendance at school.

Yet while it is easy to appreciate the force of the argument that women in some times and places have been excluded from certain forms of public discourse because they lacked linguistic and other symbolic capital, that argument invites the objection that it overlooks certain countervailing tendencies, particularly in recent times and economically advanced societies. In contemporary English-speaking countries such as Britain, the USA and Australia, it is widely reported that girls are doing better in education than boys, and in particular that they are entering adult life with higher levels of literacy. Another well-documented tendency, observed by variationist sociolinguists in a wide range of communities, is for women to lead men in the use of prestige standard linguistic variants and in 'changes from above' which involve the spread of prestige variants. In modern conditions this pattern may be linked to women's position in the labour market: many so-called pink collar occupations, such as clerical/secretarial work and school teaching, demand higher levels of literacy and standard language competence than similarly or better-paid jobs (e.g. the skilled manual trades) available to men of comparable social status.

There is, then, a body of evidence suggesting that women in most contemporary developed societies do *not* have less access to or less competence than men in the high-status languages, varieties and registers that are associated with public contexts. For some societies and some (elite) groups of women this has probably been the case for two centuries. However, during the 'second wave' of feminist militancy which began in North America and western Europe at the end of the 1960s, some feminists argued that even highly educated and literate women were socialized to favour a *style* of speaking and writing which was at odds with the demands of many public contexts. Characterized as 'unassertive' or, less negatively, 'co-operative' or 'consensual', this way of using language was accorded lesser value in the agonistically oriented western rhetorical tradition which had shaped the conventions of discourse in public sphere institutions such as Parliaments, law courts, the academy and the press. For some feminists, the remedy lay in expanding women's repertoires to encompass the assertive and adversarial styles that connoted public authority; for others, what needed to be addressed was not women's alleged deficiencies as public language-users, but the cultural devaluing of non-agonistic discourse in virtue of which they were perceived as deficient.

This debate—which in various guises has continued ever since—raises questions not only about women's material access to linguistic resources, but also about cultural attitudes and values. These too warrant attention, for, on its own, the argument that women have been excluded from public discourse by their inadequate linguistic capital is open to the criticism that it is circular: where women have not had access to the same kinds of linguistic training as men of comparable social rank, the reason has generally been, precisely, that the women, unlike the men, were not being prepared for public roles. If that is the case, lack of competence is not the root cause of women's exclusion but the effect of it, and the 'deeper' reasons for and mechanisms of exclusion remain to be accounted for. In the 1970s and 1980s, a number of feminist theorists sought to address what they saw as the deeper causes of female exclusion, adopting the kind of approach I have labelled 'symbolic'.

The symbolic silencing of women

In the 1970s and 1980s, some of the most influential theoretical accounts of women's relationship to discourse in general, and high-status public discourse in particular, were 'grand narratives' of a kind which has since fallen out of favour. The anthropologists Ardener and Ardener, for instance, promoted the idea of women as a 'muted group' (Ardener 1975; 1978). They postulated that culturally ratified forms of symbolic representation were generated by the dominant gender-group, men, on the basis of their own experience. Women's experience was different, but they were compelled to represent it in terms constructed by men. Consequently, women's reality was 'muted', experienced privately by women but unable to find public expression. Somewhat similar arguments, though with a more explicitly Whorfian edge, were developed in Spender's *Man Made Language* (1980). Generally speaking, however, these writers were not primarily concerned with differences in women's relationship to the language used in 'public' and 'private' contexts: the public/private distinction in their work was more a distinction between the intersubjective realm of culture and that of subjective female experience which remained private because it could not be verbalized in a 'man made language'.

Other feminists drew on the ideas of the post-structuralist psychoanalyst Lacan. In Lacan's neo-Freudian developmental framework, the human infant becomes acculturated as a social subject through the acquisition of a language. This entry to the 'symbolic order' is prompted by the infant's perception that it is separate from the mother's body and cannot possess it; the resulting sense of 'lack' or loss prompts the infant to identify with the symbol of patriarchal authority—the phallus—and to substitute signs, that is symbolic or linguistic entities, for the bodily satisfactions no longer available. For many Lacanians, however, boys and girls do not enter the symbolic order on the same terms because in this reworking of Freud's Oedipal narrative their relation to the phallus is different. In Lacanian theory the phallus is supposedly distinct from the penis: one is a symbol, the other an actual body part. No one of either sex can actually 'possess' the phallus. But children's observations of their own and their parents' genitals, and the meanings they attach to those observations, do make a difference. By identifying with their fathers, boys can partake more directly of the authority the phallus represents. Girls, by contrast, must recognize that their relationship to the phallus will always be indirect, and come to identify with their mothers. Becoming a feminine as opposed to a masculine subject thus entails a 'negative' form of entry into the symbolic order.

To linguists more used to accounts which are grounded in empirical observations of language-use, all this might well seem rather mystical (and implausible, given the evidence that first language acquisition proceeds in much the same way and reaches the same end-point in children of both sexes). However, some feminists have turned to Lacan's psychoanalytic framework in an effort to explain what the 'economic' approach arguably does not. Kaplan (1998 [1986]), for instance, argues that women perceive barriers to their participation in certain kinds of public discourse which cannot be accounted for in terms of the women's lack of linguistic competence to participate, nor necessarily in terms of any explicit social prohibition on their participation. For Kaplan, this raises the possibility that we are dealing with a 'deeper' cultural prohibition that women themselves have internalized. She suggests that while this may begin with the gender-differentiated process of entry to the symbolic order, it is decisively confirmed around puberty, the point at which men and women become full sexual as well as social subjects. Children, of both sexes, are typically restricted in their access to public discourse, but whereas males at puberty are permitted to enter into the domains of 'high' language, females are not granted this access, and may even experience an actual curtailment of their linguistic opportunities (it is at this stage, for instance, that some cultural taboos on female utterance take effect).

While this is a somewhat broad-brush argument, it does perhaps have the merit of introducing some considerations that the resource-based approach, with its emphasis on the material and the rational, neglects. Psychoanalysis seeks to explain the role in human behaviour of non-rational forces like desire, fear and fantasy. In its feminist forms it also seeks to explain how these forces work at the psychic level to reproduce patriarchal power-structures. From a psychoanalytic perspective the structures in question are not just social constraints that work on us from the outside, but ones we have internalized in the process of subject formation, so that they become part of our sense of who we are. This is surely not irrelevant for our understanding of the female voice in public contexts. Reading in this book about the struggles of the women MPs interviewed by Shaw (Chapter 5) and some of the university teachers questioned by Mills (Chapter 4), or pondering on the situation of the South African women described by Hanong (Chapter 11), it is difficult not to think that some part of their behaviour has its roots in fear and shame, sometimes of an intensity that is not readily explicable in terms of the practical consequences of speaking out (though this issue of consequences is one we must return to).

'Symbolic' approaches to the female voice in public contexts do not, however, have to entail highly abstract grand narratives of the kind I have reviewed so far. One consistent thread in feminist discussions of 'language and woman's place' since the 1970s has involved examining cultural representations of the female voice as expressions of what are now usually called 'language ideologies' (Woolard 1998; Cameron 2003). As I noted above, it is important not to conflate representations of gendered language with the reality of men's and women's linguistic practices; but it is also important to recognize that representations influence the understandings and the desires in the light of which human beings act. They are resources for the active process of self-fashioning which is now understood by most feminists to have a significant role in the construction of gender identity, and also distillations of the social norms which constrain that process in a given time or place. People learn what is considered normal and desirable femininity or masculinity from representations as well as from first-hand observation and experience; indeed, representations may be even more powerful in forming desires and identifications just because they are idealized. It is therefore germane to notice the prevalence of negative representations of the female voice in public contexts (today, words like 'shrill' and 'strident' come immediately to mind; in Elizabeth Cady Stanton's day the charge of indelicacy and immodesty was clearly a potent one), and the constant harping, in genres from proverbs to etiquette books, on the idea that women talk too much and in so doing make themselves unfeminine and undesirable. Speaking out in public is persistently represented as something that both unsexes and de-classes women: this may help to explain why it so often seems to engender a feeling of shame.

Making connections: Subordination, symbolic resources and social capital

But ideological representations, to be effectual, must be related to material social conditions. Judgements about the public female voice as immodest, indecent, unfeminine and so forth can only have resonance for women if they are in some way consequential in the real social world. This, perhaps, takes us back to the question of women's 'capital'—not just linguistic capital, but social capital more broadly defined—and to the issue of the consequences that may flow from speaking out. It may be asked: if we consider the totality of the social conditions any given set of women inhabit, what might they have to gain or lose by engaging in, or conversely avoiding, particular kinds of linguistic behaviour?

Consider, for instance, the observation made by Baxter (Chapter 9) that for an individual girl to claim a position of leadership in classroom discussion carries the risk that her peers will disapprove of her as 'pushy'. The ideological representation of 'pushiness' as an undesirable quality in women is plainly a factor here, but its ability to influence girls' actual behaviour must also reflect the importance they attach to female friendship as a form of social capital: a girl cannot afford to alienate her friends. The problem faced by Elizabeth Cady Stanton and her contemporaries could be analyzed in a similar way. Ideological representations of the time linked the question of women speaking in public to the issue of respectability and (sexual) reputation. Specious though this connection may seem to us (as indeed it did to many first-wave feminists), it was likely to be potent for middle-class Victorian women because their social position was in fact so dependent on maintaining their 'respectable' credentials; should those credentials be impugned, however unjustly, the sanctions women faced were real and severe.

Eckert (2000; see also Eckert and McConnell-Ginet 1999) has suggested that women are in general more dependent than men on symbolic resources for the accumulation of social capital. Referring to her work with members of the adolescent subcultures known as 'jocks' and 'burnouts', Eckert argues that young men can establish their peer-group credentials through their actions and achievements (e.g. being good at sport or at fighting), but young women are judged on the less tangible attributes of appearance, dress, demeanour, personality and speech. In consequence the young women invest greater effort in their symbolic self-presentation, attending closely to every detail that carries subcultural meaning, from the style of their jeans to the pronunciation of their vowels. Eckert believes that this pattern is not confined to adolescent subcultures. Women as social subordinates are in the same position in many communities of practice—the position, as Eckert puts it, of 'inter-lopers', continually under pressure to prove their worth and fitness to belong, but at the same time liable to be judged on different criteria from men.

The punctilious adherence of women MPs to the official rules of Parliamentary debate, reported by Shaw (Chapter 5), looks like an example of female 'interlopers' using symbolic resources in an effort to claim legitimacy as members of the House of Commons. And it might also be argued that the notion of the 'interloper' helps to explain the seemingly disproportionate anxiety felt by some women university lecturers about lecturing (Mills, Chapter 4), or by women theology students about asking questions at lectures (Jule, Chapter 6). Given that the academy is historically a masculinist institution, very markedly so in the case of a theological college, perhaps these women's anxiety reflects a sense that as 'interlopers' they have more to lose than men by giving a performance in the role of 'lecturer' or 'student' that is not 'correct' in every symbolic particular. Alternatively (though the 'alternatives' are not mutually exclusive—they could be seen as interacting to produce a classic 'double bind'), might women's reluctance to speak out in certain contexts or in certain ways be a symbolic resource for displaying legitimacy as a member of the category 'women'? Under some conditions, is silence itself (the silence that signifies modesty, or respect for one's betters, or the kind of enigmatic femininity that may be imbued with erotic meaning) a form of symbolic capital that women may have something to gain by deploying?

Yet feminists must consider not only what women have to gain or lose by making certain choices about when, where and how to speak, but also the collective interests of *men*, and the way some of them behave in defence of those interests. Women's sense of being 'interlopers' in public contexts is not just a hangover from the days of 'separate spheres', but not infrequently a product of the way they are treated by men, whose resistance to the dilution of their historical privileges is real enough. As Walsh (2001) has noted, it is a mistake to suppose that the mere entry of women in more than token numbers to masculinist institutions automatically normalizes the female voice in those institu-tions, for, on the contrary, the perceptible threat it represents to masculine hegemony may lead to an intensification of sexism and the creation of new exclusionary practices. We should not overlook the contribution made by crass sexism and outright misogyny to the contemporary situation of women speaking in public. In December 2004, for example, an academic study of British women MPs' experiences made newspaper headlines by exposing the astonishingly sexist behaviour of some male Parliamentarians: it revealed among other things how much harassment of a crudely sexualized nature is directed against women when they rise to speak in the House of Commons.[4] This may be the 21st century, but we ignore at our peril the stubborn persistence of such practices.

Conclusion: Causes and remedies

The main conclusion I would draw from this discussion is that the extent to which women participate in public discourse and the terms on which they do so cannot be explained by any single theory positing any single cause. Not only do 'material' and 'symbolic' constraints on women language-users work together, the precise way in which they work in any given time and place depends on their articulation with other, non-linguistic ideologies and practices. It seems clear, for instance, that the exclusion of women from public speech in the 19th century was closely bound up with ideologies of female domesticity and sexual respectability, and the numerous social practices through which those ideologies were expressed; 300 years earlier, by contrast, women's limited access to education looms larger in the picture than any explicit ideology of 'separate spheres'. Such historical differences (and there are also cross-cultural ones) confirm the importance of 'looking locally'; but they also point to the importance of looking *widely*, by which I mean placing women's situation as language-users in the broader context of their whole social situation rather than treating language as a realm unto itself.

For feminists, theorizing any problem affecting women is a political as well as an intellectual enterprise: it is proper to ask not only 'what explains the existence and nature of this problem?' but also 'what is to be done?' If it is accepted that the problem of the female voice in public contexts is a variable and multi-stranded one, it follows that the remedies will also be varied. But it is crucial to assess potential remedies in relation to the whole social and political context. Changes in women's linguistic situation are meaningful only in relation to that wider context: on their own they do not necessarily constitute 'progress'.

Recall, for instance, the argument that a progressive feminist approach to the status of women's speech in public contexts would involve challenging the masculinist values of the public sphere and asserting the value of women's ways of speaking. In the last two decades, something like this has happened: the co-operative and 'emotionally literate' discourse in which women are supposed to excel has been redefined as a valuable commodity in many public institutions (Cameron 2000). But arguably this has done little to advance the interests of women: what has motivated it is not a commitment to gender equality, but a desire to interpellate individuals as 'enterprising' subjects—self-reflexive, socially skilled, psychologically adaptable and, in the case of workers, able to satisfy the increased demand of contemporary consumer capitalism for their expressive and emotional labour.

The ability to speak and be heard in public contexts has been an important demand in many political struggles because it has been seen as a means to every other political end. To be of use for feminist purposes, then, theoretical accounts of the female voice in public contexts must be attentive to the question of ends: what goals women are trying to achieve and how their positioning as language-users either helps or hinders that process. Both problems and solutions need to be located in relation to the larger picture; and it needs to be acknowledged that the picture is neither simple nor static.

Notes

1. 'Western' systems of thought, politics and governance are not necessarily confined to the (geographical) west. Most importantly for present purposes, the 'western' notion of what constitutes the 'public sphere' will tend to have some influence in any modern democracy.
2. In the early modern period, reading was taught before writing rather than simultaneously with it: usually instruction in writing did not begin until the pupil had been learning to read for a year. Thus if an early modern person could sign his or her name, historians take that to imply that s/he could read, though not necessarily that s/he could write extended texts.
3. It should of course be acknowledged that for members of British minority communities where English is not the first language, educational and professional success does require the acquisition of a second language, namely English.
4. The study in question, also alluded to by Shaw (Chapter 5), was conducted by Joni Lovenduski, Margaret Moran and Boni Sones under the title 'Whose secretary are you, minister?'.

References

Anon [TE] (1632) *The Lawes Resolution of Women's Rights*. London: John More.
Anon (1696) *An Essay in Defence of the Female Sex: Written by a Lady*. London: R. Clavel.
Ardener, Shirley (ed.) (1975) *Perceiving Women*. London: Malaby.
Ardener, Shirley (1978) *Defining Females*. London: Croom Helm.
Armstrong, Nancy and Leonard Tennenhouse (eds) (1987) *The Ideology of Conduct: Essays on Literature and the History of Sexuality*. New York: Methuen.

Bourdieu, Pierre (1991) *Language and Symbolic Power*. Introduced and edited by John B. Thompson; trans. Gino Raymond and Matthew Adamson. Cambridge: Polity.

Cameron, Deborah (2000) *Good to Talk? Living and Working in a Communication Culture*. London: Sage.

Cameron, Deborah (2003) 'Gender and language ideologies'. In Janet Holmes and Miriam Meyerhoff (eds) *The Handbook of Language and Gender*. Malden, MA: Blackwell.

Donovan, Josephine (1980) 'The silence is broken!' In Sally McConnell-Ginet, Ruth Borker and Nelly Furman (eds) *Women and Language in Literature and Society*. New York: Praeger.

Eckert, Penelope (2000) 'Gender and linguistic variation'. In Jennifer Coates (ed.) *Language and Gender: A Reader*. Oxford: Blackwell.

Eckert, Penelope and Sally McConnell-Ginet (1999) 'New generalizations and explanations in language and gender research'. *Language in Society* 28, 185–201.

Gurko, Miriam (1974) *The Ladies of Seneca Falls: The Birth of the Women's Rights Movement*. New York: Schocken Books.

Jones, Ann Rosalind (1987) 'Nets and bridles: Early modern conduct books and sixteenth century women's lyrics'. In Armstrong and Tennenhouse (eds) *The Ideology of Conduct: Essays on Literature and the History of Sexuality*. New York: Metheun.

Kaplan, Cora (1998 [1986]) 'Language and gender'. In Deborah Cameron (ed.) *The Feminist Critique of Language*. London: Routledge.

Kennedy, George (1998) *Comparative Rhetoric: An Historical and Cross-Cultural Introduction*. New York: Oxford University Press.

Kramarae, Cheris (1981) *Women and Men Speaking: Frameworks for Analysis*. Rowley, MA: Newbury House.

Kulick, Don (1993) 'Speaking as a woman: Structure and gender in domestic arguments in a Papua New Guinea village'. *Cultural Anthropology* 8(4), 510–541.

Nevalainen, Terttu and Helena Raumolin-Brunberg (2003) *Historical Sociolinguistics*. London: Longman.

Rosaldo, Michelle and Louise Lamphere (eds) (1974) *Women, Culture and Society*. Stanford, CA: Stanford University Press.

Sherzer, Joel (1987) 'A diversity of voices: Women's and men's speech in ethnographic perspective'. In Susan U. Phillips, Susan Steele and Christine Tanz (eds) *Language, Gender and Sex in Comparative Perspective*. Cambridge: Cambridge University Press.

Spender, Dale (1980) *Man Made Language*. London: Routledge and Kegan Paul.

Walsh, Clare (2001) *Gender and Discourse: Language and Power in Politics, the Church and Organizations*. London: Longman.

Woolard, Kathryn (1998) 'Language ideologies as a field of inquiry'. In Bambi Schieffelin, Kathryn Woolard and Paul Kroskrity (eds) *Language Ideologies: Practice and Theory*. New York: Oxford University Press.

Woolf, Virginia (1998 [1929]) 'Women and fiction'. In Deborah Cameron (ed.) *The Feminist Critique of Language*. London: Routledge.

2
Gaining a Public Voice: A Historical Perspective on American Women's Public Speaking

Judith Mattson Bean
Texas Woman's University, USA

Introduction

To answer the question 'How did American women speakers succeed in gaining a public voice?' it is helpful to consider the history of women as public speakers. However, because public speaking is a social event involving not just a speaker but also a willing audience, this analysis should incorporate public speaking as a cultural phenomenon. Anthropological approaches and ethnography illuminate the history of women's public speaking. The ethnography of communication is concerned with recognizing recurrent speech events, their components, the relationship among components and other aspects of society, attitudes toward the event, and how communicative skills and attitudes are acquired. Pioneered by Hymes (1962), this approach places speaking within its cultural context. While it is often used to understand cultures which are very different from one's own, this approach is ideal for understanding speaking practices from the history of one's native culture. In this chapter I will consider U.S. culture of the early 1800s and how traditions of speaking were effectively challenged by early women orators.

In order to understand that period, it is necessary to examine how community speech events occur, and how speakers find audiences for speech events. To clarify what nineteenth-century women faced, I will examine the methods used to gain communicative competence, the negative attitudes they faced toward women's communicative performance, the factors leading to a woman's choosing public speaking, and some strategies of early women speakers. Finally I present a case study of a very early woman speaker who encountered barriers of race, gender, and class when she undertook public speaking in the 1830s.

A particular culture or speech community determines who that community will accept as a public speaker, not usually by law but by customs that are linked with that culture's norms of leadership, power, and range of speech events. Qualifications for public speaking vary across cultures and speech communities, and in many cultures, race, class, and gender norms also influence opportunities for public speaking. On the one hand, in cultures where formal literacy in reading and writing are highly valued and associated with access to power, those literacies are usually expected of public speakers. On the other hand, in societies that are primarily oral, qualifications to participate as a public speaker in community events are related to other norms valued by the community.

In the twenty-first century it may be difficult to recognize that democratic opportunities now available to women such as participating in government, legal proceedings, or organized religion were once closed to women either by law or by custom. Considered in relation to the history of western civilization, the emergence of women as regular public speakers is a recent phenomenon. Certainly there were exceptional women in earlier ages, but only in the nineteenth century did numerous women begin to find their audiences (speech communities) and establish enough history as speakers to expand opportunities to women in general. The study of women's public speaking and its reception by speech communities demonstrates how very slowly cultural attitudes and power structures change. A speech community reflects a culture's structure of power and authority, factors closely connected with public speaking events. A speech event may be influenced by a community's gender roles—the accepted division of labor among men and women.

Community speech events

In taking an ethnographic approach to public speaking, I consider how a speech community organizes itself and its public events (for definitions of speech community, see Saville-Troike, 2003). Nineteenth-century American culture, dominated by Euro-Americans, included many different speech communities with public speaking traditions: religious groups, governing bodies, laborers, and social reform groups, to name a few. Public speaking takes place at group events and usually requires planning, a large building, and an audience. The sponsors must feel that an audience will be interested and willing to listen to a speaker, granting the speaker at least temporary authority to speak on the chosen subject.

Public gatherings to listen to speakers occurred most often in religious settings; often the church was the only suitable place for a large audience and the space most open to women. Speaking in large buildings for public gatherings such as parliaments or courts required either membership in a society's leadership group or the permission of that leadership. Open outdoor meetings were always an option, but they rarely had the degree of authority granted to meetings held in public buildings. In addition, a few religious groups played a major enabling role for women speaking by providing implicit or explicit social support. Quaker women such as Lucretia Mott (1793–1880), Elizabeth Stanton (1815–1902), and sisters Angelina (1803–1879) and Sarah Grimké (1792–1873) employed skills learned in religious speaking. To a culture that placed high authority in Christianity, early Quaker women preachers such as Mott provided important examples and defenses for women orators. Others included Antoinette Brown Blackwell (1821–1910), perhaps best known as the first educated and ordained minister, Elizabeth Oakes Smith (1806–1893), Caroline Dall (1822–1912), Elizabeth Dow Cheney (1824–1904), and Julia Ward Howe (1819–1910) – Dall and Howe organized an association for women preachers; Smith was the minister of an independent congregation in 1877. Unitarians or Universalists were more open than most denominations to women speaking on spiritual matters. Marginalized by mainstream denominations, they acknowledged woman's spiritual equality and abilities to speak on spiritual matters to mixed audiences. In granting the use of religious spaces, leaders showed acceptance if not outright approval for women in the new role as speaker. Buildings controlled by the social reform groups that proliferated during the century also provided opportunities for women to become public speakers.

Audiences for speech events

Traditions guiding the organization of public events are based on expectations for speakers by the community's audiences. Gender was a major social division in the nineteenth century, and women were allowed the greatest opportunity to speak when they addressed only women rather than speaking to mixed gender, 'promiscuous' audiences. Women created their own audiences by organizing auxiliary reform organizations that paralleled and supported the same goals as men's groups in support of abolition of slavery, education, and temperance. However, even in speaking to their single-sex organizations, women were subjected to criticism in the press and by public leaders. Some of the most significant mileposts for women's rights were major reform conventions where women asserted their right to participate as members and speakers equally with men (examples include the London convention of abolitionists; the New York pair of conventions on temperance). Opposition was rooted in the speech community's norm of manhood as qualification for leadership, authority, and public speech.

Women's organizations provided women speakers with audiences and opportunities to gain experience. Women's associations included literary clubs, women's clubs, religious and reform organizations. Some clubs in the Boston area offered women spaces and platforms—notable were the Radical Club (1867–1880) and the New England Women's Club (NEWC) (1868–). These organizations complemented the work of the newly formed New England Woman's Suffrage Association and its Boston periodical, *The Woman's Journal*, which presented and reported on women speakers and lecturers.

Before women could be regularly admitted as speakers to other organizations, they had to be admitted as audience members, whether in lyceums (networks of lecturing societies) or reform organizations. Male lyceum committees limited female attendance at public lectures in early years. The Salem, Massachusetts lyceum required that a lady's ticket bear the name of the gentleman who was 'introducing her,' a reflection that early in the century unaccompanied single women attending public performances were usually assumed to be 'women of the streets.' Eventually, shifts in audience patterns and a growing taste for public entertainment created openings for women speakers. A re-formation of predominantly male, mixed-class audience into a middle-class, mixed-sex audience meant that lyceum audiences became increasingly stratified by class rather than by sex. Middle-class women could then respectably attend lectures unaccompanied by men, and middle-class women were increasingly invited to speak by lyceum committees.

Audiences were available to women through social reform organizations (Mattina, 1993) that defended women's public activism on traditional female attributes of piety, charity, and sympathy. Therefore, rather than challenging, they exploited stereotypical female qualities such as concern for the health and welfare of others to justify action outside the home. Women were attracted to social reform issues such as woman's rights, abolition, temperance, education, health and moral reform. Throughout the nineteenth century, temperance organizations, promoting controls on alcohol consumption, provided many women with their first opportunity to speak in public. Clarinda Howard Nichols (1810–1885) was sponsored by the Wisconsin Woman's State

Temperance Society in 1835. Health reform attracted Dall who participated in the Ladies Physiological Society. This association presented women (and men) speakers for lectures and 'conversations,' educating female audiences toward understanding their own physical nature and challenging the enforced 'innocence' fashionable in Victorian America. These efforts were less controversial for women than abolition of slavery and women's rights.

Attitudes toward women's communicative performance

An ethnographic account of women's public speaking must consider cultural attitudes about their communicative performance predicated on gender. First, the attitude that women should be silent, self-effacing, and publicly invisible meant that women who appeared as speakers could be interpreted as immodest and presumptuous. Cultural expectations made women in public more acceptable as objects on exhibition than as speaking subjects, and more acceptable as audience than as speaker. In the early nineteenth century some forms of public entertainment such as spiritualism actually did amount to public exhibition of women in both the U.S. and Britain. Women speakers were seen as being on display, 'exhibiting' the private self for public pleasure (Brodhead, 1989, p. 277). Famous women such as singer Jenny Lind (1820–1887) and author Harriet Beecher Stowe (1811–1896) could be seen as 'objects of visual consumption' for their spectators. This 'exhibitionism' impinged upon efforts of women who wanted to establish a tradition of intellectually authoritative discourse. Early women speakers often felt that the audience was there primarily out of curiosity to witness the strange anomaly of a woman speaking. Lecturers were criticized for exhibiting themselves in a manner unbecoming to 'true' women: being indecent, immodest, proud, and selfish. Sarah Hale (1788–1879), author of the satirical book *The Lecturess* (1839) and editor of a popular magazine *Godey's Lady Book*, expressed the majority view that women should remain silent in public and asserted that women held different values and should behave differently from men. She criticized author/lecturer Smith publicly and ended their friendship to protest such 'unwomanly' conduct as public speaking.

A second attitude was that women speakers were not 'true' women, but that they were 'unsexed' by engaging in public speaking. Nineteenth-century sexual-biological theories taught that women would be rendered sterile through strenuous intellectual efforts such as oratory, 'unsexing' themselves literally as well as figuratively. An influential letter by

Congregational ministers argued that women who attempted public speaking would 'not only cease to bear fruit, but fall in shame and dishonor in the dust' (1837; in Ceplair 1989, p. 211). Education leader Horace Mann (1796–1859) also asserted that 'when a woman . . . appears on the forum and makes speeches she unsexes herself' (O'Connor, 1954, p. 31). Thus, women speakers were thought to be masculinized by entering the traditional public space of males, with its strife and exposure to coarseness (even danger). Thus, a central problem in the reception of women as public speakers was the inability of many contemporaries, men and women, to see women as having both female body and 'masculine' intellect. Agonistic, confrontational speaking of public political life often involved verbal attacks, and women were thought to be unfit for the battle. An opponent of women engaging in public speaking, Catherine Beecher (1800–1878) argued that women's role in debates was 'the office of mediator, and an advocate of peace' (1837, p. 128), and that a woman should set aside her individual opinions to serve as mediator. In addition, she implies that women speaking in public on their own convictions do so at 'the promptings of ambition, or the thirst for power' (p. 101). For Beecher, a woman should not speak in public, especially when her speech might arouse opposition. In addition, some members of the speech community truly doubted that a woman could raise her voice enough to be heard by a large audience (having no technology of amplification at the time).

Ironically, a woman could be accused of either becoming 'unsexed' or being too sexually appealing. Women's public speaking was linked with doubts about a woman's 'virtue' (that is, appropriate sexual behavior). In seeking to speak their minds, women were sometimes labeled with the 'siren' stereotype that aligned destructive sexuality with the female voice. Linguist Outram (1987) describes a similar phenomenon in the discourse of the French Revolution which was constrained

> in its choice of adjectives, in the weight it puts on the gender-laden concept of *virtue*, in its whole implicit and explicit glorification of woman's sexual containment, in its identification of the female as all-powerful and all-corrupting, capable of changing the entire nature of political regimes by the use or possession of her body.
>
> (p. 132)

In the discourse of the French Revolution *virtue* was granted to the excluded (male) lower class. For aspiring women public speakers, the female body could be itself a barrier for attaining intellectual authority in discourse. For this reason, successful women speakers usually dressed conservatively, taking care that their appearance did not suggest any impropriety. Upon publishing her lectures, Dall (1855) counseled other women to wear only black. She criticized speaker Smith's fashionable appearance at a conference, describing her as a 'rare burlesque' for wearing 'white flounces' and 'crimson shawl' (Dall to Emerson, 1855).

Women were subordinated to men legally in their property and voting rights. Men were assumed to speak for women; theirs was the voice of legal, political, and cultural authority appropriate for public speaking. An audience must grant a speaker some credibility in the speech community if the speaker is to be effective. Simply gaining the opportunity to speak did not guarantee respect or authority for one's speech. Women had to prove themselves possessors of intellectual and powerful voices, not just beautiful voices suitable for emotionally expressive speaking (or singing). Because of their cultural subordination, the same problem confronted non-white, or lower-class Americans; blacks were also considered incapable of public speaking, and working-class individuals who lacked formal education also had to struggle to gain access to general public platforms beyond their own speech communities. Because of the link between educated white male leadership and public speaking, other race and class identities created obstacles to public speaking.

Choosing public speaking

Given the many negative attitudes toward women speaking in public, mainstream women had to be persuaded that they could and should participate in public activities. Most women lacked the desire to undertake a public role which brought ridicule as a result of violating gender norms. Choosing to engage in public speaking in early nineteenth-century America required commitment to changing attitudes toward women. Speeches of early women orators usually include a justification for women speaking in public because they understood that they were challenging the norms of the speech community—not just in traditions about speaking, but fundamental ideas about womanhood (Logan, 1995; Campbell, 1993). The desire to participate in reforming the culture provided a primary incentive for women to initiate public speaking; the need to earn a living was a second strong motivation.

When social attitudes were overcome, practical and private concerns—marriage relations and family financial need—also influenced a woman's decision to embark on a speaking career. Opposition to women speaking was stronger against married than single women, and against affluent women working in any capacity in contrast to those with financial need. Family members as well as friends could provide either powerful opposition or assistance for a woman's move into male domains. Usually the assent and support of men was necessary, and a few men assisted women in becoming public speakers. With greater training, power, and authority than women, men could arrange for spaces, provide private encouragement and public endorsements, or even assist a spouse with research. Many entered speaking careers as mature mothers or widows, so they needed to maintain family relations yet also secure relief from domestic responsibilities. Husbands were generally consulted, but not always followed, on a woman's final decision to assume a public role.

Because a woman's desire for self-expression or social influence had to be subordinated to family needs, financial circumstances appear as the major reason for women to take up public speaking professionally. Although some women did not need income from their speaking, most women orators relied on their oratory to support themselves. Some worked for abolitionist organizations, perhaps doing extra appearances on women's rights on weekends; others were engaged by lyceums as speakers. Margaret Fuller (1810–1850) used part of her income to support her brothers and mother in the 1840s; in the 1850s, Smith and Dall began lecturing to support their families.

Gaining communicative competence

Ethnographic approaches also consider how individuals gain communicative competence to participate in the speech community's activities. Ethnography considers how a community's organization and stratification influences access to the formal education needed for specialized forms of communicative competence such as preaching or arguing a case in court. In western civilization where there is a long tradition of [written] literacy, the opportunity to speak before an audience was often limited to those with education, though not always a formal education. However, some activities, particularly where authority was associated with spirituality, public speaking opportunities, might be available to individuals without education (Kienzle and Walker, 1998).

Women were at a disadvantage because education was divided by gender both in its availability and in its quality. Nineteenth-century school boys were trained in public speaking and encouraged to participate in speaking contests, debates, and other public speaking events. Before there was public (state) education, parents had to provide funding for private education, and most families educated only the boys. Higher education was not available for women until well into the nineteenth century. Schools for women usually lacked academic rigor, focusing on skills appropriate to entertaining, needlecraft, and caring for a family. Only rarely before the nineteenth century were women taught how to organize, develop, and present a speech for a large audience.

Topics and register

One aspect of the ethnography of communication is examining the topics of speaking considered appropriate for men and women. One subject considered inappropriate for women was the health and physiology of women. This norm was challenged by the Ladies Physiological Society, which presented lectures on women's health. Speech events also have an associated style of speaking or *register* considered appropriate for the event. The appropriate register is determined by the topic of the speech, the space in which the speech is given, and the relationship of the speaker to the audience in terms of identity factors such as race, gender, and class. If an audience has multiple identities or speech communities, a speaker may shift among registers in order to appeal to those differing groups (as we will see in Stewart's discourse). Women speakers who expressed social critique were considered 'presumptuous' and considered ignorant on topics such as the law or economy (e.g. Howe, 1881, p. 64).

When women remained in their domestic spaces, in private homes speaking for women only, their reputations were usually safe. To reduce the intense opposition to women as public speakers, some women adopted a compromise: 'conversations.' Semi-formal 'conversations,' rather than open public lectures, were acceptable because they seemed less assertive and were restricted to friends or acquaintances. Margaret Fuller's (cf. p. 28) conversations were seminars for women, but the audience also included men upon their request. Respected as a literary critic and well known for her wide learning and conversation, Fuller led discussions, then invited responses, definitions, and criticisms. Fuller's conversations were economically successful and stimulated other women to become public speakers. Drawing on powerful figures of the sibyl or the prophetess as prototypes for public roles and metaphors for self-representation, Fuller helped revise the possibilities for women's public speech by effectively combing the 'female art' of conversation with the 'manly' art of public speaking. Through the women she influenced, her inspiration for women's emergence into public discourse was extended and broadened across America in the decades after her death (Bean, 1998). Another woman stretched the genre of 'conversation' to unusual limits; educator Emma Willard (1787–1870) toured 8,000 miles in 1846 and avoided criticism by remaining seated as she spoke, making the appearance a 'conversation' rather than a lecture or speech.

Strategies of early women speakers

Given women's lack of formal education and cultural acceptance for public speaking, successful women speakers needed powerful arguments to establish their authority. Two strategies appear frequently across a wide spectrum of speakers: the use of historical accounts of activist women and the use of arguments and registers drawn from Christianity. Early American women speakers resisted allegations that they were presumptuous by demonstrating their allegiance to the dominant religion; if they did not, they were branded 'infidels' as was Fanny Wright (1795–1852) who lectured in 1827. This phenomenon is remarkable in its resemblance to the history of women's discourse during the French Revolution. Women of the counter-revolution rejected the male-marked discourse of Roman republicanism and used another 'universalistic discourse, far more adapted to women's needs as public persons, one that was provided by the Church' (Outram, 1987, p.133). The use of a universalistic discourse such as Christianity offered an automatic authority and validation (Outram, 1987, p. 31).

To counter the opposition to women speaking, a major strategy used by early women speakers was to cite historical precedents. Several books made this possible by presenting women's histories and collections of sketches of women from history who had taken active part in public discourse. Many women, such as abolitionists Angelina and Sarah Grimké, drew on Lydia Maria Child's (1802–1880) work, *The History of the Condition of Women, in Various Ages and Nations* (1835), a work that questioned rather than endorsed the traditional female roles that earlier volumes seemed to celebrate (Karcher, 1994, p. 220). Earlier works by Adams (1790) and Alexander (1779) provided additional resources for some speakers. Their long historical and broad world cultural scope provided alternate ideologies of womanhood and exempla for use in justifying women's public action. Of particular significance for these women was the precedent of the role of prophetess, a figure with which many outspoken women identified.

For reformers, opposition to the status quo and a style expressing opposition was appropriate. Caroline Healey Dall (1822–1912) challenged traditions of women's speaking styles by adopting an assertive speaking style. The press sharply criticized Dall for her 'antagonistic tone' and her confrontational style. In published lectures, Dall (1867) retorted that her critics thought she 'ought to take for granted the cheerful co-operation of the world...but it would hardly be worth while,' she said, 'for a woman to enter the desk (that is, to lecture) only to hedge it in with compromise and evasion.' She contended that 'Only by telling our brothers openly what we think of their jealousy can we ever hope to shame them out of it, ... [for] the day of opposition is not passed; ... the way of duty cannot, even in America, be trod in satin slippers' (p. 185n). Although Dall did not achieve wide acclaim as a lecturer, she was able to support her children most of her adult life through lecturing and writing. Angelina Grimké and Ernestine Rose (1810–1892) combined irony and wit with critique. Julia Ward Howe's (1819–1910) discourse was spiced with satirical comments but, rather than assuming an antagonistic stance, she presumed women's equality with men and called upon her opponents to honor democratic ideals for all.

Case study: Analysis of Maria Stewart's discourse

In order to uncover the strategies of women speakers, it is helpful to use feminist discourse analysis with its focus on performance of gender and co-construction of identities through negotiations in social interactions (Gal, 1995; Hall and Bucholtz, 1995; Baxter, 2003). To illustrate how a pioneering woman entered public speaking and resisted negative public attitudes, we will analyze an early speech event in which a woman effectively addresses class, race, and gender attitudes to create agency and authority for her discourse.

Maria Stewart (1803–1879) was an exceptional woman speaker who also met strong public criticism, not for her religion, but for her race. A free African–American who had worked only in domestic service and lost a battle for her husband's estate, she lacked financial resources, education, and organizational support, factors which help account for her brief speaking career. As an African–American woman speaking on opportunities for free blacks and women, Stewart was opposing norms of race, class, and gender in choosing to engage in public speaking. Her discourse (1832/1987a), *Lecture Delivered At The Franklin Hall, Boston, September 21, 1832*, provides an opportunity to examine how a marginalized woman developed agency through discourse. This speech event was a lecture presented in a building used regularly by the New England Anti-Slavery Society. Stewart was sponsored by

William Lloyd Garrison (1805–1879) and *The Liberator*, which published her essays. Publication provided her with a certain degree of agency and authority. Owing to the place, the race of the speaker, and the people who hosted the event, Stewart's lecture would have been interpreted as an anti-slavery speech. Her audience, to which we return below, shared her concerns and very likely provided her with some degree of authority.

Stewart's topic and register were strongly influenced by gender, religion, and race. Speaking on the topic of freedom of opportunity for free blacks and the necessity of self-help, Stewart's discourse relied on several strategies to establish agency despite the gender norms she violated in doing so. Stewart had communicative competency but no formal education or training in public speaking; she was self-educated and developed the ability to write. By all accounts she was intensely religious and, having lived as a servant in a clergyman's household, Stewart had ample opportunity to learn the discourse of Christianity. Although she grew up in the working class, she joined the small black middle class of Boston when she married a businessman. After his death, she began writing and speaking out on human rights for people of color. She described her motivation to enter public speaking when she said, 'it was contempt for my moral and religious opinions in private that drove me thus before a public' (Stewart, 1833/1987b, p. 70). No records remain to describe the particulars of Stewart's appearance or responses to it. But the discourse itself provides an example of a woman's construction of agency through strategic identification and negotiation of cultural norms in public speaking.

The choice of register for her topic was very important in a culture that expected women to remain silent on political issues, and silent in public discussions of controversial issues. Although she was not in a church nor ostensibly preaching, Stewart adopted a formal, religious register that provided some protection from opponents of women speaking. The preaching register dominated her speech, first in the opening paragraphs where she paraphrases the Bible (2 Kings 7:3–4, then 1 Samuel 17:26). In the second instance, she justifies her crossing public discourse boundaries by imagining a spiritual calling of women to action:

> Methinks I heard a spiritual interrogation – 'Who shall go forward, and take off the reproach that is cast upon the people of color? *Shall it be a woman? And my heart made this reply – 'If it is thy will, be it even so, Lord Jesus!'*
>
> (Stewart, 1832/1987a, p. 45, emphasis added)

Using 'methinks' three times in her speech, as well as formal syntax and lexicon throughout, Stewart maintained a register similar to preaching for most of the speech. In this religious register she could speak across racial divisions and, perhaps, across gender divisions *if* the audience accepted her interpretation of scripture. Stewart expressed identification with David who killed Goliath and removed the reproach from Israel, which she identifies with people of color. Although her use of Biblical discourse was typical of early women orators, Stewart's reliance on scriptural references to Africa/Ethopia was a performance of identification of race. Logan (1999, pp. 17–23), noting how Stewart recalls the Biblical promise that 'Ethiopia might stretch forth her hand unto God,' describes this strategy as Ethopianism, an ideology based on belief in the providential delivery of Africans from bondage.

The preaching register, with its implied obedience to God, was central to creating a position of authority for speaking. In doing so, she was implicitly performing elements of her gender and her religious convictions. At the same time, she reinterprets the stereotype of the obedient woman, by speaking through a divine voice which authorizes and challenges women to act.

Stepping briefly out of the formal religious register, she employs personal experience narrative and draws on discourse of common knowledge or 'custom' to describe her appeal to women in business to open employment to free black women:

> I have asked several individuals of my sex, who transact business for themselves, if providing our girls [free blacks] were to give them the most satisfactory references, they would not be willing to grant them an equal opportunity with others. Their reply has been – for their own part, they had no objection; *but as it was not the custom,* were they to take them into their employ, they would be in danger of losing public patronage.
>
> (1832/1987a, p. 45, emphasis added)

In this case, Stewart chose her words carefully to avoid opposing white women and expressing overt divisions of race in describing 'individuals of my sex.' Yet it is implied with the phrase 'our girls' and with the fear of employers that their business would suffer by employing free blacks. The reported conversation (indirect discourse) recalls situations where speakers must make special efforts to avoid expressing racist sentiments (Wetherall and Potter, in Mills, 1997, p. 145).

This use of personal experience register is brief; Stewart (1932/ 1987a) style-shifts in the next paragraph back to the formal, religious register: 'Ah, why is this cruel and unfeeling distinction? Is it merely because God has made our complexion to vary? If it be, o shame to soft, relenting humanity! "Tell it not in Gath! Publish it not in the streets of Askelon!"' (p. 46). Frequent scriptural allusions, quotations, and paraphrases allowed her message to be interpreted as a spiritual message rather than a political message. Those devices also opposed the racist discourse through which black women were equated with temptresses.

Establishing authority was especially problematic for Stewart. To speak on a political topic in public as a person of color before a mixed race audience, Stewart needed to dispel the belief that blacks were not capable of public speaking or complex thought. Throughout the early nineteenth century when slave narratives were published, for example, they were accompanied by prefaces and testimonials of white men and women who vouched for their authenticity. Having no inherent cultural power or status to bring to this speech event, Stewart needed to develop identification with diverse segments of her audience and the disparate elements of their identities in order to increase reception of her ideas. Her speech includes multiple acts of identification with white women, Christians, free black working people of the North, and all free Americans. In doing so, she draws on 'a range of "subject positions" made available in [her] culture by means of particular discourses in particular contexts' (Baxter, 2003, p. 25).

Reminding the audience of her membership in the speech community strengthened Stewart's authority. Although her use of 'my friends' may have been meant to include all of her audience, her primary identification in this speech was with other 'free people of color' (her term) of the North whose educational, economic, and occupational prospects were limited to domestic service, not by law but, as she says, by the 'force of prejudice.' This appears in frequent use of first person plural pronouns, *we, our*, as she describes the plight of free people of color in the North. Specifically, she says, 'As servants, we are respected; but let us presume to aspire any higher, our employer regards no longer' (p. 47). Four times she directly addresses the audience: 'my friends' (p. 47), 'people of color' (pp. 45, 46, three times on 47), 'My beloved brethren' (pp. 48, 49). In addition, Stewart develops identification with other groups. She refers to white women as 'ye fairer sisters' (p. 48) and she refers to abolitionists indirectly (p. 45).

Stewart would have been considered radical in her time due to her support of the ideas of Walker (1796–1830) and Garrison's *Liberator* (cf. p. 32) which supported women's rights as well as abolition. However, abolitionist support for women and slaves sometimes conflicted. In particular, Garrisonions used a discourse of gender that supported conventional notions of genteel femininity ('true womanhood') to argue that slavery destroyed the enslaved's gender identity (male or female), and thus was a shocking, degenerative force. Hoganson (1993) notes that the role of gender was 'one of the strongest and most hotly contested ideological languages employed in nineteenth-century political debate, one that brought Northern and Southern white men together around the belief that only true men could participate in politics' (p. 560). Stewart (1832/1987a) drew on abolitionist discourse, but acknowledged a conflict with it:

> I have heard much respecting the horrors of slavery; but may Heaven forbid that the generality of my color throughout these United States should experience any more of its horrors than to be a servant of servants, or hewers of wood and drawers of water! Tell me no more of southern slavery; for with few exceptions, although I may be very erroneous in my opinion, yet I consider our condition but little better than that.
>
> (p. 45)

Stewart's speech recognizes the importance of the abolitionist effort, but struggles to gain attention to a related issue: the stifling of hope and ambition in free blacks whose only employment was in service (domestic or otherwise). Ultimately, she was unsuccessful in broadening the abolitionist discourse to include expansion of opportunity for free blacks. In fact, in some states, the right to vote was taken away from free blacks in the North.

In this speech event, Stewart was opposing not only attitudes about race and gender, but also class stereotypes: the assumption that blacks were 'naturally' destined to be servants. She challenged a recently published article which argued that blacks were lazy and idle. Denying any fundamental differences of race tied to class, she also denied that the black race 'naturally' meant poverty and lower class. She also dismissed the class stereotype that race signified unique (lower-class) behavioral characteristics. She felt that, given the lack of opportunity, it was amazing that there were so many ambitious blacks, and reluctantly admitting that some 'who never were and never will be serviceable to society,' she asked, 'And have you not a similar class among yourselves? [i.e. whites]' (p. 47). She argued:

> Had it been our lot to have been nursed in the lap of affluence and ease, and to have basked beneath the smiles and sunshine of fortune, should we not have *naturally* supposed that we were never made to toil? And why are not our forms as delicate, and our constitutions as slender, as yours?
>
> (1832/1987a, p. 48)

Reflected in her repeated use of 'we' and 'our' is Stewart's strategy of identification with free blacks. Her repetition of 'as' develops contrasts between blacks confined to the working class and free white Americans who live a life of affluence and with the ideology of 'true womanhood' prevalent at the time (Sells, 1993). Furthermore, her challenge takes the form of a rhetorical question which requires the audience to defend its position.

In addition to adopting the register of the dominant religion, Stewart adopted the register of patriotic discourse, drawing on the American Revolution. First she describes free blacks as 'the American free people of color' (p. 46), then she asserts her willingness to die for free expression: 'I can but die for expressing my sentiments...for I am a true born American; your blood flows in my veins, and your spirit fires my breast' (p. 46). Responding to the assertion that free blacks were 'a ragged set, crying for liberty,' Stewart replied, 'the whites have so long and so loudly proclaimed the theme of equal rights and privileges, that our souls have caught the flame also, ragged as we are' (p. 47). And, in concluding her speech, she identifies herself and her audience with 'free citizens,' to identify with the discourse of American history and republicanism:

> Did the pilgrims, when they first landed on these shores, quietly compose themselves, and say, 'the Britons have all the money and all the power, and we must continue their servants forever? No, they first made powerful efforts to raise themselves, and then God raised up those illustrious patriots, Washington and Lafayette, to assist and defend them. And, my brethren, have you made a powerful effort?
>
> (1832/1987a, p. 49)

Thus, Stewart enacted multiple facets of her identity: race, gender, religion, and citizenship. She denied a social class identification imposed on her by her culture. She created agency by drawing strategically on valued registers of religious and patriotic discourse, and personal experience. Taken as a whole, her discourse defied stereotypes about women speakers. Most early women speakers felt the need to position themselves in relation to the resistance to their speaking in public. Stewart does so when she says, '[A woman of color] can do little besides using her influence: and it is for her sake and yours that I have come forward and *made myself a hissing and a reproach among the people'* (p. 48, emphasis added). The opposition she experienced as well as her need to support her family drove her from further public speaking.

Conclusion

Later generations of women speakers, primarily white, middle-class women faced many of the same cultural attitudes as their early nineteenth-century predecessors. They drew heavily on religious registers for their work, some engaging in preaching, establishing an organization of women preachers, and moving from preaching to suffrage work. Auto-biographies, lectures, and scholarship provide insight into how some domains of culture resist the entry of women, and also how women have succeeded in gaining public voice in those domains of power. In the U.S. the 1830s and 1840s saw the most intense debate over women's entry into public, political spaces. Pervasive, deep-seated beliefs about gender as the foundation of social order had been challenged by the politically radical female abolitionists who spoke in the 1830s.

Public speaking, despite these adverse circumstances, was rewarding for women. They associated speaking their minds in public with freedom—freedom to breathe, a transformation of self. For example, Dall (1867, p. 361) wrote, 'When a woman of good social standing struggles with convention on the one hand, and womanly affection on the other,' she wrote, 'she still stands *on the platform* somewhat as she *did at the stake*; but, on the other hand, the awakening public interest has nurtured a class of women who owe all that they have and are to the platform itself.' Asserting the dignity of intellectual labor, she claimed that women speakers 'are stronger and healthier than most women, only because they have had an object for life and thought to grasp.' In 1851 Smith eloquently described the importance of speaking to a present audience. She could end her isolation and gain the sense of community among women: 'I am happier in being thus *a voice to my kind* than I ever could be in any mere Artistic effort...I have greater hope and freedom of thought and a light and joyousness of life, which

I had never hoped to realize' (in Richards, 1981, pp. 29–30). Smith's expression here reflects a principle of feminist consciousness construction: 'In order for women to dare to speak their own truths, they must receive validation from other women... for the "social construction of reality" requires a collective effort... [and] ongoing interaction with others who co-inhabit this same socially constructed world' (Donovan, 1991, p.140). Lecturing allowed women a space for interaction with other women, not only among the audience but also in the homes they visited during lecture tours.

As women gained access to public platforms, represented women's needs, and employed their intellectual powers, they found new freedom and fulfillment. Women's speeches challenged the notion of a single woman's speaking style; rather speaking styles were governed only in part by gender. Their discourse communities, rhetorical aims, historical moment, and individual personalities combined with gender to shape flexible discourse styles across different expressive genres. Perhaps most significantly, they contributed to a redefinition of women's possibilities through transformations of public discourse conventions.

References

Adams, J. (1790). *Woman: Sketches of the History, Genius, Disposition, Accomplishments, Employments, Customs and Importance of the Fair Sex in All Parts of the World Interspersed with Many Singular and Entertaining Anecdotes by a Friend of the Sex* (London: G. Kearsley).

Alexander, W. (1976). *The History of Women, from the Earliest Antiquity, to the Present Time; Giving an Account of Almost Every Interesting Particular Concerning That Sex, Among All Nations, Ancient and Modern* (Vols 1–2) (New York: AMS Press) (Original work published 1779).

Baxter, J. (2003). *Positioning Gender in Discourse: A Feminist Methodology* (London: Palgrave Macmillan).

Bean, J. (1998). '"A presence among us:" Margaret Fuller's place in nineteenth-century oratorical culture'. *Emerson Society Quarterly*, 44(1, 2), 79–123.

Beecher, C. (1837). *An Essay on Slavery and Abolitionism, with Reference to the Duty of American Females* (Freeport, NY: Books for Libraries Press).

Brodhead, R. (1989). 'Veiled ladies: History of antebellum entertainment'. *American Literary History*, 1(2), 273–294.

Campbell, K. (Ed.) (1993). *Women Public Speakers in the United States, 1800–1925: A Bio-critical Sourcebook.* (Westport, CT: Greenwood Press).

Ceplair, Larry. (Ed.) (1989). *The Public Years of Sarah and Angelina Grimké: Selected Writings 1735–1839* (New York: Columbia University Press).

Child, L. M. (1835). *The History of the Condition of Women, in Various Ages and Nations* (Boston: John Allen).

Dall, C. to Ralph Waldo Emerson, 7 October 1855, Houghton Library, Harvard University.

Dall, C. (1867). *The College, the Market, and the Court; Or, Woman's Relation to Education, Labor, and the Law* (Boston: Lee & Shepard).

Donovan, J. (1991). *Feminist Theory: The Intellectual Traditions of American Feminism* (New York: F. Ungar Publishing Co.).

Gal, S. (1995). 'Language, gender, and power: An anthropological review'. In K. Hall and M. Bucholtz (Eds), *Gender Articulated: Language and the Constructed Self* (pp. 169–182) (London and New York: Routledge).

Hall, K. and Bucholtz, M. (Eds) (1995). *Gender Articulated: Language and the Constructed Self* (London and New York: Routledge).

Hoganson, K. (1993). 'Garrisonian abolitionists and the rhetoric of gender, 1850–1860'. *American Quarterly*, 45(4), 556–595.

Howe, J. (1881). *Modern Society* (Boston: Robert Brothers).

Hymes, D. (1962). 'The ethnography of speaking'. In Thomas Gladwin and William C. Sturtevant (Eds), *Anthropology and Human Behavior* (pp. 13–53) (Washington, DC: Anthropological Society of Washington).

Karcher, C. (1994). *The First Woman in the Republic: A Cultural Biography of Lydia Maria Child.* (Durham, NC: Duke University Press).

Kienzle, B. and Walker, P. (Eds) (1998). *Women Preachers and Prophets through Two Millennia of Christianity* (Berkeley, CA: University of California Press).

Logan, S. (Ed.) (1995). *With Pen and Voice: A Critical Anthology of Nineteenth-Century African-American Women* (Carbondale, IL: Southern Illinois University Press).

Logan, S. (1999). *'We Are Coming': The Persuasive Discourse of Nineteenth-Century Black Women* (Carbondale, IL: Southern Illinois University Press).

Mattina, A. (1993). ' "I am as a bell that cannot ring": Antebellum women's oratory'. *Women and Language*, 16(2), 1–6.

Mills, S. (1997). *Discourse* (London: Routledge).

O'Connor, L. (1954). *Pioneer Women Orators* (New York: Columbia University Press).

Outram, D. (1987). '*Le langage mâle de la vertu*: Women and the discourse of the French Revolution'. In P. Burke and R. Porter (Eds), *The Social History of Language* (pp. 120–135) (New York: Cambridge University Press).

Richards, W. (1981). *A Review of the Life and Writings of Elizabeth Oakes Smith: Feminist, Author, and Lecturer: 1806–1893.* Unpublished doctoral dissertation, Ball State University.

Saville-Troike, M. (2003). *The Ethnography of Communication: An Introduction* (3rd ed.) (Oxford, UK: Blackwell).

Sells, L. (1993). 'Maria W. Miller Stewart'. In K. Campbell (Ed.), *Women Public Speakers in the United States: 1800–1925* (pp. 339–349) (Westport, CT: Greenwood Press).

Stewart, M. (1987a). Lecture delivered at the Franklin Hall, Boston, September 21, 1832. In Richardson, M. (Ed.), *Maria W. Stewart: America's First Black Woman Political Writer: Essays and Speeches* (pp. 45–49) (Bloomington, IN: Indiana University Press) (Original work published 1832).

Stewart, M. (1987b). Mrs. Stewart's farewell address to her friends in the city of Boston. In Richardson, M. (Ed.), *Maria W. Stewart: America's First Black Woman Political Writer: Essays and Speeches* (pp. 65–74) (Bloomington, IN: Indiana University Press) (Original work published 1833).

3
Constructing Gender in Public Arguments: The Female Voice as Emotional Voice

Lia Litosseliti
City University, London, UK

Introduction

This chapter explores the discursive construction of the female voice as emotional voice in public arguments (i.e. arguments produced in public). In particular, it uses examples of argument from the British media, together with examples from work in this area within different disciplines – in order to theorise some of the diverse ways in which assumptions about gender and emotion are enacted in discourse, and shape discourse. Further, the chapter deals with the links between the discursive construction of the female as emotional and women's social positions in the public sphere. Given the political agenda of feminist linguistics, a robust analysis of such discursive construction, particularly as it is used in prevalent public arguments about social politics and ethics, is an important way of identifying and problematising these links.

I begin by setting the scene and providing a theoretical backdrop for this topic, through discussion of current thinking on gender, discourse and the construction of identities, as well as discussion of literature on emotion. I move on to illustrate and critically evaluate the discursive construction of the female voice as emotional voice, and look at specific arguments where the 'irrational female' symbolic category is drawn on by the participants. Finally, I explore some of the political implications of the 'female voice as emotional voice' stereotype, in particular how it works to sustain unequal power relationships which effectively limit women's involvement in the debates and decisions around the areas of education and war/conflict.

Setting the scene: A critical discursive feminist inquiry

Research on the relationships between gender and language, from the 1960s up to today, has been prolific, varied and diverse. Recent theoretical and analytical approaches (see Editor's Introduction for references) have moved towards a critical examination of *discourse*: language as social practice; and of how different *discourses* can be drawn on to represent, maintain, reconstitute and contest gendered social practices. Though by no means homogeneous or necessarily in agreement, the current directions in the study of gender and language put emphasis on the discursive and social context of a text in general and situated meanings within 'communities of practice' in particular, and on the discursive construction of gender identities. People use language variably, in order to 'do' gender or 'construct' different gender identities at different times, within different contexts (e.g. at home, at work, as members of groups and communities). Our identities are therefore multiple, multi-layered, contextualised, shifting, and often contradictory or dilemmatic.

It is within this context of a critical rethinking towards more complex and more nuanced questions about gender and language, as posed in much of this recent work, that I want to place my discussion in this chapter. Further, my perspective on the ideas argued in what follows is firmly rooted within **a feminist linguistics**. Feminist linguistics pursues explicitly political goals, in identifying, demystifying and resisting language use which reflects, creates and sustains gender divisions and inequalities in society (Talbot, 1998). In this light, I am proposing such a **critical discursive feminist inquiry** as one of the fundamental ways towards addressing issues of social change pertaining to the role of gender, particularly within public settings in the Western world, such as government, politics, business, the media, education and research. Although this process must acknowledge that historically women have struggled to have a voice in and access to the public arena, my focus here is on how women (and, by association, men) are positioned currently within specific public forums by particular discourses (see Editor's Introduction). These discourses are necessarily embedded within the context of female struggle for access, but at the same time can be contested, reclaimed or manipulated in ways that do not render their users powerless.

I use the term 'discourse' as language used to construct reality from a particular perspective, or a form of social practice (Fairclough, 1992; and as seen in much of the work which draws upon a Critical Discourse Analysis approach). In this chapter, I will be focusing on a particular discourse or symbolic construct, that of 'the female voice as emotional voice', and its implications within certain public arguments. Because of the many definitions of 'discourse' offered by scholars in various disciplines (see Litosseliti and Sunderland, 2002), I will use here the term 'symbolic construct' or 'symbolic category' to refer to a discourse that draws on a range of symbolic assumptions rather than on empirical observations about women's voice. I discuss this term in more detail in the following section.

The discursive construction of emotion as gendered

Over the past decade, there has been an increase in the study of emotion as well as of the relationships between gender and emotion, particularly within psychology, sociology, anthropology and philosophy (Harré, 1986; Lutz, 1990; Lutz and Abu-Lughod, 1990; White, 1990; Brody and Hall, 1993; Oatley and Jenkins, 1996).

A lot of this research has reinforced or contested the idea of trait-based sex differences (see Brody, 1997), while some studies have looked at the relationships between stereotypical beliefs about gender and emotion and the actual operation of emotion in social context (Shields, 1987 and 1995; Fischer, 1993). For example, studies in the former paradigm, particularly within psychology, have claimed that women are more emotional than men: that women experience more frequent and more intense emotions, whereas men are thought to be emotionally inexpressive and to have less intense emotional experiences. Another example would be studies (e.g. LaFrance and Banaji, 1992) that focus on emotions associated with women – arguably, sadness, anxiety and fear – and those associated with men, such as anger, pride and contempt. These are a few among many examples of studies that describe and reinforce, yet rarely challenge, gender stereotypes.

To begin with, the definition of emotion is problematic in itself. What counts as emotion and emotional experience? Are there positive and negative, rational and irrational, spontaneous and externally caused emotions? Are there differences between emotion in self-representation and in reading or evaluating others' emotional display? How is such display influenced by private/public and interpersonal/achievement parameters? While many of the (predominantly experimental) studies mentioned above have offered definitions, they have largely either ignored or been slow to examine the many situational and contextual factors surrounding the expression of emotion (see Fischer, 2000). A definition of 'emotion' or the 'emotional' in a vacuum is far from useful for my purposes in this chapter, where the focus is on the complexities of the socio-discursive construction of emotion. As Edwards argues in his analysis of emotion discourse, talk about emotion performs social, discursive actions, such as '...constructing the sense of events, orienting to normative and moral orders, to responsibility and blame, intentionality, and social evaluation. Emotion categories are not graspable merely as individual feelings or expressions, and nor is their discursive deployment reducible to a kind of detached, cognitive sense-making' (Edwards, 1999: 187).

I am, then, interested in some of the questions (here adapted from Shields, 2000) asked within more critical/constructionist approaches, that can help us theorise the discursive construction of emotion and its relationship with gender in particular: Under what social, cultural and political conditions does gender matter, what goals are involved, and what is at stake in those situations? What do women and men expect will happen to them if they do or do not experience (or express) emotion in particular ways at particular times? What does it mean to describe someone as 'emotional'? Who decides what is, or is not, emotional, and who has the power to use this label? To answer these questions, one needs to critically engage with the social currency of emotions, their socio-discursive action or effects, and issues of power, which are key in current theoretical and analytical approaches to gender and language. These are implicated in two intricately connected kinds of discursive construction through talk about 'the emotional': its association with the private, subjective and irrational; and its association with the female voice, so that qualities that define the emotional also define women (Cohn, 1987; Lutz and Abu-Lughod, 1990; Hekman, 1994; Ruddick, 1996; Cohn and Ruddick, 2004).

> As both an analytic and an everyday concept in the West, emotion, like the female has typically been viewed as something natural rather than cultural, irrational rather than rational, chaotic rather than ordered, subjective rather than universal, physical rather than mental or intellectual, unintended and uncontrollable, and hence often dangerous.
>
> Lutz (1990: 69)

The choice of the word 'association' above is significant for my argument in this chapter. A critical discursive feminist approach to gender and emotion concerns itself, not with stereotypical generalisations about gender, 'women's language' and 'gender differences', but with what speakers and writers *do* with those generalisations and assumptions within different contexts – and across different social groups, communities and cultures. A critical approach entails questioning the theoretical, methodological and ideological assumptions underlying, for example, representations of women as nurturing, passive, sensitive, intuitive, irrational and selfless, and of men as rational, active, independent and firm; and generalised claims about women using language supportively to connect or build rapport, and men using language aggressively, to initiate, 'report' and interrupt (for discussions of these claims, see, among others, Cameron, 1998; Coates, 1998; Tannen, 1990). Further, a focus on the discursive construction of identities (as specified earlier) may entail, first, a recognition that such representations make assumptions about gender as binary, fixed, monolithic, predictable and consistent; secondly, an examination of the process whereby those 'traits' associated with women have been relegated to inferior status, and their complexity has not been recognised; and thirdly, an exploration of the different ways in which people in particular contexts make use of such representations, including attempts to resist or subvert them.

This line of inquiry, then, draws attention to distinguishing between 'women's language', a symbolic category, and 'the language used by women', an empirical category (Cameron, 1998). Bearing in mind that 'the relationship between using a certain kind of language and constructing a certain kind of gender identity is almost always an indirect or mediated one' (ibid.: 953), I am focusing on how the symbolic construct 'women's language' – and assumptions, implicit values and ideologies embedded within it – is drawn on by participants in arguments, and particularly arguments produced publicly (Litosseliti, 2002a). More specifically here, I am examining assumptions, associations and in-context uses or co-constructions of the 'female as emotional' category: their employment through language, and their consequences. If we accept that gender is not a fixed, monolithic entity with distinct patterns, and that emotion discourse is a rich and variable repertoire of alternative, overlapping, inconsistent, opposable ways of talking about ourselves and about others (Edwards, 1999; see also Galasinski, 2004), then we can expect people to be drawing on this category in variable, even contradictory ways.

The female voice as emotional voice: Public contexts and public arguments

Let us consider some of the ways in which people are drawing on the 'female as emotional' category. One example can be found in the way in which writers of lesbian novels draw on stereotypically 'male' speech features, while avoiding 'female' ones, in order to frame their characters as butch; in this context, speaking too much and expressing emotion are key 'female' features to avoid in constructing a specific identity (Livia, 1995). In other cases, the 'female as emotional' category is drawn upon within professional and public contexts, where much more is at stake for the participants, and where the symbolic category is bound up with issues of power. A good example of this is the use of unemotional, disinterested language by women police officers in Pittsburgh (McElhinny, 1998), who adopted an 'economy of affect' in an effort to appear professional, impartial and authoritative. Another similar example would be the language used by the former British Prime Minister Margaret Thatcher, particularly during times of conflict, such as the Falklands War, which contributed further to her reputation as the 'Iron Lady'.

Significantly, the last two are examples of female access to established male-dominated environments [some of which are explored in detail later in this book], where women have adopted the interactional approaches that are characteristic of these institutions and environments. One explanation for this is that because leadership and authority in these environments have traditionally been associated with masculinity, consequently the language of leadership is equated with the language of masculinity (Hearn and Parkin, 1988). Other studies focusing on female priests (Walsh, 2001) and female members of the British Parliament (Shaw, 2002, and Chapter 5) also illustrate this. However, these studies, crucially, also point out that those women are judged differently to men and criticised when they use direct, confrontational language or attempt to change the speaking rules of that institution (see also Baxter, Chapter 9). There is a lot of empirical research to suggest that women are typically confronted with this 'double discourse' or double-bind (Martin-Rojo and Gomez Esteban, 2002; Wodak, 2002; Litosseliti, 2006), where they simply cannot win: it seems that, even in leading positions, women are faced with having to justify their presence and their achievements, and with being measured against different norms to men.

In terms of interaction, we could argue that this process of justification or legitimacy-gaining involves a wide variety of discursive strategies, including, perhaps unsurprisingly, a combination of what may be recognised as stereotypical 'male' and 'female' speech styles. In other words, in addition to adopting the masculinist style that is dominant in a particular environment, women may find a combination of styles and strategies as the most effective way of achieving their goals. To return to a previous example, it has been suggested that Margaret Thatcher also incorporated elements of informality and self-disclosure in her authoritative, formal, aggressive discourse (Webster, 1990). Moreover, research on 'doing' femininity and masculinity in organisations in New Zealand shows that effective women leaders typically (and skilfully) draw on a wide range of stereotypically masculine and feminine discourse strategies, to accomplish both their transactional and their relational goals (Holmes, 2000; Stubbe *et al.*, 2000; Holmes and Schnurr, 2004, and Chapter 13).

In some of my own research (Litosseliti, 2002a and 2002b), I have also illustrated how a combination of strategies informs arguments produced publicly in the mass media, by analysing what participants in those arguments do with the 'female as emotional' symbolic category. Argumentation, as a dialogic process and a prime site for the production, negotiation and contestation of discourses, is a very rich area as regards the discursive construction of emotion. First, it may take a number of forms (discussion, debate, disagreement, dispute, etc.), each of which sets up particular positions and discourses available to male and female participants – for example, of 'rationality' and 'emotion', 'truth' and 'sentiment', 'confrontation' and 'conciliation'. Secondly, those actively involved in argument typically produce, sustain or challenge versions of 'maleness' and 'femaleness' on the basis of their own and others' assumptions about gendered ways of arguing, where emotion is almost always implicated. Thirdly, public argumentation, as seen in the media, in politics and even in higher education, sets up positions of power and of powerlessness for participants.

I have previously highlighted these issues, from a critical discursive feminist perspective, in my analysis of the *Head to Head* debates in the British newspaper *The Guardian* (ibid.), and I want to reproduce a few key points here for my purposes in this chapter.

'I'm the irrational female, ignorant of how markets work.'

The *Head to Head* feature consists of correspondence on an issue of current affairs between two participants with conflicting views on that issue. One of these features (extracts below; for detailed analysis, see references above) is between Anita Roddick of the UK fair-trade cosmetics chain *Body Shop* and Stanley Kalms of *Dixons*, a UK chain of computer and electrical appliance stores. The letters are published under the headline *'Staking their claims'*, with the following sub-heading: *'What are the moral duties of business? To care for the world, or simply to make profit? In a vigorous exchange of letters, Anita Roddick of the Body Shop and Sir Stanley Kalms of Dixons spectacularly fail to agree.'*

(1a) **Roddick:** [...] You have said that what makes you happy is seeing the company's prosperity trickle down to employees. I have a broader vision: our employees want to participate in social change to give their work more meaning. That's what makes me happy – when I see employees involved, when the connection between life and work appears seamless. Is your apparently money-based view of business really so narrow?

(1b) **Kalms:** On the other hand my tribe goes back several thousand years and we have accumulated quite a lot of carefully documented wisdom. So I start from a sound ethical base – age-old values and proven rules of social obligation. No need to make them up on the hoof – instant ethics can be tiresome. [...] At Dixons we do it differently. Our writ runs to paying our staff on a Friday afternoon. 'Life and work seamless' – that is truly nonsense. Our role is to create the means, not impose the ends.

Anita, our differences may not be so sharp but I can't tell from your scattered thoughts. I believe in a focused, rational approach in which man has it within himself to improve. But it needs a reasoned acceptance of the real world. Might I suggest to you that Margaret Thatcher would be a better role model than Don Quixote.

(2a) **Roddick:** Now I know where you're coming from. I'm the irrational female imposing my world view on employees, ignorant of how markets work. But you seem to know the price of everything and the value of nothing [...] By the way, unlike Mrs Thatcher, I believe there is an alternative, so we don't tilt at windmills, we invest in them!

(2b) **Kalms:** Your attempt to monopolize the 'caring' market fails. I also care but in an ordered and studied manner, not merely based on public relations geared to selling my products [...] Your cliché-ridden response is disappointing, albeit predictable. Let me pose you a quiet question – can't you accept that your frenetic, self-righteous approach may not always be the best way to draw attention to issues that actually concern us all? [...]

(3a) **Roddick:** OH DEAR – I'm not going to play that little boys' game of 'mine's bigger than yours', but the Body Shop is Britain's most successful international retailer in 46 countries – same brand, shared values [...] How will you use your last words? More macho, retro-posturing, or will you focus on the real world – the one shared by Unipart, Co-op Bank, Nat West and BT, who relish the stakeholder challenge and welcome the debate it creates about their broader social role?

(3b)   **Kalms**: At Dixons we are not governed by abstract theories but simple common sense. I'm passionately concerned about my employees; they share in our success. In the final analysis, the consumer is king and we have millions of satisfied customers. After almost 50 years in business, I am now told I've got it all wrong. I am labeled a cynical totem of the business establishment. You ignore the empirical evidence and, like some fevered tele-evangelist, tell me I must convert to stakeholding. I must decline your invitation. Although I too have vision, I am an idealist without illusions.

I have argued that the text content (themes or repertoires) and text organisation (linguistic resources or discursive strategies) in this example set up a dichotomy between what participants describe as 'real', 'rational', 'proven', 'common sense' on one hand, and 'personal', 'felt', 'emotional' on the other. And that the deeply held associations of the former with legitimacy and authority, and the latter with an anecdotal, instinctive (or, in Kalms' words, 'scattered' and 'frenetic') approach, are drawn upon by speakers both in developing their arguments and in undermining each other's arguments. Although emotions 'are often defined in contrast to rational thought', as 'subjective, unconscious rather than deliberate, genuine rather than artificial, feelings rather than thoughts' (Edwards, 1999: 170), emotion discourse can be appropriated by the speakers to both construct ideas as irrational and treat emotions as sensible and rationally based (ibid.).

Further, as the debate progresses, both speakers make overt attempts to disrupt or defend a 'male as rational–female as emotional' dualism; in other words, the symbolic category of 'female as emotional' is available to and recognised and used by the participants, as exemplified in extract (2a): '*Now I know where you're coming from. I'm the irrational female imposing my world view on employees, ignorant of how markets work.*' Confident participants in public arguments such as this typically appropriate language, and discourses, to their advantage. In this case, Kalms draws on this category in an attempt to trivialise Roddick's views, in 1b and 2b: '*Anita, our differences may not be so sharp but I can't tell from your scattered thoughts . . . Your cliché-ridden response is disappointing, albeit predictable. Let me pose you a quiet question – can't you accept that your frenetic, self-righteous approach may not always be the best way...'.* Roddick's argument is built around the theme of 'values over price' (2a) and caring for others (*'That's what makes me happy – when I see employees involved, when the connection between life and work appears seamless'*), which she then poses in stark contrast to her interlocutor's 'old-fashioned', 'macho' approach (3a). As mentioned before in the example of women leaders in organisations, that women often 'assess others' stereotypical beliefs about gender and then strategically adopt strategies which will be most likely to achieve their ends; some of those strategies may be ones stereotypically associated with feminine language' (Mills, 2002).

However, the key point that clearly emerges from this example is that 'a hypothesised stereotype of gendered behaviour informs interaction' (ibid.). In the same vein recent research in the workplace by Holmes and Marra (2004) and Holmes and Schnurr (2004) has found that although both men and women engage in 'relational practice' at work (to do with mutual empowerment, self-achieving, creating team, preserving consensus, etc.), this is still regarded as 'gendered' work, and stereotypically 'feminine' behaviour. In the *Head to Head* extracts on p. 47, we see a similar hypothesised stereotype of gendered behaviour (in Roddick's words, the 'irrational female') informing argumentation. One effect of this is that participants are 'doing gender' or 'arguing gender' in addition to their respective argument positions (see 2a and 3a on p. 47). I have suggested, following analyses of argumentative interactions in the media and in focus groups (Litosseliti, 2002a), that in many cases this leads to additional conversational work for the women involved in argument. In a 'double-bind' (discussed earlier) of legitimising and justifying their positions, and in anticipation of symbolic constructs of gendered behaviour, women may strategically engage in extensive, inclusive, balanced arguments; and at times, even defensive and mitigated ones. In this example, Roddick is highly conscious of the 'female as emotional' construct being used against her, and is therefore making attempts to resist her positioning as an emotional, irrational and even hysterical woman. This is evident in 3a in a demonstration of documented knowledge about business: *'I'm not going to play that little boys' game of "mine's bigger than yours", but the Body Shop is Britain's most successful international retailer in 46 countries – same brand, shared values [...] How will you use your last words? More macho, retro-posturing, or will you focus on the real world – the one shared by Unipart, Co-op Bank, Nat West and BT, who relish the stakeholder challenge and welcome the debate it creates about their broader social role?'*. It is also evident elsewhere in the text (not cited) where Roddick claims that her argument is 'real' and valid, not *even if*, but *because* it is based on what she has personally experienced in doing business.

'I don't just play a passive emotional role.'

We see similar resistance to being positioned as emotional, in another *Head to Head* feature on the topic of euthanasia, which I want to illustrate here through a brief extract. This exchange of letters, entitled *Hope to Die*, is described as a 'clash over choosing death rather than life': Annie Lindsell (terminally ill at the time) wants the right to die. Dr. Andrew Fergusson is opposed to euthanasia.

> (1a) **Fergusson:** [...] the Dutch government's statistics for euthanasia in 1990 are damning: in addition to 2,300 voluntary euthanasia deaths there were more than 1,000 cases of involuntary euthanasia [...] And if the Dutch have such safeguards, why were there not 3,300 euthanasia notifications in 1990? Why only 454? [...] Once the real issues are considered objectively, a majority in a civilised society will always conclude against euthanasia. It is fundamentally wrong, always unnecessary, and cannot be policed.

> [...]

> (3b) **Lindsell:** What little breath I have is always taken away by the sheer arrogance of those who discount my knowledge, as well as my experiences. You allow that patients know their own feelings. However, like many, I also know quite a lot about the disease I live with – probably more than some GPs. I don't just play a passive, emotional role: I learn for myself, and decide as an equal partner. So please don't patronise me by implying that I don't really know my own mind, or am being pushed into wanting wider choice at the end of life.

Although a number of parameters may be at work here (a difference in participants' status being one), this public argument relies once again on a dichotomy between what is described as 'real', 'objective', documented and what is described as 'own feelings'. Annie Lindsell is explicitly resisting being positioned as passive, emotional and weak – and although it is not clear if the 'female as emotional' construct is implied in the discourse, her resistance produces a more defensive and mitigated account than her interlocutor's.

In terms of making claims about similar public arguments, it should be pointed out that the *Head to Head* feature is exaggerated, in the sense that in this particular community of practice it is polarised argument that is both expected and valued. The marketisation of public affairs media, particularly in the UK, has led to an emphasis on 'infotainment' and 'conversationalisation' of the media (Fairclough, 1995), and a preference for sensationalist and adversarial language (see Tannen, 1998, for many illustrative examples; also Chapter 7). The adversarial, polarised debate in this context is arguably more likely to give rise to explicit talk about 'the irrational female' than in more formal contexts where, for instance, saving face or appearing to be 'politically correct' are considered to be important.

Political implications of the discursive construction of women as emotional in the public sphere

I have looked at some of the diverse ways in which assumptions about gender and emotion are at play in arguments in public contexts. As a symbolic category, the 'female as emotional' may be appropriated, or drawn on differently by different participants and with different results: it can be used strategically to undermine one's argument; it may be resisted and contested in argument; it may be used blatantly or subtly to create positions and identities; it may also influence the conversational and argumentative work required by the participants. I want to finish this chapter by going back to the role of feminist linguistics in deconstructing issues of social power and inequality between males and females, and in particular what could be some of the political implications of the discursive construction of the female voice as emotional voice in the public sphere. If a critical discursive examination of public arguments is the first step in that direction, a second step would involve identifying possible links between the discursive construction and the circumstances or positions of women within public forums and institutions.

I have indicated some of these possible links in my earlier references to a 'double discourse' where men's and women's achievements are measured with different norms; to a necessity for women to both adopt and adapt such institutional norms/styles; and to the existence of masculinity and femininity at an institutional level (Mills, 2002) where masculinity is associated with rationality and professionalism. Is this double discourse partly responsible for the fact that women are still significantly outnumbered by men – across time, locations and cultures – in positions of social and political power (e.g. company presidents/CEOs, prominent politicians, judges, bishops, police chiefs, union leaders, university vice-chancellors)? And, conversely, is any social change in these areas reflected in the discourses and arguments invoked in the public sphere? For example, if there is increasing gender equality, or even arguably a feminisation of the workplace/government and so on, does this mean that in addition to female politicians adopting 'masculine' discourses, male politicians also adopt 'feminine' ones?

I will briefly look at three examples of an emerging feminist politics of emotion, where the discursive construction of the female voice as emotional voice has specific political implications for women's access to the agendas and debates that matter.

The first one comes from Fischer's 'Gender and Emotion' collection (2000), where, among other research within social psychology, Shields looks at the example of the Virginia Military Institute, a prestigious state-supported public college in North America, which at the time had been resisting pressure to become co-educational. In the related US Supreme Court case in 1996, the defendant's arguments in favour of sustaining sex-segregation relied on numerous generalisations about gender and emotion, such as women being 'more emotional' and 'less aggressive' than men, and unable to endure the 'psychological trauma' involved in that particular programme. Shields convincingly shows that these beliefs both illustrate the Western prevailing conception of emotion as internal to the person and equated to feeling, and help maintain the status quo in terms of social power. The maintenance of a status quo that disadvantages women is a key point also in other conceptualisations of emotions as political, such as the extensive feminist critique of rationality in Western thought (see, for example, Hekman, 1994).

The second example also shows that emotions are political and often exercised as a means of social control, this time in education and higher education (Boler, 1999). Boler maintains that, because emotions have engendered histories that have become cultural capital, the control of 'emotional discourse' determines the dissemination of knowledge, and its production both outside and inside the classroom. Because women are often situated on the side of the 'emotional', they find themselves in a bind: first women teachers are expected to act as caretakers and nurse-maids – roles associated with feeling but not with power – and at the same time, they are demeaned for assuming these roles. Also in the context of higher education and scholarship, she argues that feminist pedagogies are often marginalised within the academic hierarchy through association with the 'emotional', and feminist scholars are dismissed as 'touchy-feelie' types (Boler, 1998). For example, she quotes descriptions of women's studies programmes as 'therapy group' and feminism 'training ground', rather than 'serious academic programmes interested in ideas, evidence, debate'. Similarly to scholars focusing on the sociology of emotions, Boler argues that emotions are epistemological, and that rather than being opposed to reason (a prevalent Western concept), emotions enable reason. She proposes a 'feminist politics of emotion' as a theoretical, analytical and practical challenge to the historical and cultural emotional rules of patriarchy – a challenge which aims to put emotions on the political and public agenda, to publicly articulate and critically analyse them as learned hierarchies and gendered roles rather that 'natural'/'private' occurrences (ibid.).

Finally, my last example comes from work broadly within philosophy, and particularly 'anti-war feminism'. Similarly to other theories discussed in this chapter, Cohn (1993) and Cohn and Ruddick (2004) work within a framework of gender, not as a characteristic of individuals, but as a symbolic system:

> a set of ways of thinking, images, categories and beliefs which not only shape how we experience, understand and represent ourselves as men and women, but which also provide a familiar set of metaphors, dichotomies and values which structure ways of thinking about other aspects of the world, including war and security. [...] human characteristics and endeavors are culturally divided into those seen as 'masculine' and those seen as 'feminine' (e.g. mind is opposed to body; culture to nature; thought to feeling; logic to intuition; objectivity to subjectivity; aggression to passivity; confrontation to accommodation; war to peace; abstraction to particularity; public to private; political to personal; realism to moral reflection, etc.), and the terms coded 'male' are valued more highly than those coded 'female'.
>
> (Cohn and Ruddick, 2004: Chapter 21)

Within this set of assumptions, anti-war feminists set out to examine both the multiple gendered positions and identities constructed in the practice of war-making and the gendered system of meanings that shape war-making. They suggest that national security paradigms and policies are distorted by the devaluation and exclusion of 'the feminine', to the point where it becomes extremely difficult for anyone, female or male, to take the devalued position, to express concerns or ideas marked as 'feminine'. Cohn claims that this makes it easier to leave out the emotional, the concrete and the particular, to see human lives and their vulnerability and subjectivity as irrelevant, and for what she describes as 'autonomous reasoners' (those not bound by institutional constraints, gender identification and emotion) to produce the so-called objective knowledge about war and conflict (Cohn, 1993).

I find this conceptual framework very useful, because it accounts for the marginalisation of both men and women, in that the characteristics excluded or devalued as 'feminine' can be characteristics of both men and women. And, at the same time, it can help us interpret phenomena such as the exclusion of 'the feminine' during times of war from newspaper pages and television screens. In her analysis, immediately after the September 11 terrorist attacks in New York, of the first five pages of five newspapers in Britain on September 14 and 15, Madeline Bunting (writing in *The Guardian*, 2001) points out:

> *The Sun* had no women writing on the crisis on either day compared to their writing about a third of the front of the paper on the previous Friday. Likewise, the *Mail* on the Thursday, but by the Friday, it had shifted to roughly 50/50 across the front pages and comment with a strong human interest emphasis. This was still a steep decline; in comparison the previous Friday was dominated by women reporters (2,703 words to men's 874) and comment pages were written entirely by women. *The Times* and *The Guardian* showed a similar sharp drop in women writing; the former had no women in the first five pages or on the comment page on Friday and *The Guardian* had only one (1,215 words) which represented a sharp drop from the previous week, when women wrote 5,850 words. Only the *Telegraph* recorded little change in the number of articles – it was consistently low – although the word count doubled, almost all of which was accounted for by men. [...] The consequence is a curious, lopsided, mutated version of the event in which men have dominated the debate, shaping our understanding of what happened, how it happened and what should happen next. Women have been marginalised in a way which would have seemed barely possible only two weeks ago.

Interestingly, this state of affairs is explained in the article through the binary concept of gender difference, by drawing on stereotypical notions such as a female tendency to empathise and a male preference for objectifying and controlling the world from a distance. Anti-war feminists rightly question these dichotomies, given the social currency of traits such as empathy, and because they reproduce a gendered ideology or system of meanings that excludes women from decision-making about war in particular and politics in general. Moreover, in terms of the role of the media, these dichotomies ensure that women stay in the 'softer' areas of news (e.g. features and domestic stories; see, for example, Holland, 1996) and in the private rather than the public sphere. What is necessary in order to address and redress such systematic ideologies and power relations is an examination of their masking in discourse and an understanding of what and whose interests they are serving; such examination and understanding can consequently guide our political actions.

Concluding remarks

In this chapter, I have argued that gendered discourses or hypothesised gendered constructions around emotion perform social and discursive actions. My discussion was placed in the theoretical context of language as social practice and a complex constellation of situated meanings; and seen from a feminist linguistic perspective that engages critically with questions of 'gendering' or 'doing gender' and with the consequences of doing so variably in different settings.

In seeing gender as enacted in discourse, in variable and sometimes contradictory ways, I have considered examples from debates in the British press, where what is assumed and implied about 'the female voice as emotional voice' is as meaningful as what is actually publicly articulated by the participants. Although both women and men may draw on the symbolic category of 'the female as emotional', this gendered stereotype can both shape interaction and create asymmetrical positions for women and men. In terms of shaping interaction, I have suggested that participants in argument often 'argue gender' in addition to putting forward their argument positions on a topic, and may also strategically draw on a combination of gendered interactional styles. In terms of position and power asymmetries, women are often faced with a 'double-bind' situation: a process of self-accountability and justification for their views, actions and behaviours. This is reflected in women's significant conversational work, at times extensive and carefully balanced. It is also implied in discourses about the value of feminist pedagogies and the value of female (and feminist) voices in the political debate about war and security – areas which I considered briefly in concluding my discussion.

I have suggested that, to theorise the female voice in public contexts, we need to focus on discourses in different localised settings and

communities of practice; we also need to consider the interactional
goals of participants in public arguments, and the interpersonal and
power relationships between them; and we need not lose sight of the
subtle and complex links between discourses and women's and men's
social positions. These objectives are likely to be most productively
achieved through interdisciplinary frameworks and projects that ask
new questions, produce new knowledge and encourage new applications
of knowledge in this area.

References

Boler, M. (1998) 'Towards a politics of emotion: Bridging the chasm between
    theory and practice'. In *APA Newsletter on Feminism and Philosophy*, vol. 98 (1)
    (Fall, 1998).
Boler, M. (1999) *Feeling Power: Emotions and Education* (New York: Routledge).
Brody, L. (1997) 'Gender and emotion: Beyond stereotypes'. *Journal of Social
    Issues*, vol. 53 (2), pp. 369–394.
Brody, L. R. and Hall, J. A. (1993) 'Gender and emotion'. In M. Lewis and J. Haviland
    (eds) *Handbook of Emotions*, pp. 447–460 (New York: Guilford Press).
Bunting, M. (2001) 'Women and War'. *The Guardian*, 20 September 2001.
Cameron, D. (ed.) (1998) *The Feminist Critique of Language: A Reader*, 2nd edition
    (London: Routledge).
Coates, J. (ed.) (1998). *Language and Gender: A Reader* (Oxford: Blackwell).
Cohn, C. (1987) 'Sex and death in the rational world of defense intellectuals'.
    Signs, vol. 12 (4), pp. 687–728.
Cohn, C. (1993) 'War, wimps and women'. In M. Cooke and A. Woolacott (eds)
    Gendering War Talk, pp. 227–246 (Princeton, NJ: Princeton University Press).
Cohn, C. and Ruddick, S. (2004) 'A feminist ethical perspective on weapons of
    mass destruction'. In Sohail Hashmi and Steven Lee (eds) *Ethics and Weapons of
    Mass Destruction: Religious and Secular Perspectives*, pp. 405–435 (New York:
    Cambridge University Press).
Edwards, D. (1999) 'Emotion discourse'. *Culture and Psychology*, vol. 5 (3),
    pp. 271–291.
Fairclough, N. (1992) *Discourse and Social Change* (London: Polity Press).
Fairclough, N. (1995) *Media Discourse* (London: Edward Arnold).
Fischer, A. (1993) 'Sex differences in emotionality: Fact or stereotype'. *Feminism
    and Psychology*, 3, pp. 303–318.
Fischer, A. (ed.) (2000) *Gender and Emotion—Social Psychological Perspectives*
    (Cambridge: Cambridge University Press).
Galasinski, D. (2004) *Men and the Language of Emotions* (Basingstoke: Palgrave).
Harré, R. (1986) *The Social Construction of Emotions* (Oxford: Blackwell).
Hearn, J. and Parkin, W. (1988) 'Women, men, and leadership: A critical review
    of assumptions, practices, and change in the industrialized nations'. In
    N. Adler and D. Izraeli (eds) *Women in Management Worldwide*, pp. 17–40
    (London: M.E. Sharpe).
Hekman, S. (1994) 'The feminist critique of rationality'. In *The Polity Reader in
    Gender Studies*, pp. 50–61 (Cambridge: Polity).

Holland, P. (1996) 'When a woman reads the news'. In P. Marris and S. Thornham (eds) *Media Studies – A Reader*, pp. 438–445 (Edinburgh: Edinburgh University Press).

Holmes, J. (2000) 'Women at work: Analysing women's talk in New Zealand workplaces'. *Australian Review of Applied Linguistics (ARAL)*, 22 (2), pp. 1–17.

Holmes, J. and Marra, M. (2004) 'Relational practice in the workplace: Women's talk or gendered discourse?'. *Language in Society*, 33, pp. 377–398.

Holmes, J. and Schnurr, S. (2004) '*Doing femininity at work: More than just relational practice*'. Paper presented at IGALA3 conference 5–6 June 2004, Cornell University, NY.

LaFrance, M. and Banaji, M. (1992) 'Toward a reconsideration of the gender-emotion relationship'. In M. Clark (ed.) *Review of Personality and Social Psychology* (vol. 14) (Beverly Hills, CA: Sage).

Litosseliti, L. (2002a) 'The discursive construction of morality and gender: Investigating public and private arguments'. In S. Benor, M. Rose, D. Sharma, J. Sweetland and Q. Zhang (eds) *Gendered Practices in Language*, pp. 45–63 (Stanford: Center for the Study of Language and Information, Stanford University).

Litosseliti, L. (2002b) 'Head to Head: The construction of morality and gender identity in newspaper arguments'. In L. Litosseliti and J. Sunderland (eds) *Discourse Analysis and Gender Identity*. 'Discourse Approaches to Politics, Society and Culture', vol 2, pp. 129–148 (Amsterdam: Benjamins).

Litosseliti, L. and Sunderland, J. (2002) (eds) *Discourse Analysis and Gender Identity*, 'Discourse Approaches to Politics, Society and Culture', vol. 2 (Amsterdam: Benjamins).

Litosseliti, L. (2006) *Gender and Language: Theory and Practice* (London: Arnold).

Livia, A. (1995) ' "I ought to throw a Buick at you": Fictional representations of butch/femme speech'. In K. Hall and M. Bucholtz (eds) *Gender Articulated*, pp. 245–277 (New York: Routledge).

Lutz, C. (1990) 'Engendered emotion: Gender, power, and the rhetoric of emotional control in American discourse'. In C. Lutz and L. Abu-Lughod (eds) *Language and the Politics of Emotion*, pp. 69–91 (Cambridge: Cambridge University Press).

Lutz, C. and Abu-Lughod, L. (1990) (eds) *Language and the Politics of Emotion* (Cambridge: Cambridge University Press).

Martin-Rojo, L. and Gomez Esteban, C. (2002) 'Discourse at work: When women take on the role of manager'. In G. Weiss and R. Wodak (eds) *Critical Discourse Analysis: Theory and Interdisciplinarity* (London: Palgrave Macmillan).

McElhinny, B. (1998) ' "I don't smile much anymore": Affect, gender and the discourse of Pittsburgh police officers'. In J. Coates (ed.) *Language and Gender: A Reader*, pp. 309–327 (Oxford: Blackwell).

Mills, S. (2002) '*Third Wave Feminist Linguistics and the Analysis of Sexism*': plenary talk at IGALA2 conference, 12–14 April 2002, Lancaster, UK. Also as pre-print in Discourse Analysis Online [http://www.shu.ac.uk/daol/].

Oatley, K. and Jenkins, J. (1996) *Understanding Emotions* (Cambridge, MA: Blackwell Publishers).

Ruddick, S. (1996) 'Reason's "femininity" '. In N. Goldberger, J. Tarule, B. Clinchy and M. Belenky (eds) *Knowledge, Difference and Power*, pp. 248–273 (New York: Basic Books).

Shaw, S. (2002) *Language and Gender in the House of Commons*. PhD thesis, University of London.

Shields, S. A. (1987) 'Women, men and the dilemma of emotion'. In P. Shaver and C. Hendrick (eds) *Review of Personality and Social Psychology*, vol. 7 (Beverly Hills, CA: Sage).

Shields, S. A. (1995) 'The role of emotion beliefs and values in gender development'. In N. Eisenberg (ed.) *Review of Personality and Social Psychology*, vol. 15, pp. 212–232 (Thousand Oaks, CA: Sage).

Shields, S. A. (2000) 'Thinking about gender, thinking about theory: Gender and emotional experience'. In A. Fischer (ed.) *Gender and Emotion—Social Psychological Perspectives* (Cambridge: Cambridge University Press).

Stubbe, M., Holmes, J., Vine, B. and Marra, M. (2000) 'Forget Mars and Venus, let's get back to earth: Challenging stereotypes in the workplace'. In J. Holmes (ed.) *Gendered Speech in Social Context: Perspectives from Gown & Town*, pp. 231–258 (Wellington: Victoria University Press).

Talbot, M. (1998) *Language and Gender* (London: Polity).

Tannen, D. (1990) *You Just Don't Understand: Women and Men in Conversation* (London: Virago).

Tannen, D. (1998) *The Argument Culture* (New York: Virago).

Walsh, C. (2001) *Gender and Discourse: Language and Power in Politics, the Church and Organisations* (London: Routledge).

Webster, W. (1990) *Not a Man to Match Her* (London: Women's Press).

White, G. (1990) 'Moral discourse and the rhetoric of emotions'. In C. Lutz and L. Abu-Lughod (eds) *Language and the Politics of Emotion*, pp. 46–68 (Cambridge: Cambridge University Press).

Wodak, R. (2002) 'Interdisciplinarity, Gender Studies and CDA: Gender Mainstreaming and the European Union': plenary talk at IGALA2 conference, 12–14 April 2002, Lancaster, UK.

Part II
Researching the Female Voice in Public Contexts

4
Gender and Performance Anxiety at Academic Conferences

Sara Mills
Sheffield Hallam University, UK

Introduction

This chapter analyses the factors which lead to some women experiencing 'stage fright' or 'performance anxiety' when speaking in public, particularly in the presentation of papers at academic conferences.[1] Performance anxiety is often considered something which women are more likely to experience than men when speaking to an audience. It is considered that the discursive rules operating in this setting are more in line with stereotypically masculine norms of speech. It is my contention that particular types of gender identity and preconceptions about the masculine nature of public speaking may be activated or challenged in the process of giving academic papers. Thus, women do not necessarily suffer from performance anxiety, and indeed many older women do not suffer from stage fright at all. But those who do may have internalised some sense of the discourse considered appropriate to the context and consider themselves unable to draw on this masculine discourse with ease. Some of the reasons for this may be: their marginal position within the university; their assessment of their expertise or status in relation to the audience; their assessment of their own personality and whether they feel that this is open to change. What seems to play a role in performance anxiety is the degree to which the individual has internalised or resisted stereotypical views of the gendered nature of the public sphere and public speaking. In order to test out these ideas, in this chapter, I discuss the results of a questionnaire which I sent to academics to investigate the factors which they considered to contribute to performance anxiety.

The impetus for this chapter was an incident which I observed at an academic conference, where a female colleague who is generally confident, sometimes to the point of being overbearing, gave a paper to a small group of feminist theorists. From being initially confident, she gradually became more incoherent, to the point that she seemed unable to read her notes and became increasingly unable to pronounce the title of her paper which was the focus of much of her extempore introduction. She eventually recovered her composure, but after the paper had been given several colleagues discussed with me their own experiences of stage fright and the contexts where this was most likely to occur. From this discussion and from subsequent discussions with other female academics, it seemed clear to me that performance anxiety is the result of an assessment of the situation (often a mistaken assessment) and not some inbuilt weakness on the part of the individual, although that is often how it is experienced by the individual. Most of the people I discussed this with stated that they feared that their level of expertise was less than their audience and that even when they had prepared well, they did not feel that they could talk authoritatively. Some of the women with whom I discussed this were fairly senior within their universities and were researchers with international reputations. Furthermore, another female colleague discussed with me the fact that at a conference she had experienced a hostile response to a paper that she had given – male colleagues had aggressively asked her questions in a way which she felt aimed to destroy her argument. She felt personally undermined, and her confidence was so shaken by the experience that she subsequently felt very uneasy about giving papers at all. These two anecdotes crystallised for me the way that an individual's projections about an audience's response conditions the way that one performs in a particular context. Gender seemed to play a role in this complex dialogic process and it is the complexities of the role of gender at an indexical and at a stereotypical level which form the main focus of this chapter.

New models of gender

In order to analyse the role of gender in performance anxiety, it is necessary to consider briefly the theoretical advances in feminist linguistics which have changed the way that gender is conceptualised (see Editor's Introduction). Rather than analysing males and females as separate groups, and making sweeping generalisations about the way that all women speak in public, there has been a move to a more 'local' way of analysing gender and a less monolithic model of what 'women' do in language (Baxter, 2003; Eckert and McConnell-Ginet, 2003; Holmes and Meyerhoff, 2003). Thus, what feminist linguists are concerned with now is the way that women and men construct their gender identities within particular contexts. What has also become a focus of attention in recent feminist linguistics is recognising that gender is not coterminous with sex, but a type of 'coding' of styles and practices which individuals may draw on or resist in the course of their interactions; in the process of negotiating with these styles, individuals construct their gendered identity.

Furthermore, Butler suggests that 'the materiality of sex is constructed through a ritualised repetition of norms' (Butler, 1993: p. x). Thus, gender identity is a repeated performance of the normative behaviour associated with a particular sex. What we need to add to Butler's model of gender is the way that these norms are contested and/or affirmed in interaction; they are not fixed but hypothesised by individuals depending on their assessment of the context (Mills, 2003).

Whilst there has been a move to more performative and contextualised understandings of the way gender identity is constructed, that does not mean that it is impossible to make generalisations about the way gender works. Many women experience difficulty speaking in public, and this may be partly due to what is perceived as allowable for women to do. It is only in recent times that women have begun speaking within the public sphere in large numbers within both business and academic contexts; therefore, it is not surprising if some women still view speaking in public as a masculine practice.

Masculinity and public speaking

There is nothing intrinsically masculine about the public sphere; but it does seem to be indirectly gender-indexed, that is the styles of speech prevalent within the public sphere are indirectly associated with speech styles associated with masculinity. Giving academic papers is part of one's role within an institution as a lecturer; as such it is an activity which is scrutinised by others and which is rule governed, and which may or may not accrue benefit to the individual if they give what is seen as a good performance. In a sense, individuals can accrue some social capital to themselves, in Bourdieu's (1991) terms, by performing well and giving effective academic papers. Thus, the process of giving academic papers takes place within an environment where power circulates in that there is a:

> set of resources and actions which are available to speakers and which can be used more or less successfully depending on who the speakers are and what kind of speech situation they are in.
>
> (Thornborrow, 2002: 8)

Giving an academic paper is not a simple matter of transmitting evidence or information to an audience; it is also a question of displaying professional competence, claiming expertise for oneself, ranking oneself in relation to others, establishing a place in the hierarchy of the professional body or academic community and at the same time it is also a matter of producing and presenting oneself as a particular type of gendered individual. To give a competent paper, you should show yourself able to speak fluently and confidently without hesitation and nervousness, you should be able to structure an argument, and show that you have done the necessary research and can critique this body of work in order to construct your argument, which builds on this research but makes some claim to originality and authority – you must be able to demonstrate that you can deal with difficult, intellectually challenging subject matter. Therefore, in giving a paper you are proving that you have the authority to assert by positioning yourself within a research field (demonstrating your familiarity with and mastery of a body of research), and at the same time you are proving that you are authoritative by speaking in an authoritative way (making claims directly, not using epistemic modality such as 'perhaps' or 'might', not hedging on the force of a claim, speaking clearly and not visibly suffering from nerves), that is speaking in the way that is approved of within this kind of context. In addition, not only do you have to prove that you can read from a script, OHP or power point, but you have to show that you can respond in an unscripted way to the 'grilling' by members of the audience after the paper has been given. And perhaps it is this feedback on the performance or your assessment of what that feedback might be like which informs one's sense of one's position in relation to a research community and one's ability to speak authoritatively. Since it is an assessment of your ability, based on a projection of others' assessments of you, hypothesised stereotypes of gender necessarily play a role (Mills, 2003).

The values and style associated with public speaking are indexically linked with those associated with masculinity. Thus assertiveness, confidence, verbal skill, verbal play and authority are all values which seem to index both successful public speaking and stereotypical masculinity (Johnson and Meinhof, 1997). Even the pitch of the voice is seen to contribute to authoritativeness since, as Kiesling (2003) argues, low pitch tends to index indirectly stereotypical masculinity and power. But it should be stressed that this is a stereotype of what masculine speech is like; many men feel just as uncomfortable with these speech norms as some women do. The stereotype should not be seen as something that all men draw on when constructing themselves as gendered individuals, but neither should it be seen as having no effect whatsoever. As Bourdieu (1991) has shown, we hypothesise these norms of femininity and masculinity, and even when we do not model our own behaviour on them, they nevertheless inform our judgements about what is appropriate within a particular context. The functions of masculinity and femininity differ from context to context, but individuals will draw on these hypothesised norms, assuming that in some sense the stereotypes exist outside themselves (Mills, 2003). If we assume that:

> identity is something that people do during the business of everyday interaction ... the kinds of identification that are resources for social action are available, and have their nature defined, through systems of meaning which have cultural and ideological histories, then the type of identity which is constructed for women and which women construct for themselves during the process of giving an academic paper is one which is forged out of a history of association of public speaking with masculine discursive norms.
>
> (Weatherall and Gallois, 2003: 495)

Women therefore have to make choices about how to present themselves, whether they adopt the masculinist norms of speaking, or try to adopt such norms and fail through behaving in a stereotypically feminine way – that is, suffering from performance anxiety.

One's assessment of the success of a paper is often based on one's sense of how others respond to the paper; this notion of a 'discourse of approval' seems to play a vital role (Baxter, 2003). Therefore, the questions or informal discussions with individuals at the end are important in constructing a sense of whether our presentation has been successful. Holmes' (1992) research showed an interesting difference in the way that men and women in audiences expressed their approval/disapproval of presentations; whilst there seemed to be little difference in her data in the percentage of supportive statements which were made by women and men in audiences, there seemed to be a significant difference in the number and kind of aggressive questions which were asked at the end of papers by members of the audience, with males asking more aggressive questions than women. Keinpointner (1997) argues that such aggressive questioning should be seen as acceptable within an academic context, because only through such behaviour can one refine an argument. However, such questioning may be interpreted as aggressive, and as aimed at undermining you as an individual rather than as constructive criticism of the academic content.

There is an assumption amongst both people writing about performance anxiety and the academics that I questioned that stage fright is necessarily problematic and that what we need to do is to try and eliminate it, because it displays lack of confidence (Antion, 2004; Barkley, 2004; Janof, 2004). This only holds if we assume that in the public sphere we have to appear invulnerable, and that the type of discourse which is appropriate in the public sphere is one which is smooth, seamless and polished. This seems to me a particularly masculine view of the talk associated with the public sphere and it seems to find its epitome in the speech of Tony Blair, the British Prime Minister. Fairclough (2000) has shown that a great deal of effort is expended on presenting Tony Blair as invulnerable and verbally confident, through coaching by aides. Many have remarked that one of Tony Blair's greatest attributes is his ability to speak well. Shaw (2002; also Chapter 5) has shown that women MPs seem to be significantly ill at ease with the discursive conventions of the House of Commons, most notably when they have to assert themselves during debates. The speech styles prevalent in the House of Commons tend to be extremely aggressive, but the level of aggression is highly ritualised and constrained. Thus, within the House of Commons the type of speech style which is seen to be appropriate is one which seems to correlate very closely with a stereotypically masculine form of speech.

This dominance of masculine discursive norms also seems to hold true in other public contexts, for example in the courtroom where confident language seems to index certain attributes such as honesty and integrity (Cotterill, 2003). Walsh (2001) has shown how the influx of women workers into a range of professions has led to changes in the types of speech style considered appropriate in certain contexts. But she asserts that rather than more feminine speech styles being used, women priests and MPs have considered it necessary for their own professional identity to take on wholesale the speech norms of the environment in which they work. If they try to use stereotypically feminine norms of caring and co-operation, they then constitute, Walsh argues, a kind of private sphere within the public sphere. McElhinney (1998), in her analysis of women police officers, has shown that they have to adopt the masculinist speech norms associated with their particular profession in order to be seen as professional. She argues that:

> institutions are...often gendered in ways that delimit who can properly participate in them and/or how such participation can take place...Workplaces are gendered both by the numerical predominance of one sex within them and by the cultural interpretation of given types of work which, in conjunction with cultural norms and interpretations of gender, dictate who is understood as best suited for different sorts of employment.
>
> (McElhinney, 1998: 309)

She goes on to argue that:

> because masculinity is not referentially or directly marked by behaviours and attitudes but indexically linked to them (in mediated non-exclusive probabilistic ways) female police officers can interpret behaviours that are normatively or frequently understood as masculine...as simply "the way we need to act to do our job".
>
> (McElhinney, 1998: 322)

That is to say, the link between assertive non-emotional forms of speaking are linked in a non-indexical way to masculine norms of speech. Thus, when the women officers use these speech styles they see them as displaying professionalism, rather than as displaying masculinity. Here the discursive norms for professionalism and masculinity are closely correlated.

However, although in the case of Parliament and the police force it seems as if the discursive norms are fairly static and unchanging, within other areas of the public sphere there do seem to be changes, because of the appointment of women to positions of power within organisations or because of changes in ethos. For example, within the business environment, workplaces can be more or less masculine or feminine and this can condition the speech norms which are judged appropriate (Holmes and Stubbe, 2003; see also Chapter 13). Within more feminine workplaces, more relaxed, feminine speech styles are considered acceptable and, as Holmes and Stubbe (2003) argue, there may be a leakage of the social world into the world of work, so that the workplace appears more hospitable to women.[2] However, although there is a tendency for less masculine forms of speech style and comportment in those workplaces considered feminine, Holmes and Stubbe state that there is no neat division in the styles used, as women and men:

> seem to draw creatively on a wide range of discursive resources to perform their roles as effective managers in these differently gendered workplace contexts.
>
> (Holmes and Stubbe, 2003: 593)

In a similar way, Kendall (2003: 604) argues that:

> women in positions of institutional authority who linguistically downplay status differences when enacting their authority are not reluctant to exercise authority, nor are they expressing powerlessness; instead they are exercising and constituting their authority by speaking in ways that accomplish work-related goals while maintaining the faces of their interlocutors.

Thus, feminine speech norms here do not necessarily signal powerlessness. Women may simply find that the most effective way for them to operate within a work environment is to use feminine speech norms, because of the way 'masculine' speech is viewed.

What many of these analysts fail to examine is the way that feminine or masculine discourse is judged by others. Thimm *et al.* (2003) have shown that competence in the workplace is often associated with males, whilst females are judged on their co-operativeness. If that is the case, then women will be judged negatively if they use masculine norms, and this may lead to them finding a particular discursive style ineffective in a particular context. They may then choose to use a different style. As Kendall (2003: 604) asserts:

> Women and men do not generally choose linguistic options for the purpose of creating masculine and feminine identities; instead, they draw upon gendered linguistic strategies to perform pragmatic and

interactional functions of language and thus constitute roles in a gendered way.

Within the business environment it is quite clear that a range of speech styles are considered appropriate depending on the norms and ethos of the particular environment, but within the context of the academic paper, there seems to be little room for manoeuvre. At some feminist conferences, a relaxation of the norms of strict masculinist presentation became the norm during the 1980s and 1990s, but most papers given now to large audiences follow the conventions of a read-from script paper followed on occasions by aggressive questioning.

Strong women speakers

Rather than assuming that women are simply more prone to stage fright because of an essential difference between men and women, I take a social constructionist viewpoint, arguing that in certain contexts gender plays a particular role. This may be due less to individual predispositions, than to the fact that the act of speaking in public and claiming expertise in a subject has in the past been coded as masculine; that is, gender indirectly indexes these elements. Because of this gendering of the context, gender may have an impact on individuals when they transgress traditional gender roles – for example, women who speak in public. However, this gendering of the context may not always have an impact; it is important to recognise that many women do in fact enjoy speaking in public and do not suffer from performance anxiety. Bucholtz (1999) has criticised some earlier feminist research as 'good girl research', arguing that it has studied normatively white middle-class women being normatively feminine. Bucholtz's argument is that we should study groups of women behaving in other than stereotypical ways, and there is now a wave of research which focuses on women who do not abide by feminine discursive norms (see Eckert and McConnell-Ginet, 2003; Holmes and Meyerhoff, 2003). For example, Harness Goodwin (2001, 2003) has analysed the way that girls in school playgrounds can be assertive and verbally aggressive particularly when the activity is one in which they have expertise and where they wish to exclude other participants. Research into the speech norms of Afro-American women has shown that they do not appear to be constructed in their speech in the same way that stereotypically white middle-class women have been described as behaving (Bucholtz, 1996; Morgan, 1999; see also Chapter 12). In my own work, I have been interested in the way that many women do not in fact appear to find it difficult to speak in the public sphere or to be assertive themselves verbally (Mills, 1999). Women like the British ex-Prime Minister Margaret Thatcher, American Secretary of State Condaleezza Rice and Pakistani ex-Prime Minister Bennazir Bhutto have challenged the convention that women are uncomfortable speaking within the public sphere, and politicians such as Irish EU representative Mary Robinson have reconfigured the aggressive masculine mode of political speaking by combining forcefulness with a soft-spoken style. Halberstam (1998) in her work on 'masculine' women has analysed the way that some women do not simply accept the stereotypical norms of behaviour, but rather challenge them by consciously adopting behaviour conventionally associated with masculinity and with men. In sum, there has been a trend in language and gender research to focus on women who adopt masculine norms in speech and thereby challenge the notion that these are in fact masculine norms and that women are necessarily associated with lack of assertiveness.

Gender and confidence

As I have argued above, speaking in public generally involves claiming competence for oneself and projecting oneself as confident. Confidence itself is a nebulous concept, even though the way that it manifests itself physically upon the body makes it appear very material. Many of the respondents to the questionnaire remarked that they either did or did not feel that they had confidence as if it were an attribute of their personality which they were born with, rather than a positive evaluation of oneself which develops through an assessment of one's position in relation to others. For example, one of the female academics I questioned stated:

> I am a totally non-public person (a near-recluse, I think!) – my ideal communication situation is one to one. I know I could approach absolutely anyone on that basis.

Once one has made this assessment of the type of personality that one is, and the communicative context in which one is comfortable, it may lead to one not feeling confident outside that sphere. Another female academic I questioned stated that she found giving papers difficult:

> Because I am an introvert rather than an extrovert and so find it difficult projecting myself. This is probably a perceptual problem.

I can probably talk in public much better than I think I can, and sometimes I know I have been very successful. I always prefer talking to smaller groups in more intimate settings, where I feel much more 'at home'.

This use of the phrase 'at home' is particularly telling here, suggesting that this woman finds herself in a context which in some ways clashes with the norms associated with being a woman, or at least conforming to a particular stereotype of feminine behaviour. But interestingly, rather than seeing this as a social or institutional problem, she considers this to be an individual problem of her 'introversion'.

Baxter (2003) has shown that the confidence of the students that she studied seemed to be constructed in a curiously circular process whereby those who were considered popular students were approved of by others and were consequently given the time and space to express their opinions; because of this approval they assumed that they were popular and thus behaved confidently. Those who were not popular were also those who were not confident, again in a circular process. A similar process seems to be at work in the giving of academic papers, and it is this circularity of the feedback and one's assumptions of the approval or disapproval of one's audience which seems crucial in the process of deciding whether or not you 'are' a confident person in general.

This notion that confidence is experienced when we make a positive evaluation of our audience's assessment of us leads to a reconceptualising of power relations so that we can see them, as Thornborrow puts it, as emerging 'in the interplay between participants' locally constructed, discursive identities and their institutional status' (Thornborrow, 2002: 1). Thus, it is clear that neither gender identity nor confidence are fixed and part of our personalities, but are worked out in the process of assessing the local norms and judgements of ourselves which we consider to be in play within particular contexts.

Discussion of the data

I sent out 25 copies of a questionnaire by e-mail attachment, to male and female academics and asked them to forward it to other colleagues. This questionnaire aimed to elicit responses about whether the person experienced performance anxiety and, if so, how it manifested itself and what factors led to the anxiety. It also asked questions to those who did not experience anxiety about why they felt that this was the case.

I received back 20 responses from females and 14 from males.[3] My initial assumption was that I would not find a great deal of difference between the responses of male and female academics, largely because within the research paradigm current in gender and language studies there is great emphasis on women and men within similar contexts performing in similar ways (Eckert and McConnel-Ginet, 2003; Holmes and Meyerhoff, 2003). I considered that if I did find a gender difference, it would not be about who suffered from performance anxiety but rather in the way women and men conceptualised it. In fact, I did find that there was a great deal of difference in the ways that performance anxiety was experienced and conceptualised: female academics were much more willing to admit that they suffered from it, whilst male academics minimised the extent to which they experienced perform-ance anxiety and several of them suggested that they did not suffer from it at all.

The two key factors which seem to contribute to performance anxiety as reported in the questionnaires are assessment of power relations (principally an assessment of the expertise of audience in relation to the speaker) and an assessment of the person's right to speak in that context. Gender seems to play a role albeit indirectly in the process whereby people make assessments of others' judgements of their authority.

I will discuss the responses of the female academics first and then go on to analyse the male academics. I had assumed that those women who had received positive encouragement from family and friends in relation to public speaking would find giving academic papers easy, but one of the female respondents stated:

> Despite always being told I'm wonderful in front of an audience by my parents, being advised how to handle such nerve-racking situations, being told that I come across to others as a very confident person, being told not to worry because it will be fine if I just relax I still cannot shake off the nerves, self-consciousness, worry, etc.

Here there seems to be a conflict between what this person considers to be an inherently stressful situation, others' assessments of her ability to deal with that situation and her own ability to perform.

Nearly all of the women academics remarked that greater experience led to a decrease in performance anxiety and the older academics were more prone to suggest that they did not suffer from stage fright. However, one woman stated that she found chairing small groups more difficult than giving papers:

> When I am chairing the small groups I am involved in I have learned that I cannot control the contributions of others but I can do preparation into making sure that there are appropriate places for the contributions of others; this minimises participant frustration. Lately I have not been as anxious about chairing meetings. This has been chiefly about doing some thinking about what it is I can and cannot control and not deluding myself that I have it in my power to control the outcome of a meeting. However I need to have confidence in the formal structure of the meeting and the soundness of the principles underpinning it to be free of anxiety. When I thought that I would fail if I hadn't controlled everything I was more nervous because I was fearful that others would blow MY enterprise off course (which of course they would because why should they either identify or identify with my priorities?). I find most of the meetings I chair exciting because I am less frightened of surprises than I used to be.

It is particularly interesting that this academic is concerned about keeping everything under control, and that she characterises her colleagues as not necessarily in sympathy with her aims to the point that she is worried about her enterprise being 'blown off course'. Despite the fact that this is a small-group setting, the lexical set that she draws on is significant, for she uses words such as 'frightened', 'fearful', 'anxiety', 'fail', 'nervous' and 'surprises' in the same context as 'power', 'control' and 'confidence', suggesting that speaking authoritatively may provoke feelings of inadequacy, particularly in contexts where you hypothesise that colleagues might be 'frustrated' with you. It is also significant that this academic cannot see that her colleagues should 'identify with [her] priorities'. An interesting parallel can be drawn to the comments of another woman academic who stated that she suffered from performance anxiety:

> Particularly where there are very large audiences such as a formal lecture theatre or auditorium where there are ranked seats, or if I know I am going to address senior people. I sometimes find that my mouth goes very dry and that I do become extremely aware of my situation. I imagine doing something disastrously wrong which will 'blow my cover' as a serious academic!!

This notion of being exposed, or of others discovering that you are not a 'real' academic, runs through many of the comments made in the questionnaires by female academics and highlights the fact that many of them feel that their position is marginal within the institution.

Many of the women remarked that the cause of their nervousness was their colleagues' judgement of them; for example, one respondent whose first language is not English stated:

> I know I am in some way evaluated by my colleagues. I feel they expect too much from me and I think they overestimate my capabilities – or probably I underestimate my capabilities. I am afraid of making mistakes in English or of being banal and tend to avoid situations where I must run the risk.

This concern about not measuring up to others' assessments occurs in another female academic's comments:

> For research talks, I think the worry is about how my peer group will receive the work – so far, I've always had very positive receptions so this isn't based on any past bad experiences. Also, I worry about whether I will do justice to the research in my explanation of it (although, in reality, I'm better prepared for research talks than for any other public speaking).

What is significant here is that these women recognise that their assessment of their own competence does not match reality; however, that does not prevent them from continuing to doubt their abilities and assuming that their colleagues negatively evaluate their work.

Many of the women comment on a number of factors from their personal histories which might account for their experiencing performance anxiety. One woman academic stated:

> I have never really enjoyed public speaking though it has got much easier over the years... In recent times my worst experiences have been chairing meetings when I have had to deal with aggressive colleagues. I do not like conflict situations – either in private or public and my instinct is to run away! However, what is especially strange and characteristic about my response is that it appears to be invisible to the outside world! People always say I look calm and in control; I give little indication of what I feel – even though on occasions I have been close to passing out! I think there are also

issues of 'not speaking out' in my family background. I have never been listened to at home and have little confidence that people will want to listen to what I say! My class background also makes me uncomfortable speaking in a professional register: my speaking and writing registers are very different and I feel weird using jargon speaking – though sometimes I can 'speak' this 'language'.

Here, there is a perception that her class position clashes with her adopting 'a professional register', as does her family history which seems to undermine her claims to speaking in her own right. These factors are brought to account for her nervousness in front of a public audience.

A further element which was seen to contribute to performance anxiety for many of these women was the use of technical equipment, which often indirectly indexes masculine expertise. One female academic stated:

Our first year lectures are video-linked – we teach in one lecture theatre and it is transmitted at the same time to a remote lecture theatre since we don't have a single lecture theatre big enough for the class. I dread having to do these lectures – partly because of worries that the equipment may not work (the technicians always disappear after the equipment has been set up), but also because I hate having to use anything more than an OHP when lecturing. It's also very uncomfortable having to lecture to a remote audience since you don't get the usual feedback (I can see them on a monitor, but it's not the same as having them in front of you).

Once a particular activity or context has been indirectly indexed as masculine, women may find that they experience anxiety when engaging in it. Thus, as in many of the other responses, this technical apparatus prevents the interaction being like a small group discussion, which seems to be a more feminine private sphere interaction. Tellingly, one female academic stated that she tried to reconceptualise the public sphere so that it was more like the private sphere:

I try to persuade myself that it is going to be an enjoyable experience, and that I know the people I am talking to. In other words, I try to envisage how I feel when I am talking one-to-one or to someone I know, and transfer this to the public situation. In the right mood, this works well!

What is striking about these responses is that all of the women responded at some length, giving details of the symptoms that they experienced and reasons why they felt that they experienced them. Many of them discussed explicitly their feelings of marginalisation and fear in relation to their colleagues. This is in marked contrast to the comments made by the male academics I questioned. The male respondents' comments were much more terse than those of the female academics and they used humour more. One remarked that the only solution to performance anxiety was to 'prepare good content'. Another remarked that he did not suffer from stage fright because of his 'former career as a stand-up comedian . . . failure holds no terrors'. Another male academic stated that he did not suffer from anxiety because 'some unkind people (my wife) might say it is because I have an ego the size of a house'. Here, this respondent, though attributing this opinion to his wife and therefore avoiding claiming it himself, can assert his own ego stability, at the same time as indirectly asserting that performance anxiety only affects those whose 'ego size' is less than his. Several simply stated that they suffered no anxiety at all, or if they did it was only at the level which everyone experienced. Another stated that he did not suffer from much anxiety because he had experience of speaking in public contexts, particularly within his trade union:

> familiarity with the experience overcomes the fear. You know you've done it before and that it won't kill you! Focusing on your 'message' helps a lot.

Another minimised the experience of anxiety, suggesting that the only problem that he had was occasionally not remembering words:

> Mostly I don't have problems, but I see that people unused to speaking in public do have them. So I suppose habit, practice, deliberately acting out a role, tricks one picks up such as not moving one's feet (and other conscious control over signs of insecurity) and sweeping the audience with a glance so they all think you're looking at them individually.

This seems to be asserting a strong identity for himself at the same time as drawing attention to the fact that his confidence is in fact an act, a set of 'tricks' that he has mastered.

Those men who did admit to experiencing performance anxiety still suggested that it should not be seen negatively. One male academic admitted that:

> After the 'exposure' of an event I feel a desire to go and hide and look desperately for positive feedback. I can agonise for weeks about having said 'the wrong thing'.

Nevertheless, he commented that the questionnaire was 'too negative' as:

> Public speaking can also bring a sense of exhilaration of well being, of self-confidence and enjoyment.

Several other male academics agreed that nervousness should not be seen as a problem; one stated that, 'It isn't overwhelming and I associate it with being focused and ready to speak.' Another said:

> I don't see [these symptoms] as problems. I think it's natural to feel keyed up before speaking in public.

This minimising of anxiety surprised me and so did the male academics' minimising of the physical reactions associated with performance anxiety. Whereas female academics discussing the symptoms described them in great detail, most of the male respondents stated that they suffered only from occasional hesitation. It seemed important for the males to represent themselves as confident and not suffering overly from performance anxiety, whereas the women academics seemed relatively untroubled at representing themselves as experiencing potentially humiliating symptoms.

Conclusions

In a sense, these responses surprised me, as I was expecting that the differences between males and females would be minimal. I had expected women and men perhaps to conceptualise their experience of performance anxiety differently, but I had not expected such a polarisation of response. The males seem to be presenting themselves as stereotypically masculine individuals – confident, at ease and even exhilarated by public speaking (only two of them admitted to experiencing performance anxiety). Thus, it seems that either the males in this study did not suffer from anxiety to the same extent as the females, or they were not prepared to admit that they suffered anxiety, possibly because confidence in the public sphere seems so integral to the construction of masculine identity. It seems from this small sample that the women questioned, on the whole, were more likely to interpret the situation of hostile questioning as personally threatening, or were more likely to view the audience reaction as potentially hostile. It may well also be the case that women consider that they are 'allowed' to talk about inadequacy, because of the discursive norms of femininity which in some ways 'approve' of self-revelation and the discussion of short-comings, whereas it is more difficult for men to admit to inadequacy and lack of confidence.

It is clear from these responses that confidence is a circular process whereby you judge your audience's assessment of your performance, and there may well be gendered frameworks which influence the assess-ment of your own value and confidence. However, the construction of gender is a process rather than something achieved once and for all, and there were significant numbers of the older women respondents who stated that they felt that, with experience, they had become more confident in public speaking. Thus, whilst it is clear that gender does play a role in our experiencing of performance anxiety, gender itself manifests itself or is displayed to others in different ways dependent on contextual factors.

What seems to play a major role in the variation in gender performance is the degree to which hypothesised stereotypes of gendered behaviour within particular gendered contexts lead to assumptions about our own position within the academic community and within the public sphere.

Notes

1. I use the terms 'performance anxiety' and 'stage fright' interchangeably, although I feel that there are subtle differences between them. I feel that the term 'stage fright' is slightly more derogatory than 'performance anxiety' and seems to be suggesting that experiencing difficulties in speaking in public is due to personal inadequacy and weakness rather than being due to more general, higher-level structural problems in the way women are integrated into the public sphere.
2. We may want to argue that these values are not in fact feminine but egalitarian; or we may want to see them as more about a certain informality becoming acceptable within certain types of workplace. We may then want to question whether it is useful to describe these values as feminine or mascu-line. However, it does seem sensible to retain these terms and the distinction between them, since participants in studies of the workplace themselves tend to use this system of classification to describe their workplaces.

3. This questionnaire should be seen as indicative of certain views, but obviously because of the small scale of the survey I will not be generalising to women as a whole or men as a whole, nor would I want to make any claims for its validity outside the confines of this group of academics. These findings do nevertheless have some value in suggesting the way in which individuals might think about performance anxiety and its relation to their gender identity.

Bibliography

Baxter, J. (2003) *Positioning Gender in Discourse: A Feminist Methodology* (Palgrave: Basingstoke).

Bourdieu, P. (1991) *Language and Symbolic Power* (Cambridge: Polity).

Bucholtz, M. (1996) 'Black feminist theory and African American women's linguistic practice' in Bergvall, V., Bing, J. and Freed, A. eds, *Rethinking Language and Gender Research* (London: Longman).

Bucholtz, M. (1999) 'Bad examples: Transgression and progress in language and gender studies', pp. 3–20, in Bucholtz, M., Liang, A. C. and Sutton, L. eds, *Reinventing Identities: The Gendered Self in Discourse* (Oxford and New York: Oxford University Press).

Butler, J. (1990) *Gender Trouble: Feminism and the Subversion of Identity* (London: Routledge).

Butler, J. (1993) *Bodies that Matter: The Discursive Limits of Sex* (London: Routledge).

Cotterill, J. (2003) *Language and Power in Court* (Basingstoke: Palgrave).

Eckert, P. and McConnell-Ginet, S. (2003) *Language and Gender* (Cambridge: Cambridge University Press).

Fairclough, N. (2000) *New Labour, New Language* (London: Routledge).

Halberstam, J. (1998) *Masculine Women* (London: Routledge).

Harness Goodwin, M. (2001) 'Organising participation in cross-sex jump rope: Situating gender differences within longitudinal studies of activities,' pp. 75–106, in *Research on Language and Social Interaction* (34/1).

Harness-Goodwin, M. (2003) 'The relevance of ethnicity, class and gender in children's peer negotiations', in Holmes, J. and Meyerhoff, M. eds, *The Handbook of Language and Gender* (Oxford: Blackwell).

Holmes, J. (1992) 'Women's talk in public contexts', pp. 131–150, *Discourse and Society* (3/2).

Holmes, J. and Meyerhoff, M. eds. (2003) *The Handbook of Language and Gender* (Oxford: Blackwell).

Holmes, J. and Stubbe, M. (2003) ' "Feminine" workplaces; stereotype and reality', pp. 573–600, in Holmes, J. and Meyerhoff, M. eds, *The Handbook of Language and Gender* (Oxford: Blackwell).

Johnson, S. and Meinhof, U. (1997) *Language and Masculinity* (Oxford: Blackwell).

Keinpointner, M. (1997) 'Varieties of rudeness: Types and functions of impolite utterances', pp. 251–287, *Functions of Language* (4/2).

Kendall, S. (2003) 'Creating gendered demeanors of authority at work and at home', in Holmes, J. and Meyerhoff, M. eds, *The Handbook of Language and Gender* (Oxford: Blackwell).

Kiesling, S. (2003) 'Prestige, cultural model and other ways of talking about underlying norms and gender' in Holmes, J. and Meyerhoff, M. eds, *The Handbook of Language and Gender* (Oxford: Blackwell).

McElhinney, B. (1998) ' "I don't smile much anymore": Affect, gender and the discourse of Pittsburgh Police Officers', in Coates, J. ed., *Language and Gender: A Reader* (Oxford: Blackwell).

Mills, S. (1999) 'Discourse competence; or how to theorise strong women speakers', pp. 81–90, in Hendricks, C. and Oliver, K. eds, *Language and Liberation: Feminism, Philosophy, Language* (New York: State of New York University Press).

Mills, S. (2003) *Gender and Politeness* (Cambridge: Cambridge University Press).

Morgan, M. (1999) 'No woman, no cry: Claiming African American women's place', in Bucholtz, M., Liang, A.C. and Sutton, L. eds, *Reinventing Identities: The Gendered Self in Discourse* (Oxford: Oxford University Press).

Shaw, S. (2002) *Language and Gender in Political Debates in the House of Commons*, PhD thesis (London: Institute of Education).

Thimm, C., Koch, S. and Schey, S. (2003) 'Communicating gendered professional identity: Competence, co-operation and conflict in the workplace', in Holmes, J. and Meyerhoff, M. eds, *The Handbook of Language and Gender* (Oxford: Blackwell).

Thornborrow, J. (2002) *Power Talk: Language and Interaction in Institutional Discourse* (Longman: Harlow).

Walsh, C. (2001) *Gender and Discourse: Language and Power in Politics, the Church and Organisations* (Harlow: Longman).

Weatherall, A. and Gallois, C. (2003) 'Gender and identity: Representation and social action', in Holmes, J. and Meyerhoff, M. eds, *The Handbook of Language and Gender* (Oxford: Blackwell).

Useful websites on stage fright/performance anxiety

Antion, T. (2004) 'Stage fright strategies', www.antion.com/articles/stagefright.htm.

Barkley, S. (2004). 'Stage fright in the observation process', www.plsweb.com/resources/articles/coaching/2004/03/11.

Janof, T. (2004) 'Overcoming stage fright', International Cello Society, www.cello.org/index.

Johnson, M. (2004) 'The solo performer: Stage fright', www.mjblue.com/pfright.html.

Maliga, L. (2004) 'How to overcome stage fright', http://utut.essortment.com/howtoovercome_rgxd.htm.

Scott, A. (2003). 'Stage fright', www.ostrichink.com/sept2003/stage.html

5
Governed by the Rules?: The Female Voice in Parliamentary Debates

Sylvia Shaw
University of Middlesex, UK

Introduction

Speaking out is the business of parliamentary debate. In possibly no profession other than politics does success depend so strongly upon an individual's ability to speak effectively in public and often adversarial contexts. Parliaments have been almost exclusively the realm of male politicians until the latter half of the twentieth century, and as they are governed by rules devised to constrain the debate discourse they provide a unique context within which to examine the relationship between language use, gender and power in public institutions. Here I investigate the female voice in the archetypal parliamentary context: the British House of Commons. This parliament is often characterised as an adversarial 'bear pit' where opposition parties face each other and fight out issues in a confrontational manner. I also consider some of these findings with a comparative analysis of data from a much newer political assembly, the Scottish Parliament.

Previous research into language, gender and political debates includes Edelsky and Adams' (1990) investigation into gender, language and floor apportionment in U.S. televised debates. Walsh (2001) asks whether women uncritically accept pre-existing discursive practices in institutional contexts that have been previously dominated by men (such as parliaments and the Church of England), whether they seek to change them, or whether they shift between these two positions. Wodak (2003) investigates female role construction in the European Union (EU) parliament, and Harris (2001), Ayala (2001) and Christie (2003) have used the adversarial context of the British House of Commons to investigate and develop theories of linguistic politeness. In this chapter, I aim to find out what makes women speakers powerful or powerless in parliamentary settings. In particular I relate the female voice to the rule-governed nature of parliamentary discourse and explore the ways in which these rules are negotiated differently by men and women within the House of Commons.

Most of the women Members of Parliament (MPs) I have interviewed speak of a 'terror' of speaking within the House of Commons debating chamber. Many male MPs probably share this sentiment, but they do not face the sexist barracking and negative media representations commonly directed at women MPs.[1] There are overt indications that women and men are not treated equally in this context: for example, male MPs in the debating chamber have made 'melon weighing' gestures (intended to represent a woman's breasts) while a woman MP makes a speech; the media characterise the 1997 intake of new Labour MPs as 'Blair's babes'; and women have been assigned to stereotypical 'women's' portfolios and topics. It has been claimed that 'institutions are organised to define, demonstrate and enforce the legitimacy and authority of linguistic strategies used by one gender – or men of one class or ethnic group – whilst denying the power of others' (Gal, 1991: 188). This means that women's language and behaviour are more likely than that of male colleagues to be affected by contradictory expectations and institutional constraints. As the House of Commons was an exclusively male forum until the latter stages of the twentieth century, it is likely that men from the dominant ethnic and class groups in Britain will be the most powerful participants, and that men and women are participating on unequal terms: 'organisations and structures institutionalise the predominance of particular masculinities, thereby empowering and or advantaging certain men over almost all women and men' (Lovenduski, 1996: 5). Here I adopt the idea that particular settings can be the domain of some groups and not others as expressed in Bourdieu's notion of linguistic habitus (1991) which he describes as a 'linguistic sense of place' that:

> governs the degree of constraint which a given field will bring
> to bear on the production of discourse, imposing silence or hyper-
> controlled language on some people while allowing others the
> liberties of a language that is securely established.
>
> (1991: 82)

Similarly, Freed's notion of 'gendered spaces' suggests that the setting and communicative tasks together become an index (Ochs, 1992) of a gendered style and that 'certain social activities and practices may themselves become symbolically gendered if they are regularly and consistently associated with women or men' (Freed, 1996: 67).

I found that to be constructed as powerful speakers in debates MPs must be conversant with both formal and informal rules in their 'communicative tasks'. Debates consist of not only formal written rules which relate to the 'ideal' or canonical form of debates but also sets of rules that have come to be accepted over time and form part of the 'actual' debate rules (Edelsky and Adams, 1990; Shaw, 2000). The ability of an MP to assimilate, use or 'play' with these rules relates to their power in the debating chamber, and are part of what constructs them as 'core' or 'peripheral' members of this Community of Practice (CoP) (Eckert and McConnell-Ginet, 1992). A CoP can be thought of as a group of people who come together to engage in a particular set of activities or 'practices'. Individuals belong to multiple, changing CoPs upon different terms of participation and the relationship of a 'core' member of this CoP to the rules is complex and variable. To signal their membership they must be faultless in their adherence to some rules (such as those governing the use of formal address terms) but yet have the ability to transgress other rules for their own advantage.

The research study

The methodology adopted for this research aims to be qualitative, highly contextualised and reflexive (Stacey, 1988; Furnow and Cook, 1991). A detailed ethnographic description (according to Hymes (1972, 1974) ethnography of speaking framework) was undertaken to contextualise the parliamentary discourse. An ethnographic approach is particularly useful in identifying interactional norms in relation to gender as it:

> highlights speaker competence, local understandings of cultural practice, and cross-cultural variation. It therefore contributes to the feminist project of calling attention to women's abilities and agency, whilst reminding scholars that gendered language use is not everywhere the same.
>
> (Bucholtz, 2003: 48)

This research aims to be 'anti-essentialist' in that it recognises the diversity of women's identities and linguistic practices. However, gender is seen as one of the factors that may affect an individual's membership of, and participation within, this CoP. I therefore view gender as both a flexible and a fixed category. The flexibility comes from the fact that gender is not viewed as a 'given' social category reflecting a pre-existing identity, but rather as constructing and maintaining an individual's identity in the ongoing process of talk. The fixity comes from the way in which men and women are constrained by 'institutional arrangements based on sex category' (West and Zimmerman, 1987: 146) typical of this type of institutional context. This means that women 'actively work out their subject positions and roles in the process of negotiating discursive constraints' (Smith, 1990: 86).

The linguistic analysis is based upon transcriptions taken from a 60-hour corpus of video data from different House of Commons speech events between 1997 and 2001. Additionally semi-structured interviews with MPs gave insights into my interpretations of the transcribed events. A range of discourse analytic approaches were used to investigate the different linguistic practices which were identified as possibly constituting speakers as powerful participants in debates. As mentioned above, power in debates is strongly related to an individual's ability to adhere to or transgress rules. Here I discuss examples from the data that relate specifically to the ways in which the female voice negotiates rules in debates and the ways in which this disadvantages women in comparison to their male colleagues.

Rule-breaking in debates

Introduction

Previous research into political debates suggests women do not transgress rules to gain advantage in debates as much as their male counterparts. Edelsky and Adams' (1990) research into U.S. televised debates showed that male candidates transgressed rules governing turn length and time restrictions more than their female opponents and thus gained an advantage by maximising their own televised talk time whilst minimising that of their opponents. Christie's (2003) work on language, gender and politeness in political debates found that women MPs in House of Commons debates conform to transactional discourse norms. Women MPs in Christie's data corpus were not repetitive and managed to be sufficiently brief, whereas male MPs were admonished by the

Speaker (moderator) 30 times for breaching these rules. My own research on floor apportionment supports these claims (Shaw, 2000 and in p. 92). I found that in five debates 38 illegal interventions were made by male MPs, and only 4 by female MPs. Here I focus on two key ways in which women MPs may 'lose out' by their relationship to the debate rules. First, through their greater difficulty with acquiring the rules of parliamentary debate and secondly through their tendency to conform to debate rules when their male counterparts break them for interactional advantage.

Gaining an advantage by adhering to the rules

In political debates rules exist to permit the 'equalization of turns' and to preserve the rights of a speaker so that only one person speaks at a time. The debate can be viewed as the 'most extreme transformation of conversation – most extreme in fully fixing the most important (and perhaps nearly all) of the parameters that conversation allows to vary' (Sacks, Schegloff and Jefferson, 1974: 731). In the House of Commons, the formal rules of debates are listed in *Erskine May's Treatise on the Law, Privileges, Proceedings and Usage of Parliament* and are enforced by interventions made by the moderator or 'Speaker' of the House of Commons. Rules must ensure interactional equality and also maintain 'order' within the chamber. The maintenance of 'order' is to avoid confrontation that could possibly lead to the breakdown of the debate through heated arguments within the chamber. The line drawn in front of both government and opposition benches shows the historical importance of these rules: MPs must stay behind the line to ensure that they are more than a sword's length apart and cannot engage in bloody dueling across the chamber. Today the emphasis of the rules is more on preventing verbal rather than physical dueling and the preservation of 'order' guarantees the orderly progression of the debate and preserves MPs' speaking rights.

MPs must be able to adhere to some formal debate rules such as those governing 'parliamentary language' in order to be powerful speakers in debates. The failure of an MP to acquire the rules governing these linguistic practices may construct a speaker as a junior or peripheral member of the CoP. The rules governing parliamentary language ensure that exchanges do not become too personal and confrontational and include the rule that all speeches should be addressed to the Speaker and not directly to a political opponent. In order to achieve this indirect mode, all turns should be initiated with the address term

'Madam/Mister Speaker' and MPs must only address or refer to other MPs in the third person according to the office they hold, and not by using the pronoun 'you'.[2] These linguistic constraints (together with restrictions on using taboo language and directly accusing another MP of being a liar) form the set of rules that make up what is known as 'parliamentary language'. As noted earlier, the ability of an MP to acquire these rules is part of what constructs them as a powerful or 'core' member of this CoP. The transcript below shows a newly elected woman Labour MP[3] failing to use the correct forms of address in her speech in the debate on the Stephen Lawrence Inquiry:[4]

Transcript one

Transcription Key: (.)=micropause of under a second; (1)=timed
                    pause in seconds
                    underline=emphasis on word or syllable
                    [ ]=utterances overlapping with the line above
                    JH=John Hayes (Conservative male MP)

Female MP:	the problem the police faced (.) was the fact that	1
	they were institutionally racist (.) institutionally	2
	incompetent and institutionally corrupt and I	3
	would say that corruption is the twin brother	4
	of racism (.) and it affects us all and this why	5
	the debate is so important (.) and the Lawrence	6
	inquiry is so important for white people as	7
	well as black people	8
JH:	would the right Honourable Lady give way	9
Female MP:	yes	10
JH:	I'm very grateful to the Honourable Lady (.)	11
	the Honourable Lady is telling this House is	12
	she the police suffers from institutionalised	13
	corruption (.) leaving aside that outrageous	14
	claim (.) doesn't she realise that by blaming an	15
	institution collectively (.) by assuming there is	16
	some unconscious collective guilt (.) she is	17
	letting off the hook (.) those officers who are	18
	certainly guilty of these charges (.) because	19
	they are hiding behind the very sort of	20
	collective allegations that she makes	21

Female MP:	thank you (.) well if we can look at the issue	22
	you raise by perhaps taking another –ism and	23
	another institution (.) just to see whether (.)	24
	the point you make is correct or not (.)	25
Female MP:	oh I'm sorry	26
Speaker:	o o order the Honourable Lady must use the	27
	correct parliamentary language	28
Female MP:	Mr Deputy Speaker I suffer from an inability	29
	to get that into my mind even after two years	30
	in this house (.) yes um the Honourable	31
	Gentleman er opposite um will perhaps look	32
	at another example we can use another –ism I	33
	was saying and a another institution lets take	34
	sexism (.) and lets take (.) er parliament lets	35
	take the House of Commons (.) lets look	36
	across the benches here (.) and in fact when	37
	the Home Secretary rose to his feet there was	38
	one woman opposite and twenty-six men (.)	39
	on the opposition benches (.) now surely you	40
	would not deny that that means we have an	41
	institution which is biased against women (.)	42
	would the Honourable Gentleman deny that	43
	I presume he would not (.) now equally	44
	equally (.) so you would say (.) well I sorry	45
	the Honourable Gentleman	46
Speaker:	order the Honourable Lady must think carefully	47
	before she chooses her words (1)	48
Female MP:	absolutely right er (.) Mr Deputy Speaker er	49
	the Honourable Gentleman just said yes he	50
	would deny that there is a discrimination	51
	against women when effectively there are no	52
	women well two women at this moment in	53
	time sitting on the benches opposite	54

(Speech Continues)

The MP uses the more informal address form 'you' four times in this extract (lines 23, 25, 40 and 45). The Speaker intervenes twice (lines 27 and 47) in order to tell the MP giving the speech to use correct 'parliamentary language'. This is a powerful speech, critical of both the police for being institutionally racist[5] and parliament itself for being institutionally sexist. One interpretation of the persistent use of this informal address form is that the MP is flouting the parliamentary rules. Her apologies for the rule-breaking (lines 26, 29–31 and 49) could be interpreted as sarcastic and her intention could be to show that the 'correct' formal address term is archaic and awkward. This resistance to the parliamentary rules would seem all the more appropriate here as the topic of her speech is highly critical of public institutions in general and the House of Commons in particular.

However, the MP makes it clear when interviewed that the rule-breaking was not intentional, and that she sees this rule-breaking as her own inability to master the interactional constraints of the debate floor. Furthermore, an error she made later in the same debate (when she presses an MP to 'give way' but then forgets her intervention) has a lasting effect upon her attitude towards speaking in debates:

Interview extract one

> *MP*: I was pleased with my speech and I even thought oh maybe I've got the hang of this Commons thing and maybe that's why I was very insistent on him on this MP giving way because I felt that I was easily an equal with him in the chamber to have an argument about it [...] but I have never felt carefree about speaking in the chamber again because it's the fear thing if that kicks in you don't have the logic to fall back on it becomes a psychological thing the 'oh that's happened' it is very difficult to get round it and when I speak to other (women) MPs about it they all say yeah that's how I've always been in the chamber and I think maybe that I am. I didn't start off that way a lot of MPs start off that way.
>
> *Interviewer*: Which is a shame because your speech in that debate shows you are a good speaker.
>
> *MP*: Oh well I can't any more I am not any more I find it makes you want to write things down more which is a bit of a killer for speaking because you know you don't speak freely.[6]

The consequences of breaking these rules are great as the MP has lost confidence in her speech-making abilities and has decided to speak with more caution in the future. The factors contributing to this reaction are undoubtedly complex and partly relate to the emotive nature of the topic of the debate itself as well as the specific role that this MP plays within the debate. However, this transgression of the rules may be particularly difficult for this MP because of the masculinised nature of the 'habitus' of this CoP. Not only are women more 'visible' than men in this forum (Puwar, 2004) but they may have to work harder than men to gain respect and be seen as equal colleagues. As Eckert and McConnell-Ginet point out in relation to their own findings:

> Such data suggest an extension of the generalization that women have to do much more than men simply to maintain their place in the standard language market [...] women may have to use linguistic extremes in order to solidify their place, wherever it might be.
>
> (1999: 195)

The 'linguistic extremes' for women MPs could be strict adherence to the debate rules. The pressure upon a woman MP to perform faultlessly when she rises to stand in the chamber may therefore be greater than upon her male counterparts.

Although women may have more pressure upon them to conform to the rules, there is no definite evidence to suggest that they break such rules regarding parliamentary language more than male MPs. However, it is surprising that there were no examples in the data corpus of newly elected male MPs failing to use the correct parliamentary language. The behaviour of the Speaker(s) and that of newly elected male MPs would have to be examined more closely in order to investigate this. Anecdotally there are reports that the Speakers of the House of Commons favour old members over new, have their favourite MPs, and choose to be pedantic about some rules but not about others. I found that in five debates the Speaker corrected the use of parliamentary language much more than s/he corrected MPs who spoke out of turn. It is also possible that the Speaker(s) call women MPs 'to order' more than men. An analysis of the behaviour of all newly elected MPs may also reveal a different explanation. One female MP I interviewed claims that *'men who are nervous are more likely just to stay out and not be there. There are lots of men never ever speak at all'.*[7] If this is the case male MPs may be avoiding making the kind of public error discussed above by non-participation within the chamber.

The House of Commons seems to be a particularly punishing forum in which to make mistakes of this kind. The Scottish Parliament is a CoP that shares many of the procedural characteristics of the House of Commons, but differs in some key respects. It is a relatively new parliament (opened in 1999) and has a higher proportion of women Members of the Scottish Parliament (MSPs).[8] Furthermore, women were founder members and it was designed with democratic and egalitarian notions of representation to the fore (Mitchell, 2000). Although most of the rules governing the interaction are the same as the House of Commons, one difference is that members can address each other by their first names. The transcript below shows Margo MacDonald asking the First Minister[9] a question in 'First Minister's Question Time'.

In this example Margo MacDonald starts her turn by making a joke (if we can return from Mars...on line 1). Then she starts to ask the First

Transcript two[10]

MM=Margo MacDonald (SNP), PO=Presiding Officer, FM=First Minister (Henry MacLeish)

MM: <u>than</u>k you Presiding <u>Offi</u>cer (1) if we could return to	1
<u>ear</u>th and leave Mars be<u>hind</u> (.) I wonder if the First	2
Minister re<u>calls</u> with me that following the <u>win</u>ter crisis	3
(.) in the NHS	4
PO: [no I'm sorry] you haven't asked (.) <u>or</u>der	5
MM: oh I know (.) he <u>knows</u> what my first question <u>was</u> though	6
I think	7
PO: no no order you <u>must</u> read out your first question	8
MM: oh (.) <u>right</u> we'll go through the <u>form</u> (laughs) to <u>ask</u> the	9
First Minister	10
MSPs: [laughter]	11
MM: how he plans to (1) recruit the required number of nurses for	12
<u>hos</u>pitals to cope with seasonal ad<u>miss</u>ions this winter (1)	13
FM: er Margo (.) I'm really sorry that the procedures of the	14
House <u>force</u> me to answer your <u>first</u> question and then we	15
can get onto the <u>real</u> business after that (turn continues)	16

Minister a question but does not follow the correct procedures[11] (lines 2–4). The Presiding Officer (moderator) says she must read her question first (line 5) to which she replies that it is not necessary because the First Minister knows what her question is (line 6). The Presiding Officer insists she must read the question correctly (line 8) and she does so (lines 12–13). When the First Minister responds to the question he apologises to the MSP (using her first name only) for having to follow the procedures (lines 14–15).

This example provides a striking contrast with the transcript from the House of Commons. The woman MSP either forgets to ask the initial formal question or does not do so because she regards it as an unnecessary procedure. In either case she challenges the fundamental procedures of the chamber by contradicting the correction of the Presiding Officer. She is right in saying the First Minister knows her question already, he does. So in omitting to read out the initial question she is transgressing the accepted and official norms before agreeing to 'go through the form' which she clearly regards as unnecessary. This exchange also shows the lack of formality in the Scottish Parliament when compared with the House of Commons as first names are used, and the Presiding Officer even apologises for having to enforce the rules (line 14). The data from the House of Commons suggests that MPs are unlikely to challenge the Speakers' authority in this way (although some male MPs directly challenge debate rules when intervening or filibustering, discussed later). Furthermore the Speaker's style when intervening is much more authoritarian and direct than the intervention made by the Presiding Officer. The woman MP in the first transcript invokes negative consequences by transgressing the rules but there is no indication that this is case in the example from the Scottish Parliament. On the contrary it is the rules that appear misguided rather than the MSP's transgression of the rules.

This comparison[12] suggests that it is the particular culture of the House of Commons CoP and the way in which linguistic rules are enforced by the Speaker which makes the woman MP's transgressions so awkward. In contrast, the apparent lack of concern the woman MSP shows for Scottish Parliament rules suggests that she feels in a strong enough position to challenge the Presiding Officer when she transgresses the rules. In turn, the Presiding Officer is much less authoritarian than the Speaker in the House of Commons. Women MSPs were also found to illegally interrupt other MSPs, use adversarial language and to use humour to manipulate the 'key' of speech events, whereas these practices were extremely rare amongst women MPs in the House of Commons (Shaw, 2002). It is likely that the involvement of women in the Scottish Parliament from its origins, the higher proportion of women MSPs, and even possibly such factors as the design of the debating chamber may contribute to a more egalitarian culture than exists in the House of Commons.

Gaining an advantage by breaking the rules

Floor apportionment

The extent to which an MP is able to control the resource of the debate floor as evidenced by linguistic exchanges is one element that relates to the amount of power an MP has in debates. In an analysis of floor apportionment in debates (Shaw, 2000), it was found that there was nominal equality between male and female MPs with respect to 'legal' turns that follow the rules of debate. Women and men took equal amounts of legal debate turns and 'give way' interventions (in relation to their numbers in parliament). However, women MPs made far fewer illegal interventions than men MPs. Speaking or shouting from a sedentary position whilst another 'legal' speaker holds the floor is one of the most common transgressions in debates, and one that is often tolerated by the Speaker. Illegal interventions can be collective shouts of disapproval or approval (for instance cheering), individual short interventions (such as 'rubbish!') or substantive individual interventions that interfere with the 'legal' debate floor. The transcript below shows how the focus of the debate can be dawn away from a 'legal' speaker and the floor 'hijacked' by illegal intervenors.

A combination of legal and illegal interventions in this transcript result in the female speaker (who has all the legal rights to the floor) struggling to maintain her status as the main speaker. The transcript also shows the lack of interventions by the speaker to stop these transgressions and enforce the rules. As male speakers made 90 per cent of all the individual illegal utterances in five debates this suggests that this type of rule-breaking has to some degree been accepted as a masculine 'norm' in debates. As illegal interventions account for a high proportion of all the interventions made in the House of Commons, and women do not participate in these type of interventions, men

Transcript three[13]

Transcription Key: CMP=Current MP (with legal rights to the floor);
IMP=intervening MP; C=Conservative; L=Labour;
m=male; f=female

CMP f(C):	it is very significant that this has not taken	1
	place (.) there is an <u>e</u>lement in <u>my</u> view of	2
	de<u>ceit</u> in the way in which this legislation	3
	(.) has been protect er presented in this	4
	house	5
IMP m(L):	would the right honourable lady give way	6
CMP f(C):	I will	7
IMP m(L):	(Give way) has the Hon. Lady been asl<u>ee</u>p	8
	for the last two years the European <u>Court</u> of	9
	Human Rights have <u>ord</u>ered us to change	10
	our laws (.) we <u>have</u> to we have to <u>change</u>	11
	the <u>law</u>	12
IMP m(C):	rubbish (1)	13
IMPm(L):	(Give way contd.) the honourable gentleman	14
	from his lazing position says rubbish (.)	15
	unfortunately life is <u>life</u> (.) and <u>life</u> says we've	16
	got to change the <u>law</u> and we're <u>doing</u> it (.)	17
	it's not there is <u>no</u> hidden agenda there	18
IMP m(C):	of course there is	19
IMPm(L):	(Give way contd) oh <u>r</u>ubbish Winterton (.) you	20
	really are a <u>silly</u> man (1)	21
MPs:	[laughter]	22
CMP f(C):	gentlemen (.)	23
IMP m(C):	no more silly than <u>you</u>	24
CMP f(C):	I'm really I'm as aware as <u>he</u> is that there's been	25
	a debate on the issue from that perspective and	26
	that the honourable gentleman opposite has	27
	made his (.) contri<u>bu</u>tion to some extent but	28
	that does not <u>alter</u> the fact that we are still here	29
	debating (.) what is going in this case to be	30
	do<u>mes</u>tic legis<u>lation</u> (turn continues)	31

(Shaw, 2000: 411)

dominate the debate floor and women are disadvantaged by their reluctance to transgress these rules.

Filibustering

The practice of filibustering is probably the most extreme example of rule-breaking in the data corpus. Filibustering is the practice by which a group of MPs from one party attempts to speak for so long in a debate that there is no time left for the debate to be resolved, or for the following debate to be started. It is a tactic which 'plays with' and challenges the debating rules for political gain. It is also a process that manipulates the serious 'key' of debates into an ironic one: everyone in the chamber (including the Speaker) knows that an MP is breaking the rules by talking about irrelevancies and minor details, but they are unable to do anything about it. Filibustering is also a highly collaborative enterprise undertaken by a number of MPs from one party who help each other to prolong the speeches by intervening and suggesting further topics with which to prolong the debate. There are three examples of filibustering in the 60-hour data corpus and women MPs do not take part in any of them.

The ability to resist and challenge the Speaker's authority is perhaps the strongest expression of an MP's dominant behaviour in debates. Filibustering MPs regard themselves as being powerful enough to disregard the Speaker's interventions. Furthermore, the irony mentioned earlier exploits the fact that everyone in the chamber is aware that the MP is breaking the rules, but nothing can be done to stop him. An example of this ironic tone is when the filibustering MP repeatedly emphasises the 'importance' of what everyone present knows is an utterly unimportant point. In one of these filibusters the video recording clearly shows an MP laughing and sniggering behind his papers when his filibustering colleague makes an obvious deviation from the topic of the amendment, and when he defies the Speaker's interventions. This covert humour is a highly collaborative enterprise in which the amusement is shared by the MPs taking part in the filibuster (and other members of their political party). The collaborative and gendered nature of filibustering seems (like humour (Shaw, 2002)) to help to establish and maintain the 'fraternal networks' (Walsh, 2001: 19) made manifest in 'bonds based on competitive mastery and subordination'. The fact that women either cannot or will not engage in this linguistic practice only serves to underline their position as peripheral members of this CoP.

Conclusion

These examples show that women MPs may be more conscious of adhering to debate rules than their male colleagues. One explanation for this could be that women MPs consciously choose to behave differently by rejecting the male, elitist, old-fashioned traditions of the House of Commons. This would mean that women MPs are *choosing* not to break the rules in debates. Given the interactional advantage contingent upon rule-breaking this would seem ill-advised, but it could be that women MPs are actively seeking to alter the culture and norms of the debating chamber. Alternatively, the different behaviour of men and women MPs could be a result of the coercive forces within the CoP which mean that women are made to feel like 'interlopers' (Eckert, 1998) in the community, subject to negative sanctions like sexist barracking and negative stereotyping. It is likely that both these explanations play a part in explaining men and women MPs' differential linguistic practices. In an analysis of the marginal position of women priests in the Church of England, Walsh (2001) finds that their position is partly the effect of their own belief in women's 'civilizing difference' and partly the effect of sexist reactions to them by male priests and by the media. As noted in the introduction Walsh finds that 'what *is* clear is that their language and behaviour is more likely than those of male colleagues to be fractured by competing, and often contradictory norms and expectations' (2001: 201).

Women MPs in interviews expressed contradictory views. They identified practices such as barracking and cheering as male activities in which they consciously did not participate.[14] They also expressed the belief that women MPs behave differently from men: *'we're doing things differently and we know we're doing things differently'*.[15] However, some of the interviewees expressed contradictory attitudes in this respect. Having identified 'male' practices and stated they did not engage in them, they also claimed that they had to *'ape the men's behaviour because that's the only way you're going to get anywhere'*.[16] The fact that women MPs do not have consistent reactions to the avoidance of these 'male' linguistic practices suggests that women MPs' *choice* of non-participation in these practices cannot fully explain the differences found.

Eckert (1998) suggests some explanations for the importance of women's adherence to norms and rules. In her research on phonological variation in two CoPs of U.S. high school adolescents ('Jocks' and 'Burnouts') she finds that: 'the constraints on girls to conform to an exaggerated social category type are clearly related to their diminished possibilities for claiming membership or category status' (1998: 73). This conformity may be realised by other forms of linguistic behaviour such as conforming to or transgressing linguistic rules, and related to different types of CoPs. Eckert argues that women moving into prestigious occupations and especially elite institutions 'are generally seen as interlopers and are at greater pains to prove that they belong' (1998: 67). With this 'interloper' status, women are more subject than men to negative judgements about superficial aspects of their behaviour (such as dress or style of speech).[17] The way in which women can 'prove their worthiness' is 'meticulous attention to symbolic capital' (1998: 67). She notes that:

> While men develop a sense of themselves and find a place in the world on the basis of their actions and abilities, women have to focus on the production of selves – to develop authority through continual proof of worthiness.
>
> (1998: 73)

Women MPs' desire to adhere strictly to the rules and their desire to avoid rule-breaking can therefore be viewed as one of the ways in which women MPs make sure they are 'beyond reproach' in a CoP which views them as 'outsiders'.

There is evidence to suggest that women MPs' lack of participation in male discursive practices may be due to coercive forces leading them to have a marginal 'interloper' status within the CoP. Some women MPs recognise their status as that of 'interloper':

> My strategy was to try and be an insider. When quite clearly I was never going to be an insider in the House of Commons my strategy was to build up my strength outside.[18]

Women MPs are constructed as outsiders by sexist barracking, which is common, and their exclusion from cross-party exchanges expressing solidarity. This may serve to strengthen the 'fraternal networks' (Walsh, 2000: 301) against women MPs. Negative sanctions outside the chamber are also pertinent, as the media characterisation of women MPs as 'Stepford wives', 'clones' and 'Blair's babes' clearly have an effect on the women themselves[19] and are taken up and used against women MPs through barracking within the chamber. The imposition of these negative sanctions upon women MPs may mean that they can only pay 'meticulous attention to symbolic capital' rather than attention to their actions and abilities in order to prove their worthiness (Eckert, 1998: 67–73).

These coercive forces may therefore result in women MPs avoiding rule-breaking or norm-challenging practices in order to satisfy the requirements of their 'interloper' status by being 'beyond reproach' with respect to the formal CoP rules. Women MPs may also be constructed as outsiders because of the contradictory and impossible expectations upon them. For example, they are expected to be just like (or just as able as) male politicians, but they must also prove that it makes a difference when more women are elected (Dahlerup, 1988: 279). Additionally, the ideological salience of such ideas as a women's 'consensual' style of speech or the critical mass theory[20] can only fracture their behaviour further. In one study (Childs, 2000, 2004), women MPs claimed that they are 'less combative and aggressive, more collaborative and speak in a different language to men' (2004: 14). In my interviews with women MPs I found that they were often reluctant to characterise a women's style of speech but that women's language was nevertheless described as being 'less hectoring' but 'equally forceful'. One MP comments:

> One of the good things about women and debating is that we all listen to each other and we're all constructive, but actually when you have that sort of debate I didn't enjoy it.[21]

This sort of contradictory position is typical of the stance that women MPs have in relation to gendered 'styles' and their own participation in House of Commons speech events. Furthermore, women MPs who believe there are male and female styles put themselves in an uneasy position in relation to their own performances in debates – what place in the 'bear pit' for a consensual style? It has been noted that there has been a recent shift towards a perception of 'female verbal superiority' (Cameron, 2003: 458) where private rather than public communication skills are highly valued. However, it is difficult to see how the strong traditions of adversarial public speaking in the House of Commons can be undergoing a process of 'conversationalization' (Fairclough, 1992) of public discourse. As Holmes (1992: 144) points out, 'there is no obvious incentive for adult males to give up highly valued talking time in public contexts'.

Dahlerup (1988) and Walsh (2000; 2001) view institutional change as contingent upon the 'critical acts' undertaken by the female minority group.

> Even a small number of women can make an impact upon dominant discursive norms, if they pursue a 'critical difference' approach, whereas the voices of large numbers of women can be assimilated, if they choose to adopt a policy of accommodation to pre-existing norms and practices.
>
> (Walsh, 2000: 273)

The most significant factor in changing the position of the minority is the 'willingness and ability of the minority to mobilise the resources of the institution to improve the situation for themselves and the whole minority group' (Dahlerup, 1988: 296). Walsh (2001) finds that groups like the Northern Ireland Women's Coalition (NIWC) in the Northern Ireland assembly have helped to promote an alternative set of linguistic norms for political debates through an organised campaign focussed upon increasing the presence and treatment of women in the assembly. However, women MPs in the House of Commons expressed uncertainty at their ability to instigate political solidarity beyond the divisions created by party allegiances:

> I think it would be good if we could get women of all parties together but I don't think it will happen [...] the men would use it and say 'Oh look there's a group of women they must be weak to need that'. You just can't afford to draw attention to the fact that you're a woman.[22]

Given these constraints it is difficult to see how women MPs can undertake a critical difference approach and challenge their interloper status. Nevertheless, women MPs in the House of Commons may benefit from understanding how they are governed by the rules of this particular institutional language game, and what the real costs and rewards of their existing strategies might be.

Notes

1. Interviewees identified sexist barracking that was typically directed at women's physical appearance or intellectual capabilities. Similarly negative media characterisations often took up the idea that new women MPs could not think for themselves. For example, they were described as 'Stepford wives' (Interview data from Shaw, (2002)).
2. For example, when addressing an opposition MP the address term should be 'The Honourable Lady/Gentleman' and when addressing an MP in their own party, the address term should be 'My Honourable Friend'.
3. I have preserved the anonymity of this MP because although she granted me permission to use her interview data she did not know I would publish it with an analysis of her speech in this way.
4. This debate on 29th March 1999 discussed the finding that the metropolitan police was 'institutionally racist' in its failure to investigate the murder of a black teenager, Stephen Lawrence.
5. The full speech can be found in the Hansard Report for Monday 29th March 1999 at http://www.publications.parliament.uk.
6. Shaw (2002), Appendix 2, interview transcript E pages 347–348.
7. Shaw (2002), Appendix 2, interview transcript C pages 332–333.
8. At the time this data was collected, women occupied 37 per cent (48 MSPs) and men 63 per cent (81 MSPs) of the seats in the Scottish Parliament.
9. The 'First Minister' is the leader of the government party (in this case Labour), and is the equivalent of the Prime Minister in the House of Commons.
10. From First Minister's Question Time: (07/12/00).
11. In question times, the first question (which has been written and submitted in advance) must be read by the questioner. This is a formality as the questioner invariably wants to ask the Minister or First Minister the supplementary questions that follow (for which the Minister/First Minister has not had time to prepare).
12. A full comparison of the two parliaments was undertaken as part of the larger study (Shaw, 2002).
13. This extract is from the Sexual Offences Bill: Amendment one on the age of consent on 01/03/99. The female Conservative MP is Teresa Gorman, the male Labour MPs is Gerald Bermingham, and the interrupting male Conservative MP is Nicholas Winterton.
14. Shaw (2002), Appendix 2, Interview B, lines 80–85.
15. Shaw (2002), Appendix 2, Interview A, line 433.
16. This statement was made by Jackie Ballard (Shaw 2002, Appendix 2, Interview B, lines 94–95, p. 326). Another female Labour MP expresses this contradictory attitude, at first claiming that '*we're doing things differently and we know we're doing things differently*' and that '*we have to hold our nerve and not turn into the men*' but then stating that '*I think gradually we'll be sucked into behaving the way they* (the men) *behave because that's what they want, the establishment*' (Shaw (2002), Appendix 2, Interview A, p. 321, lines 433, 439–40, 459–461).

17. The observation that women are 'interlopers' who are more subject to the negative effects of gender stereotyping can be related to Kanter's (1977) idea of tokenism, and Yoder's (1991: 183) observation that studies of tokenism in gender inappropriate occupations have found that women 'experience performance pressures, isolation, and role encapsulation, but men do not'.
18. Shaw (2002), Appendix 2, Interview D, lines 92–94.
19. Shaw (2002), Appendix 2, Interview A, lines 255–275, 400–408.
20. The critical mass theory claims that a qualitative shift will automatically take place in an institution when women's representation reaches about 30 per cent (Kanter, 1977). It is a very influential theory even though many researchers (e.g. Yoder, 1991, Kathlene, 1994) have shown that simply increasing the numbers of a minority does not eradicate sexism.
21. Shaw (2002), Appendix 2, Interview B, lines 38–40.
22. Shaw (2002), Appendix 2, Interview B, lines 187–194.

References

Ayala, S. P. De (2001) 'FTAs and Erskine May: Conflicting need?'. *Journal of Pragmatics*. 33, 143–169.

Bourdieu, P. (1991) *Language and Symbolic Power*. Cambridge: Polity and Blackwell.

Bucholtz, M. (2003) 'Theories of discourse as theories of gender: Discourse analysis in language and gender studies' in Holmes, J. and Meyerhoff, M. (eds) *The Handbook of Language and Gender*. Oxford: Blackwell, 43–68.

Cameron, D. (2003) 'Gender and language ideologies' in Holmes, J. and Meyerhoff, M. (eds) *The Handbook of Language and Gender*. Oxford: Blackwell, 447–467.

Childs, S. (2000) 'The new Labour women MPs in the 1997 British Parliament', *Women's History Review*. 9 (1), 55–73.

Childs, S. (2004) 'A feminised style of politics? Women MPs in the House of Commons'. *British Journal of Politics and International Relations*. 6 (1), 3–19.

Christie, C. (2003) 'Politeness and the linguistic construction of gender in parliament: An analysis of transgressions and apology behaviour'. *Sheffield Hallam Working Papers: Linguistic Politeness and Context*. http://www.shu.ac.uk/wpw/politeness/christie.htm.

Dahlerup, D. (1988) 'From a small to a large minority: Women in Scandinavian politics'. *Nordic Political Science Association*. 11 (4), 275–298.

Eckert, P. (1998) 'Gender and sociolinguistic variation' in Coates, J. (ed.) *Language and Gender: A Reader*. Oxford: Blackwell, 64–75.

Eckert, P. and McConnell-Ginet, S. (1992) 'Communities of Practice: Where language, gender and power all live' in Hall, K., Bucholtz, M. and Moonwomon, B. (eds), *Locating Power: Proceedings of the Second Berkeley Women and Language Conference*, Berkeley Women and Language Group. Berkeley, CA, 88–99.

Eckert, P. and McConnell-Ginet, S. (1999) 'New Generalisations and explanations in language and gender research'. *Language and Society*. 28 (2), 185–201.

Edelsky, C. and Adams, K. L. (1990) 'Creating equality: Breaking the rules in debates'. *Journal of Language and Social Psychology*. 9 (3), 171–190.

Fairclough, N. (1992) *Discourse and Social Change*. Cambridge: Polity Press.

Freed, A. (1996) 'Language and gender in an experimental setting' in Bergvall, V., Bing, J. and Freed, A. (eds) *Re-thinking Gender and Language Research: Theory and Practice*. London and New York: Longman.

Furnow, M. M. and Cook, J. A. (1991) *Beyond Methodology: Feminist Scholarship as Lived Research*. Bloomington and Indianapolis: Indiana University Press.

Gal, S. (1991) 'Between speech and silence: The problematics of research on language and gender' in di Leonardo, M. (ed.), *Gender at the Crossroads of Knowledge: Feminist Anthropology in the Postmodern Era*. Berkeley, CA: University of California Press, 175–203.

Harris, S. (2001) 'Being politically impolite: Extending politeness theory to adversarial political discourse'. *Discourse Studies*. 12 (4), 451–472.

Holmes, J. (1992) 'Women's talk in public contexts'. *Discourse and Society*. 3 (2), 121–150.

Hymes, D. (1972) 'Toward ethnographies of communication: The analysis of communicative events' in Giglioli, P. (ed.) *Language and Social Context*. Harmondsworth: Penguin, 21–44.

Hymes, D. (1974) *Foundations in Sociolinguistics: An Ethnographic Approach*. Philadelphia: University of Pennsylvania Press.

Kanter (1977) *Men and Women of the Corporation*. New York: Basic.

Kathlene, L. (1994) 'Power and influence in state legislative policy making: The interaction of gender and position in committee hearing debates'. *American Political Science Review*. 88 (3), 560–576.

Lovenduski, J. (1996) 'Sex, gender and British politics' in Lovenduski, J. and Norris, P. (eds) *Women in Politics*. Oxford: Oxford University Press, 3–18.

May, T. E. (1989) *Erskine May's Treatise on the Law, Privileges, Proceedings and Usage of Parliament*. London: Butterworths.

Mitchell, J. (2000) 'New parliament, new politics in Scotland'. *Parliamentary Affairs*. 53 (3), 605–621.

Ochs, E. (1992) 'Indexing gender' in Duranti, A. and Goodwin, C. (eds) *Re-thinking Context: Language as an Interactive Phenomenon*. 358–358.

Puwar, N. (2004) 'Thinking about making a difference'. *British Journal of Politics and International Relations*. 6 (1), 65–80.

Sacks, H., Schegloff, E. A. and Jefferson, G. (1974) 'A simplest systematics for the organization of turn-taking in conversation'. *Language*. 50, 696–735.

Shaw, S. (2000) 'Language, gender and floor apportionment in political debates'. *Discourse and Society*. 11 (3), 401–418.

Shaw, S. (2002) *Language and Gender in Political Debates in the House of Commons*. Unpublished PhD Thesis: University of London.

Smith, D. (1990) *Texts, Facts and Femininity: Exploring the Relations of Ruling*. London: Routledge.

Stacey, J. (1988) 'Can there be a feminist ethnography?'. *Women's Studies International Forum*. 11, 21–27.

Walsh, C. (2000) *Gender, Discourse and the Public Sphere*. Unpublished PhD Thesis: Sheffield Hallham University.

Walsh, C. (2001) *Gender and Discourse: Language and Power in Politics, the Church and Organisations*. London: Longman.

West, C. and Zimmerman, D. H. (1987) 'Doing Gender'. *Gender and Society*. 1, 125–151.

Wodak, R. (2003) 'Multiple identities: The roles of female parliamentarians in the EU parliament' in Holmes, J. and Meyerhoff, M. (eds) *The Handbook of Language and Gender*. Oxford: Blackwell, 573–599.

Yoder, J. (1991) 'Re-thinking tokenism: Looking beyond numbers'. *Gender and Society*. 5, 178–192.

6

Silence as Morality: Lecturing at a Theological College

Allyson Jule
University of Glamorgan, Wales

Introduction

The New York Times recently reported that religion, in the last twenty years in particular, has edged its way into the forefront of American life. More specifically, there are currently 70 million evangelical Christians now living in the United States, making it the most popular religious subgroup in the entire Western world. Of all Americans, Fifty three per cent cite religion as key to how they vote (and how they did vote most recently in November 2004) – the highest the religion factor has ever been in American voting history. It is therefore now considered 'a normal thing' to discuss religion within American society (Goodstein, 2004, p. 2). Paglia (1992) discusses the power and significance of American-style evangelical[1] Christianity in her essay, 'The joy of Presbyterian sex', saying there are 'Protestant looks, Protestant manners, Protestant values' central in American society. Because of Canada's proximity to the US and because of the vast influence America currently wields in Canada, an exploration of evangelical Christianity as part of under-standing gender public performances is brought forward here.

I am investigating here the ways Evangelical Christian men and women appear to perform gender roles, drawing on the notion of 'linguistic space' in particular because it is a concept which I believe allows for a focus on community participants and on who participates and gains status by speaking aloud in a public context. In my search for an understanding of the female voice in such public settings, I link religious identity and heritage to the female voice or, in this case, religious affiliation to the lack of a female voice. I locate my research inside a Canadian-American evangelical graduate theology college because such a location allows for a discussion of religious identity and lived practice as part of the currently experienced American 'Protestant manners, Protestant values' influencing Canadian society in general (Stackhouse, 2002).

One of the most observable influences of feminism on Canadian Christianity in the last thirty years is the increase of women in theological education and in positions of leadership within the church (Mutch, 2003). However, their presence in co-educational university lectures while they are in training for positions in church leadership reveals traditional power discrepancies as deeply embedded. Being male may include speaking in public as specifically demonstrative of masculine morality, and being female may include the avoidance of speaking in public as specifically demonstrative of feminine morality. Because theology has long been the domain of men, women in today's theological education may experience an unusual set of patriarchal conditions when in comparison with those in mainstream university education where women's place and equality are perhaps more solidly assumed.

Women enter theological training en route to ordination – that is, en route to becoming ministers or pastors as leaders in churches. However, many of today's North American evangelicals see ordination as something still reserved for men, with women limited to more supportive roles in church life. While debates within evangelical Christianity concerning the ordination of women are vigorous and dynamic (Grenz and Kjesbo, 1995; Scanzoni, 1996; Reuther, 1998; Storkey, 2001; Porter, 2002), it is interesting to see that more and more women do pursue theological graduate degrees at all. Regardless of the range of views on women's roles in the church, increasing numbers of women today enrol, graduate in theological education, and go on to careers in many evangelical churches (Grenz and Kjesbo, 1995; Busse, 1998; Hancock, 2003; Mutch, 2003); indeed there is growing feminist thought within modern evangelicalism itself, in spite of strong anti-feminist lobby groups on the American religious right, such as *Focus on the Family* or *Concerned Women for America*, which promote and push 'traditional values' as central to being Christian (Coontz, 2003).

Female silence in the classroom

Lecturing is a major part of university life. My need to appraise this specific teaching method emerges from my general interest in silence inside classrooms as public settings, silence that is something uniquely and often experienced by those born female (Jule, 2004a, 2004b). I identify this amount of talk as 'use of linguistic space' and believe that there are certain classroom teaching methods which legitimate and encourage verbal participation of some students while serving to maintain silence among others. I use the lens of linguistic space because I find it useful in describing ways of participating in classroom experiences. Who speaks? That the young girls in primary classrooms who explored Mahony's (1985) work were often silent while the young boys did more talking aloud in public contexts has influenced my views of the female voice in public spaces in other age groups. The nature of the female voice in public contexts seems to me one that is burdened by expectations of female silence, whether it is young girls in primary education or women following postgraduate programmes.

Much research concerned with gender and its role in influencing classroom experiences points to the influence of a masculinist discourse which values what is male or masculine over what is female or feminine. Even current feminist linguistic research, while increasingly concerned with specific events and situations rather than questions of difference, still cannot escape the tendency of boys in classrooms to speak in certain circumstances when girls in those same circumstances do not speak. Research in classrooms often focuses on the teacher's lack of awareness of who speaks and on how teachers themselves over-talk during lessons and give more of the remaining linguistic space in these public contexts to those students born male (Bousted, 1989; Kelly, 1991; Thornborrow, 2002; Baxter, 2003; Jule, 2004a; Sunderland, 2004). Girls have often been seen as 'passive, background observers to boys' active learning' (Spender and Sarah, 1980, p. 27). Such feminist sociolinguistic work suggests that the amount of talk used by male learners signifies as well as creates their social power and/or that female learners may collude in such power relations by being silent – that is, the girls themselves appear to like it that way.

We know that teachers and college professors talk more to their male than to their female students, beginning in the first years of schooling and continuing on into postgraduate work (Swann and Graddol, 1989; Kelly, 1991). Sadker and Sadker (1990) suggest that female college students in particular are invisible members of the class and that this invisibility is reinforced specifically through male-dominated/masculine speech and through persistent female/feminine silence so that women in many college classrooms are also marginalized from discourse. That women in theology colleges may be further silenced because of their belonging to a particular religious identity tells us something about the relationship of gender to other variables so that related 'situations and events' create part of a larger tapestry of gendered experience (Bing and

Bergvall, 1998). There are many forces at work in each situation so that the teasing out of gender or the focus on it inevitably intersects with other influences, such as religious identity.

Lecturing as teaching method

Lecturing is a common teaching method at the college level. It is a formal method of delivering knowledge: an expert prepares the lecture well in advance, allowing for considerable research, study, and rumination. University lectures are part of people's daily schedules; both the lecturer and the students are usually present for obligatory reasons. The lectures are meant to disseminate knowledge for the set purposes of fulfilling the requirements of a given course. Depending on the nature of the course material or on whether the class/module/lecture is mandatory or optional, lectures may well constitute up to thirty hours of a given module in any one term (up to three hours per week for ten weeks of an undergraduate module or class in most institutions). Such lectures occur with such frequency that personal involvement of the participants appears limited; lectures are experienced as a necessary practice in the university experience.

Barthes (1977) considered the university lecture in terms of politics, of belonging, and as a location to rehearse 'performance discourse'. While the lecturer is lecturing, the students are often silently attending to the ideas and writing notes on specific new vocabulary or content pertaining to the lesson material. The ideas expressed are usually that of the lecturer. Much freedom is allowed concerning his or her politics, his or her power/ego issues, and his or her ability at discursive performance. As such, the lecturer has enormous control over the mood and the dynamics of the room. Lecturing as teaching method works by conveying information through summary and elaboration – and all at the discretion of the lecturer. During a student question period, students have an opportunity to publicly interact with the lecturer, briefly taking on the role of performer themselves and signalling investment, interest, and involvement by asking a question aloud in the public context.

Goffman's (1981) ideas on the lecture differentiate between 'aloud reading', which is often perceived as more scholarly, and what he calls 'fresh talk', which is perceived as more informal though not necessarily more engaging. 'Aloud reading' is a scripted lecture, one where the lecturer presents the material with a heavy reliance on prepared notes. 'Fresh talk' lectures are those lectures where the lecture speaks more 'off the cuff', without the benefit of prepared notes. Lecturers may use a combination of both styles, while some may be more consistent in using one or the other. Barthes (1977), Goffman (1981), and Frank (1995) all recognize the lecture as a multi-layered discourse performance. In spite of more collaborative seminar-style classes, the university lecture persists as a marker of scholastic participation; both attending lectures and performing lectures are part of the academic experience. Spoken delivery is usually understood as candid and dynamic, more 'real', than listening to a lecture on tape or reading the notes of a lecture silently at home. A valuable, charismatic academic lecturer is certainly one to be encountered if at all possible. As a result, the pedagogy of the lecture is 'intensely personal', even if it is personal in precisely impersonal, academic ways (Frank, 1995, p. 30).

Lecturing as power

A lecture is a mark of the lecturer's authority. It is the lecturer who holds the power – or at least this is the idea. However, Lacan (1968), and specifically his work on 'the other', highlights the role of the performance as a specific role of power and status. There is in any community one who is performing the central lead role and there are many others who perform the roles of audience. The performer is 'the subject' of significance, while in other ways the performer may be 'the object' of observation and significance: there are various ways to interpret speaking and listening. In any case, power and powerlessness are performed and are performed in understood ways. The university lecturer, however, may well be both 'the subject' (the performer) and 'the object' (the one who is observed by others). Lacan's ideas have influenced my own understanding of power relations in classrooms and propel these questions: Who is performing? Who is observing? Which action (performing or observing) signals and evokes power? Which evokes less power? It may be that performing the role of speaker signals masculine power: the male lecturers speak and are honoured because of their speaking, while women students are rehearsed into supporting the male or masculine performance.

Feminism offers various responses to these questions but it may be fair to say, in the light of the vast feminist scholarship concerning pedagogy, that power largely lies in the teacher's or lecturer's hands. The teacher performs and observes and both signal power. 'Holding the floor' is the teacher's prerogative and is something which demonstrates the class's point of reference; that is, in this case, power is revealed in and created through the language practices of the lecturer. The lecturer is perceived as valuable, the one 'knowing'. The students or audience members are the ones seeking the knowledge; they are observing. What is said in lectures implicitly and explicitly hints at the lecturer's views and opinions, including religious and moral ones. The students serve to support these views. The lecturer performs power, status and significance; the students perform attentive and supportive audience roles.

Lectures in a theology college reveal a particularly religiously inflected context. I wonder if lecturing, followed by student question periods as is the pattern in the college I studied, alienates the female students because the oppositional feminine/masculine tendencies are condoned by oppositional feminine/masculine patterns of behaviour within evangelical Christianity. The prevalence of lecturing done by mostly men at this theology college positions it as a masculinist tool, one that may rehearse female students into feminine positions of silence while rehearsing male students into masculine speech and their future roles of leadership. If so, then the use of lectures in this theology college works to reinforce and support hegemonic masculinity (Connell, 1995) – a masculinity which insists on feminine subservience and feminine 'reverent awe' (Gilligan, 1982). Because of the transference of information or knowledge that lecturing presupposes, silence of students during question–answer time (a time in which they could speak) may affirm the possibility that those silent are performing a specific and understood role which that behaviour signifies; perhaps women are quiet in such settings because their religion values their silence.

Morality as gendered

In Gilligan's (1982) *In a Different Voice*, she explores various themes of gendered language patterns: a woman's place in society, gendered patterns in dealing with crisis and intimacy, and gendered patterns of expressing morality. To Gilligan, morality appears closely if not entirely connected with one's sense of obligation and one's view of personal sacrifice. She goes on to suggest that masculine morality is concerned with the public world of social performance and influence, while feminine morality is concerned with the private and personal realm. As a result, the moral judgements and moral behaviours and expressions of men tend to differ from those of women. In the light of Gilligan's ideas, it may be possible to suggest that students within an evangelical subculture are encouraged to perform gender so that masculine behaviour is connected to public displays of influence, and so that feminine behaviour is connected with intimate, more private displays. Men are rehearsed into the role of performer; women are rehearsed into the role of silent audience member – all for apparently moral reasons. Women's silence demonstrates to others and to the women themselves their devoutness to God, seen in their ability to be supportive. Their silence is their way of being 'good'.

One would think that the current presence of women in theological education, the rise of feminist theology, and the growth of women's ordination would have significantly changed the nature of theological education. However, recent research into the lives of evangelical women who chose theological education indicates that the lived experiences of these women are often painful and are consistently confusing (Gallagher, 2003; Ingersoll, 2003; Mutch, 2003). With various other religious experiences possible (including none at all), some women appear to remain and invest in their evangelical subculture because they experience something meaningful and worthwhile. Women who study theology say they are often dismissed as feminists for pursuing theology and are often marginalized as a result of this label. Still others feel marginalized and limited and highly nervous about their possible future contributions to church life; they anticipate problems even if they have not yet experienced any (Mutch, 2003). Canadian women in theological education report that being a woman in ministry requires 'commitment of conviction' which is carried out within a constant 'context of challenge' (Busse, 1998). Most cite both loneliness and stress as parts of their career choice and as parts of their theological education experiences. Nevertheless, women continue to enrol, and to graduate and to go on to seek ordination in various evangelical denominations. Why such struggle?

The debate in theological education settles mainly on how, or if, a woman can represent Christ in the church. Some see the role of minister or pastor to be a literally male one: that is, to represent Jesus Christ as Son of God. As such, women who choose to enter theological training at an evangelical college do so with a burden of explanation. How can they, as women, represent a male figure? Unlike their male classmates, they will have to grapple with the possibility that their sex (being born female) will be a distraction and a continual controversy throughout their chosen careers.

The research study

This theology college

For one year, I worked on a research project at a postgraduate theology college. My project was to focus on the views of feminism among devout Christians living in the area. (The results of that interview study are discussed elsewhere (Jule, 2004c, 2004d).) However, as one trained in ethnographic methods and feminist linguistics, the year took on a slightly different focus for me, one that worked alongside the interview study. As a visiting scholar, I was able to sit in on any class of interest, either as a regular attendee or as a drop-in/on-off visitor. As such, what emerged was an ethnographic experience, one where I became a participant observer, seeking the patterns of belonging in this community.

The particular theology college explored is located on the University of British Columbia's large campus in Vancouver, Canada.[2] The college markets itself as 'an international graduate school of Christian studies' (school website). It also advertises itself as a 'trans-denominational graduate school', not affiliated with any specific Christian denomination, though it clearly articulates evangelical Christian ideas, such as 'to live and work as servant leaders in vocations within the home, the marketplace, and the church'.

Forty per cent of the student population is Canadian with an equal number (40 per cent) from the United States; the remaining 20 per cent are from other areas including Britain and Australia as well as several who travel from parts of Asia, Africa, and Latin America. There are 350 full-time students and approximately 350 part-time students. Because the college is for graduate students, most are over the age of twenty-five and all have one degree behind them. Their first degree need not be theology; students come from a variety of fields, including education, medicine, law, arts, sciences. There are roughly 60 per cent male and 40 per cent female students.

Students choose from a variety of Masters programmes, including a Masters of Divinity, the degree needed for ordination in most evangelical churches. Though the college is a well-respected one internationally, there are no doctoral programmes offered. Some students continue on to pursue a qualification as Doctor of Theology at larger theology colleges, such as Oxford, Harvard, Yale, or Princeton. Most, however, enter this theology college to gain ordination and to serve as clergy in the evangelical community. Hence, this college is the way women, called to evangelical ministry, train for their careers in church leadership.

The college employs nineteen full-time faculty members: seventeen are male, two are female. The first woman was hired in 1991; the other was hired in 2000. The imbalance of male to female faculty members, particularly in the light of the male:female ratio represented in the student body, was part of understanding the gender roles in this community. The large lecture classes at the college were taught exclusively by male faculty; the classes taught by the two women were smaller grouped classes and were not core requirements. I believe that the religious views of this community greatly influence the low numbers of women in faculty positions. If women in theology are highly questionable, then perhaps only a certain kind of woman would persist to the level of scholastic achievement.

Methodology

The study used ethnographic methods, alongside the quantitative method of measuring linguistic space. That is to say, I was a participant observer over the full year; I sat in many offered theology classes, acting as both a student and a researcher, and kept a detailed observation diary. I selected two classes in particular to focus on because these two shared the male:female ratio that existed in the college at large. If I was going to measure in some quantitative way the breakdown of linguistic space in these lectures, then I wanted to be sure I had similar sample groups in terms of the male:female distribution as well as in terms of the class size. Both classes were compulsory; both filled the lecture hall with 200 students. I also had semi-structured interviews with both lecturers; their brief comments are recorded here. In addition, I spoke with five women who were in each class, asking them why they had not asked questions during the question sessions in these lectures. Their comments are also included in the findings. The study is an ethnographic one in the sense that I attempted to capture a qualitative as well as a descriptive quantitative record of student experiences in these college lectures.

The classes

I sat in on two of the large lectures, both consisting of approximately 200 students, both core classes. Both classes were held once a week during the Fall term. Both classes ran for three hours with one or two breaks. Both lecturers were male. The male lecturers were known as senior scholars in their fields; both were well published and well known in evangelical circles. All lectures in the core classes held in the main lecture hall (such as two in focus here) are taped onto audiocassettes and sold in the college bookstore; hence, classroom lectures in this college serve the purpose of instruction as well as supplementary income for and promotion of the lecturer and the college itself.

It was clear that both lecturers, Dr MacKay and Dr Jones,[3] had lectured on their material before, perhaps for years. Dr MacKay was well over fifty-years old; Dr Jones was in his late forties. Both were of British extraction and their accents identified their ethnic background and their training. Both lectured from prepared outlines previously given to students. I chose these two classes because of the similarities in class size and in their use of lecture-style, but mainly I chose to examine these two classes because both represented the 60:40 ratio of male students to female students as seen in the college more generally.

Findings

The male lectures

Dr MacKay began each class with approximately five minutes of announcements, such as where to collect marked assignments, before beginning his lecture. Dr MacKay had three tutorial assistants who marked weekly essay submissions. Sometimes one of the tutorial assistants (all of whom were male) would speak about these details before Dr MacKay would ascend the podium. A microphone was usually clipped onto the lapel of his suit by a sound technician so as to record the lecture as well as to allow the entire lecture hall to hear adequately. The lecture would then begin with a two- or three-minute prayer by Dr MacKay himself. He would lecture without visible notes, though students followed along in the student packs where each lecture was provided in outline form – something purchased at the beginning of term. Most students appeared to use the lecture outlines to follow along and to write steady notes throughout, filling in each section of the page. Dr MacKay spoke in a clear, steady voice; he rarely used humour or personal anecdotes and demonstrated more 'aloud reading' style of performance discourse. At the end of the three hours (including one half-an-hour break), twenty minutes would be given over to questions from the students. For the twelve weeks of lectures in Dr MacKay's class, not one woman asked a question. Three to five male students would ask suitable questions, all higher order questions spoken into standing microphones. Each week, different male students would ask questions. Their questions would last between one and five minutes. Dr MacKay's responses would follow suit, generally running four to eight minutes. No female students spoke publicly during the entire term.

Dr Jones's class, however, appeared less formal than Dr MacKay's. Dr Jones did not wear a suit and often arrived late and with scattered papers. Nevertheless, Dr Jones also had the aid of three tutorial assistants who often started the class on time for him with announcements of assignments or sometimes reminders of college activities (such as the

Christmas banquet ticket sales). Dr Jones usually began his lectures with a joke or humorous anecdote from his family life. Eventually an opening quick thirty-second prayer was said, and Dr Jones would begin his lecture. Dr Jones used PowerPoint images which would include particular Bible passages under examination in the lecture or photographs of Biblical sites or maps. Dr Jones used more 'fresh talk' as part of his performance discourse. Students took copious notes; the class outline indicated the general lecture topic per week. Dr Jones gave a very long one-hour break. During the hour, Dr Jones would retreat to his office; the students ate their lunch or went to the library. Dr Jones also gave time for questions, sometimes ten minutes but averaging seven minutes most weeks. In the twelve weeks spent sitting in on Dr Jones's lectures, one woman asked a twenty-second question. It was brief and answered quickly, but it stood out to me as indication of some accessibility for women in the less formal, more 'fresh talk' lecture.

In my opinion, Dr Jones was the more engaging of the two lecturers, though in casual conversations with students they noted very little difference. The content of each class seemed of more significance to the students than the personality or delivery style of the professors; all students were aware and in awe of the distinguished academics in their midst. When I asked both lecturers (casually and privately) if they noticed that only men asked questions during question times, Dr MacKay said he had not noticed this; Dr Jones said he had noticed this 'years ago'. He also said, 'Women don't like to ask questions in public.'

The female students

Five female students attended the lectures of both Dr MacKay and Dr Jones. As such, I asked them through email correspondence why they had remained silent in both classes throughout the full term. One of the respondents, Ruthie, was the one woman who asked a question to Dr Jones. Her response as to why she did so is recorded here first:

Ruthie: I was actually really nervous when I got up to ask Dr Jones that question but I really wanted to know and he didn't seem to be getting close to saying it. I have noticed though that most lectures at [...] respond to people who are most like themselves so I think the guys asked the questions all the time because they respond better to the men as professors. I ask questions all the time in the classes I take lead by women. I think this is because I relate to them better.

Bethany: Dr MacKay is fairly aggressive and if you don't sound intelligent he makes no excuses for you. It's his pedagogy, not his personality as such. He is just very masculine and old-school. I don't know why I didn't ask a question in Dr Jones's class. Maybe I did feeler weaker – I am weaker! They are the experts.

Judith: I didn't feel that I had a firm enough grasp of the subject matter to even phrase a question. I'm just learning.

Lydia: I never ask questions in such a large space. I'd have to get up and stand by the mic and I'd never do that. Besides, I didn't know what I would have asked. It was all new to me. I would rather tell someone else to ask for me than do it myself. I usually wait it out and usually my question gets answered without my having to ask it.

Joy: I noticed the way they both leapt to answer the questions and I didn't want to defend my question – though I can't remember having one I wanted to ask. I also think that the men knew what they were talking about and so I was in learning mode, not speaking mode.

Discussion

Both Dr MacKay and Dr Jones clearly use most of the available linguistic space during their respective lectures. This is not surprising, considering the method of instruction. However, of the remaining linguistic space, men used disproportionately more. This is the surprise. The women did not speak. For the entire term, the women attended and listened, but they did not say anything. Why was this? Perhaps the responses given by the women themselves offer some possible reasons as to why they remained silent.

Most significantly in Dr MacKay's lectures, the male students used 100 per cent of the student linguistic space – all of it. In Dr Jones's classes, the male students used almost the same amount: they monopolized the linguistic space. Only one woman, Ruthie, said anything: she asked one brief question. It was the male students in both classes who talked during the question–answer period. They seemed to perform their masculinity by posing questions during this time, while the female students seemed to perform differently: they were silent throughout. Clearly not all the male students asked questions; some of them also remained silent all term. However, all of the female students were silent; they almost never spoke at all (exception being Ruthie). Instead, the women appeared as consistently supportive listeners. When the women responded to my observation that they had not asked questions during the term they spent with Dr MacKay and with Dr Jones, in general they seemed not to see themselves as equipped or ready, as seen in the comments made by Bethany and Judith, or not able to perform in such a circumstance, such as expressed by Lydia and Joy.

Is their silence a bad thing? There are various ways to interpret the meaning of silence, as explored to a great extent by Jaworski (1993). And in the light of Lacan's (1968) ideas, the silence could signal the role of the observer. There are multiple interpretations of what the silence means. In certain contexts, silence can indubitably be powerful (e.g. Bousted, 1989). However, regardless of the interpretations of the silence or the value attached to the speaking to role, the linguistic space is occupied by the men in the room and not by the women. If who speaks signals who is significant, who has the status, then the men's roles position them into power.

Given the prominence of evangelical voices in current American and Canadian life, it is not surprising that I, as a social science, would have an interest in exploring the intersection of gender and language with religious communities. Many other researchers have undertaken studies on the relationship of evangelical faith and femininity, most recently Gallagher (2003) and Ingersoll (2003). Both of these scholars offer robust research on gender and the evangelical subculture, and both suggest that evangelicalism appears a salient religious experience to many, even with (or perhaps because of) the necessary adherence to traditional Christian teachings concerning gender roles. Evangelicalism's ability to thrive in the midst of larger secularism and current religious pluralism is in part because it is a religious subculture that appears to accommodate cultural engagement along with conservative theological orthodoxy (Gallagher, 2003). These women participate by being quiet and this role is one supported by their religious community.

Evangelicalism and evangelical theological education thrive not because they are effective in establishing some market niche (which they have certainly done in America today, according to Gallagher, 2003), but they thrive because evangelicalism is somehow relevant and useful to the people involved. In particular, the 1980s and 1990s saw anti-feminism emerge in American society, specifically inside evangelical circles (what is termed 'the backlash'). And in spite of early feminist claims made by mostly evangelical women in the 1800s and early 1900s, the current American Christian 'right' has begun to assert political pressure on issues concerning the family in direct opposition to feminist causes. In short, evangelicals now articulate a view of society which rejects liberalism and equality in favour of certainty and moral conservatism.

Their views emerge from a belief that men lead as benign but clear patriarchs who can and must insulate their families from the complexity of secular life; women serve as supporters of their efforts (Gallagher, 2003). As a result, both men and women achieve morality and a resulting peace of mind by behaving in stereotypically masculine and feminine ways: men to lead, women to submit to male leadership and male significance.

It may well be that women choose evangelicalism precisely as a way to find meaningful communities and to reduce the stress of navigating more complex gender roles within society (Busse, 1998). Gallagher (2003) suggests that women remain in evangelicalism precisely because of the set roles for women, not in spite of them. Such women find the clarity 'empowering' (p. 11). These set roles for women are traditional and conservative. The rhetoric of a strong masculine Christianity appeals to men as well as to many women. Even organizations within evangelicalism which support and promote female ordination do so within the set dogma, offering differing interpretations of key scriptures concerning the role of women but not differing interpretations of gendered behaviour. Men are to be strong and rational, and women are to support male 'headship', even if they are ordained and in the positions of leadership.

These realities within evangelical circles, specifically that one could be a female ordained minister and still remain committed to submission as a key moral and gendered behaviour, suggest that women in this Christian college must manage the contradictions within these ideas. These women have proceeded to pursue theological education not for reasons of liberation or female emancipation from male domination in the church, but as a way to serve the church with their gifts of service and support. Though some women may have difficulty in such a context, most appear to remain and further invest themselves precisely because of a sense of calling. They remain in their 'context of challenge' because of their 'commitment of conviction' (Busse, 1998). They work out their gender roles within a specific framework of male leadership and domination. Even if ordained, these women must see their roles as supportive and not leadership-driven.

That lecturing is used in this theology college suggests a clash between conservative/spiritual masculinity and pro-feminist/social justice masculinity seen within the larger university experience (Clatterbaugh, 1990; Skelton, 2001). Such a domination of linguistic space is what Skelton calls 'the school and machismo': that the ways males experience or exploit educational opportunities are 'skills' which males in society 'learn to develop' (p. 93). Men are rehearsed for speaking roles; women are rehearsed for listening roles. Christian evangelical men are trained for public, voiced leadership; Christian evangelical women are trained to listen and support male leadership.

Conclusion

I agree with Paglia (1992) in that there are distinctive 'Protestant looks, Protestant manners, Protestant values' and that these codes of belonging to Protestant evangelical Christianity are attractive and seductive to many men and women. That women choose to belong and to support a religion which views stereotypically gendered roles as desirable might explain their alarming silence throughout the classes I observed. The women remained silent all term. I believe that such specific 'manners' and 'values' are parts of their being seen as devout in this community.

Women's roles are supportive roles, even if appearing to reach for the top levels of church governance by enroling in Masters of Divinity programmes. The Protestant looks, manners, and values seem to include feminine silence. Though the evangelical world has competing debates within it concerning the role of women, it appears to be the case at this college that the female presence in positions of power has not meant a challenge to traditional roles at all. Women in such communities seem to largely function as supportive listeners to the larger male-dominated linguistic space of the lectures.

A masculine style of seeking public influence and participation as a way to be moral seems also at work at this college; the men acted the part of knowing, belonging to, and participating in power, while the women served the part of consistent and supportive audience. These patterns are so commonly seen in other pedagogical research inside classrooms that the findings are not surprising. What this research points to are cultural and historical threads which have perhaps appeared to some as patriarchal oppression but which may reveal women consciously or subconsciously colluding in such circumstances. Women choose to be quiet. Have they been conditioned to expect or even want the men to dominate, or has masculinist discourse positioned the women to collude in male dominance? Such questions can only be answered with yet more research but this study suggests that both are strong possibilities.

Many women remain in evangelical Christianity; women appear to participate in theological education by being silent. Lecturing is a pedagogical tool and a popular teaching method in universities today.

Therefore, many women continue to serve well as audience members in their own educational experiences. These are the Protestant manners and values. The lecturer as performer is well received and well supported by college life in general. The male privileging of this style is not currently being challenged. Based on my extended observations over the year, my view now would be that both men and women who belong to specific religious groups defend gendered behaviour as moral and even 'natural'. The popularity of evangelicalism, particularly in American life, now requires more feminist scholarship in the search for understanding women's experiences in evangelical public life and the reasons why they collude by remaining silent.

Notes

1. The term 'evangelical' is used to refer to those of Protestant faith who are 'Pentecostal', 'fundamentalist', or 'mainline liberal' – terms articulated by Gallagher, 2003. She also suggests evangelicals are generally anti-feminist and anti-big government; they hold these views because of their perceptions of what 'the Bible says' and they promote the 'Good News' to convince others of their views.
2. There are several theology colleges on the University of British Columbia's campus. The one examined here will remain nameless for reasons of anonymity. The names are fabricated to protect anonymity. Also, 'Doctor' is the title used for professors in Canada, indicating a PhD as well as professor status. To be called 'Professor' usually indicates no PhD and, hence, less credentials. 'Doctor' is the more senior title.
3. The names are fabricated to protect anonymity. Also, 'Doctor' is the title used for professors in Canada, indicating a PhD as well as professor status. To be called 'Professor' usually indicates no PhD and, hence, less credentials. 'Doctor' is the more senior title.

References

Barthes, R. (1977). 'Writers, intellectuals, teachers'. In *Image-Music-Text*. trans. S. Heath (Ed.). New York: Hill. 190–215.
Baxter, J. (2003). *Positioning Gender in Discourse*. Basingstoke, UK: Palgrave Macmillan.
Bing, J. and Bergvall, V. (1998). 'The question of questions: Beyond binary thinking'. In J. Coates (Ed.), *Language and Gender: A Reader*. Oxford: Blackwell. 495–510.
Bousted, M. (1989). 'Who talks?' *English in Education*, 23, 41–51.
Busse, C. (1998). 'Evangelical women in the 1990s: Examining internal dynamics'. MA thesis. Briercrest Bible Seminary, Caronport, Saskatchewan.
Clatterbaugh, K. (1990). *Contemporary Perspectives on Masculinity: Men, Women and Politics in Modern Society*. Washington, DC: Westview Press.
Connell, R. (1995). *Masculinities*. Cambridge: Polity Press.

Coontz, S. (2003). *The Way We Never Were: American Families and the Nostalgia Trap*. New York: Basic Books.

Frank, A. W. (1995). 'Lecturing and transference: The undercover work of pedagogy'. In J. Gallop (Ed.), *Pedagogy: The Question of Impersonation*. Bloomington, USA: Indiana University Press.

Gallagher, S. K. (2003). *Evangelical Identity and Gendered Family Life*. London, UK: Rutgers University Press.

Gilligan, C. (1982/1993). *In a Different Voice*. Cambridge, USA: Harvard University Press.

Goffman, E. (1981). *Forms of talk*. Philadelphia: University of Pennsylvania Press. 160–196.

Goodstein, L. (2004). 'Politicians talk more about religion, and people expect them to'. *The New York Times*. Weekend, 4 July, p. 2.

Grenz, S. and Kjesbo, D. M. (1995). *Women in the Church*. Downers Grove, IL, USA: Intervarsity Press.

Hancock, M. (Ed.) (2003). *Christian Perspectives on Gender, Sexuality, and Community*. Vancouver, BC: Regent College Publishing.

Ingersoll, J. (2003). *Evangelical Christian Women: War Stories in the Gender Battles*. New York: New York University Press.

Jaworski, A. (1993). *The Power of Silence*. London, UK: Sage.

Jule, A. (2004a). *Gender, Participation and Silence in the Language Classroom: Sh-shushing the Girls*. Basingstoke, UK: Palgrave Macmillan.

Jule, A. (2004b). 'Speaking in silence: A case study of a Canadian Punjabi girl'. In B. Norton and A. Pavlenko (Eds), *Gender and English Language Learners*. Virginia: TESOL Press. 69–78.

Jule, A. (2004c). 'Gender and religion: Christian feminism'. Paper presented at the Religion and Society Conference, Point Loma University, San Diego, California (March 23–26).

Jule, A. (2004d). 'God's daughters? Evangelical women speak for themselves on feminism'. Poster presented at IGALA3, Cornell University, Ithaca, NY (June 5–7).

Kelly, J. (1991). *A Study of Gender Differential Linguistic Interaction in the Adult Classroom*, 3 (2), 137–143.

Lacan, J. (1968). *The Language of the Self: The Function of Language in Psychoanalysis*. trans. A. Wilden. Baltimore: Johns Hopkins University Press.

Mahony, P. (1985). *Schools for the Boys?: Co-education Reassessed*. London: Hutchinson.

Mutch, B. H. (2003). 'Women in the church: A North American perspective'. In M. Hancock (Ed.), *Christian Perspectives on Gender, Sexuality, and Community*. Vancouver, BC: Regent College Press. 181–193.

Paglia, C. (1992). 'The joy of presbyterian sex'. In *Sex, Art, and American Culture: Essays*. New York: Vintage Books. 26–37.

Porter, F. (2002). *Changing Women, Changing Worlds: Evangelical Women in Church, Community and Politics*. Belfast, UK: The Blackstaff Press.

Ruether, R. R. (1998). *Introducing Redemption in Christian Feminism*. Sheffield, UK: Sheffield Academic Press.

Sadker, M. and Sadker, D. (1990). 'Confronting sexism in the college classroom'. In S. Gabriel and I. Smithson (Eds), *Gender in the Classroom: Power and Pedagogy*. Chicago: University of Illinois Press. 176–187.

Scanzoni, L. D. (1996). 'Women's place: Silence or service?' *Eternity* 17 (February), 14–16.

Skelton, C. (2001). *Schooling the Boys: Masculinities and Primary Education*. Buckingham, UK: Open University Press.

Spender, D. and Sarah, E. (Eds) (1980). *Learning to Lose: Sexism and Education*. London, UK: The Women's Press.

Stackhouse, J. G. (2002). *Evangelical Landscapes*. Grand Rapids, MI: Baker Book House Company.

Storkey, E. (2001). *Origins of Difference: The Gender Debate Revisited*. Grand Rapids, MI: Baker Book House Company.

Sunderland, J. (2004). *Gendered Discourses*. Basingstoke: Palgrave Macmillan.

Swann, J. and Graddol, D. (1989). 'Gender inequalities in classroom talk'. *English in Education*, 22 (1), 48–65.

Thornborrow, J. (2002). *Power Talk*. London, UK: Longman.

7
Gender and the Genre of the Broadcast Political Interview

Clare Walsh
De Montfort University, UK

Introduction

My inspiration for this chapter was Fairclough's (1998: 157) comment that the dominant ethos on the British Broadcasting Corporation (BBC) Radio 4's flagship news programme *Today* is 'white, *male* and English common sense' (my italics). *Today* was created in 1957 as a news magazine programme with a format of two key co-presenters and now has a regular audience of six million listeners. It is broadcast from 6 to 9 a.m. six days a week and comprises a series of topical interviews, interspersed with news bulletins and regular items on sport[1] and business. The BBC has come to regard it as Radio 4's pre-eminent current affairs programme, a view shared by the media in general. For instance, *The Sunday Times* described it as 'a leader in the making and breaking of news stories' (5 May, 2000). This high-profile status and agenda-setting role means that *Today* acts as a very important platform for politicians who seek to have their voices heard in the public domain.

In the first part of this chapter, I will outline evidence which suggests that, like other media whose staple is hard news, there is indeed, and has been since its inception, a dominant male 'voice' on the programme. This has led to a privileging of a masculinist style of political interviewing and a concomitant marginalising of the female voice, whether in the role of interviewer or interviewee. I will illustrate this by analysing data from interviews conducted by the longest-serving male presenter, John Humphrys, who joined the programme in 1986. I will then go on compare his interviewing style with that of Sue MacGregor, a female presenter of similar age and professional experience, who presented the programme from 1984 until her retirement in 2002. Bell and van Leeuwen's (1994) framework for analysing broadcast political interviews will be applied to data collected during the 2001 British general election campaign (May–June, 2001). I will conclude by suggesting that MacGregor's chosen strategy of resistance to the programme's dominant masculinist ethos, her adoption of what I have elsewhere termed a 'critical difference stance' (Walsh, 2001: 7) that offers an alternative female voice, appears to have had an adverse effect on perceptions of her competence as a political interviewer and that this, in turn, had material consequences for her professional status as a presenter. By contrast, the normalising of what has become an increasingly adversarial style of political interviewing on the programme has, I would argue, contributed to a wider political culture in Britain which has alienated many female *and male* listeners/voters from the whole political process.[2]

The *Today* programme as a masculinist community of practice?

Eckert and McConnell-Ginet's (1992) concept of 'communities of practice' aims to account for the complex way in which individuals negotiate identities for themselves, including their gendered identities, in relation to dominant discursive norms. *Today* is one such community of practice which has ways of talking, beliefs and values that have, over time, become normative. Van Zoonen (1998: 33) points out that evidence from studies in a range of cultural contexts throughout the 1980s and 1990s testify to a masculinist culture in the newsroom. Traditionally, hard news, in particular, has been seen as a male preserve. In her recent autobiography, MacGregor (2002: 221) claims that when she joined *Today* in 1984 it 'still bore a heavy mantle of male supremacy'. Interestingly, this situation does not appear to have changed with the arrival of the programme's first female editor, Jenny Abramsky, two years later. MacGregor claims that Abramsky continued the practice of favouring her two male colleagues, Brian Redhead and John Humphrys, with the top political story of the day (MacGregor, 2002: 237), lending support to my claim that women in public life can, and do, embrace masculinist discursive practices in ways that can serve to marginalise female co-workers (Walsh, 2001: 72). Such editorial decisions helped to confirm MacGregor's subordinate role as permanent female 'side-kick', a situation which was not helped by Redhead's attitude towards her:

> as I grew in confidence he would hand out some devastating put-downs. Any stumble on my part would be noticed and marked with

a grin. Once he thrust a piece of paper with the word 'Fool!' written on it in front of me as I finished a live interview.

(MacGregor, 2002: 229)

Her autobiography offers other telling insights into her professional life. For instance, because she had been brought up in South Africa, MacGregor records how she had been sent there to cover her personal impressions of the country in the lead-up to the historic 1994 election and how she had also been asked to cover the Queen's visit there a year later, but, much to her disappointment, it was Humphrys who was sent to cover the election itself (MacGregor, 2002: 288).

This pattern in which MacGregor was given 'soft news' stories, while her male colleagues were given a higher proportion of 'hard news' items, continued until her retirement, despite her efforts to challenge this situation. In his book written to mark the fortieth anniversary of *Today*, Donovan (1997: 119) notes that an analysis of the allocation of the prestigious 8.10 a.m. slot for the whole of 1996 revealed that 'Humphrys does the big set-piece interview on two out of every three programmes he does, [James] Naughtie does it on almost half of his but MacGregor does it on less than a third of hers.' Figures for the first six months of 2001 indicated that the only change that had occurred in this situation five years on was that Humphrys' share of the major interviews had increased by 10 per cent (cited in MacGregor, 2002: 307). This was true despite the fact that the Chief Executive of BBC News told Donovan that it was 'basic policy that there is an equivalence between them all' (Donovan, 1997: 307). Donovan discovered that this equivalence did not extend to pay, since MacGregor was being paid almost £20,000 less than her male colleagues. As MacGregor (2002: 309) notes: 'the message was clear: women are still valued less than men'.

The broadcast political interview – an inherently adversarial genre?

Several media commentators have referred to the inherently combative nature of the broadcast political interview in which interviewers seek to hold politicians to account (Heritage and Greatbatch, 1991; Bell and van Leeuwen, 1994; Harris, 2001; Thornborrow, 2002). A post-structuralist view of discourse would suggest, however, that there is nothing inevitable or immutable about this generic convention. That such conventions are historically and culturally contingent is evident from Blumler and

Gurevitch's (1995) observation that a dramatic shift has occurred in Britain from a 'sacerdotal' approach to reporting politics, an approach which prevailed until the 1950s, to one that is openly 'disdainful'. For instance, *The Independent* newspaper has paid tribute to *Today* for its 'sharp questioning and trophy wall of ministerial heads' (24 October, 2000). The latter comment provides an indication of the extent to which an aggressive and contestatory style of political interviewing has become normalised on the programme. In his book *Devil's Advocate* (1999), Humphrys makes it clear that he embraces this style with considerable relish, as is evident from the following extended metaphor he uses to describe it:

> I'm not a fox-hunting man myself, but I imagine that the buzz those characters get when they've finally run the exhausted and terrified beast to ground after a thrilling chase is not entirely different from that moment after some good studio sport when you say, 'Secretary of State, thank you,' and he says 'thank you' back through gritted teeth and tries to smile.
>
> (Humphrys, 2001: 235)

The danger of viewing political interviewing as a deadly game, however, is that, as Fairclough (1998: 151) notes, genuine political discussion can become subordinated to 'gladiatorial contest'.

Humphrys does not so much exhibit the 'quizzical, amused, slightly sceptical' attitude which is characteristic of the 'honest broker' role referred to by Kumar (1977: 134), but instead has made widely known his attitude of hardened cynicism towards *all* politicians. This manifested itself on a number of occasions during the British general election of May–June 2001. For instance, a revealing pronoun slippage occurs in an interview with the then Leader of the House, Margaret Beckett, on the issue of voter turnout: *'They're* not supporting William Hague by not voting for you. *We-we're* absolutely entitled to say *we're* fed up with all of you, if that is our view, and *we* are not going to vote as a way of showing *our* protest' (*Today*, 5 June 2001). In Curran's (1982: 215) words, Humphrys is not so much a non-partisan as an *anti*-partisan. Far from reflecting 'ordinary conversation', as Fairclough (1998: 160) suggests, his approach to political interviewing is more like the stylised and hectoring mode of debate that prevails on the floor of the House of Commons (see Shaw, Chapter 5).[3] The extended version of 'Yesterday in Parliament' may have moved to

Radio 4 longwave, but Humphrys has ensured that its tone has not. This is not, however, an interactional style that is exclusive to male interviewers. I would suggest that MacGregor's replacement on the programme, Sarah Montague, has adopted an adversarial approach to political interviewing that is closer to Humphrys' than to MacGregor's.[4]

Analysis of John Humphrys' style of political interviewing

Bell and van Leeuwen (1994: 143) identify a recursive generic pattern for the political interview (as shown in Figure 7.1):

Greeting [(Soliciting Opinion) (Checking) (Challenging) (Entrapment)] Release

---

Figure 7.1 A summary of Bell and Leeuven's account of the generic components of a political interview.

Not all of these elements will be present in all political interviews, but they argue that, however combative the interview, it should end as courteously and co-operatively as it began, since they are 'games that have no final victor or vanquished' (Bell and van Leeuwen, 1994: 157). Thus the release stage is a way of allowing the interviewee to save face at the end of the interview. Yet the extract below of an interview between Humphrys and ex-Conservative Prime Minister Sir Edward Heath during the 2001 general election campaign reveals how Humphrys violates this rule by ending instead with what is effectively an 'entrapment' question disguised as a release question:

Extract (1) BBC Radio 4, Today programme, 21 May 2001

JH: When you said to *The Independent* that you thought that the majority of the electorate had been turned off by the right-wing take-over of the Party under Mr Hague, what did you mean by that?

EH: Well what I meant was that ah (long pause)

JH: And you referred to Mr Hague in your interview with Boris Johnson in *The Spectator* as 'a laughing stock'. I mean that's a bit unkind, wasn't it?

EH: ((laughs)) He-well he got <u>that</u> wrong and he realised it because what I said was that they were laughing at people in the House when eh he made his statement.

JH: So how do you rate eh Mr Hague as a leader?

EH: Well I never make judgements about our [leaders

JH: [((incredulous laugher))
         Well, go on mmh, but?

EH: But, he's there and we support him.

JH: So eh are you not prepared to say on the eve of an election 'I think
         he's a jolly good bloke and he's-he's the best prime minister the
         country could have?'

EH: What I'm prepared to say is that he's our leader and we'll support
         him and we'll do our utmost to make sure he wins the election.

JH: And some might say <u>that</u> is rather damning with faint praise.

EH: No, I don't think so.

JH: Not that there was any praise in it. You just said he's our leader,
         didn't you? You didn't say he was a good leader?

EH: Well, he's got (0.3) some very strong qualities of determination
         and perseverance.

JH: What about his weaknesses?

EH: (long pause) About his what?

JH: HIS WEAKNESSES.

EH: Well, we all have weaknesses and we don't want to deal with those
         at a time of an election...

JH: All right. Well, straightforward question. Who'd make the best
         prime minister: Tony Blair or William Hague?

EH: (perceptible pause) I don't make judgements like that.

JH: (perceptible pause) Sir Edward Heath, thanks very much indeed.

The opening question in this extract appears to be a straightforward
checking question, but its berating tone and its presupposition of a split
within the party give it the force of a challenge. Humphrys then takes
advantage of Heath's hesitation to introduce a pseudo-extension ('And
some might say that is rather damning with faint praise.') This is
signalled by the conjunction 'And', and a rising intonation, but which
in fact effects a subtle, though significant, topic shift from the issue of
the Party's future policy direction to that of Mr Hague's personal
credibility. Given that the alleged charge against Hague is that he is 'a
laughing stock', the evaluative gloss 'I mean, that's a bit unkind' can
only be interpreted as ironic, especially since it is delivered in a heavily
ironic tone and is embedded in a tag question that cues a positive
response. By contrast, given the preceding co-text, Humphrys' next
question, 'So, how do you rate Mr Hague as a leader?', cues a negative
response. He then goes on to 'ventriloquize' the kind of ringing

endorsement, albeit delivered in a mock upper-middle-class voice, that Heath so spectacularly fails to deliver.

Indeed, the entire interview is characterised by what Clayman and Heritage (2002) refer to as 'global hostility', manifested in this instance in an overall mocking question content. None of the questions asked genuinely solicits information, since Heath's comments have already appeared in two other media sources, but instead the questions act as prompts for an on-air *performance* of a hesitant and evasive script, full of meaningful pauses and understatements, a performance which is calculated to damage the credibility of William Hague, the then Conservative Leader. Bell and van Leeuwen (1994: 155) describe entrapment questions as questions that 'seek to drive interviewees into a corner' and which they cannot answer either way without appearing to contradict themselves. This is true of the statement delivered with a questioning intonation: 'You didn't say he was a good leader?', since the reply 'Yes, I did say he was a good leader' would be contradictory, whereas the alternative, 'No, I didn't say he was a good leader', would be overtly damaging to Hague.

Humphrys' use of a metalinguistic gloss that identifies his final question as a 'straightforward' one gives it the superficial appearance of a release question, but, given his reputation as a pugnacious interviewer, it is likely to have aroused Heath's suspicions sufficiently to generate an ambiguous pause. Clearly, as an ex-Conservative leader, Heath was extremely unlikely to have endorsed Tony Blair's leadership, but to have endorsed Hague's would have meant contradicting the cautious modality he employs throughout the interview. This then forces him to resort to a very non-committal, uncooperative and thus highly politically damaging response. After a ritual 'thank you', Humphrys moves swiftly on, using Heath's final evasive reply as the contentious ground for a follow-up interview with the then Conservative Chairperson, Michael Ancram, in which he says: 'But it is quite extraordinary, isn't it, that erm, that a former Conservative prime minister is not prepared to say during an election campaign: "Our man would make a better prime minister than the other guy?" ' It is less extraordinary, however, when one has followed aurally the carefully laid stages of the trap that Humphrys set for Heath. This analysis challenges Bell and van Leeuwen's (1994) claim that political interviews are contests in which there are ultimately no winners or losers.

Humphrys (2001) admits that he regularly engages in fraternal 'banter' with *male* politicians, such as the ex-Conservative Chancellor Kenneth Clarke and the current Deputy Prime Minister John Prescott.

This entails a register shift to 'chat' that, Tolson (1991) claims, is increasingly embedded in even serious broadcast talk. One such 'chummy' exchange occurs in what was otherwise a very confrontational interview with Kenneth Clarke, one of the candidates in the Conservative leadership campaign that followed their election defeat.

Extract (2) BBC Radio 4, Today programme, 18 August 2001

KC: I was in fact actually complaining that I was getting pursued on holiday by people who recognised me eh because they happened to be Englishmen on the same [trip...

JH: [The price of fame.

KC: Eh eh the price of fame, absolutely. You must suffer the same thing. It's like having your radio report on all the time John ((JH: heh heh)). Eh but I've now forgotten what the main point of your question was

As well as providing a harmonic moment of homo-social bonding in the midst of what is almost invariably an adversarial interview, such register shifts are likely to enhance the media capital of the male politicians in question, since it humanises them and foregrounds their sense of humour. The marked absence of such 'chatty' and good-humoured exchanges in interviews between a key political presenter like Humphrys and female politicians therefore effectively denies them access to an important resource by which a politician can reduce the distance between his/her public persona and the 'lifeworld' of the overhearing audience.

Furthermore, there is evidence to suggest that Humphrys subjects female politicians to even more hostile questioning than is true of their male counterparts. For instance, his hectoring of the then Secretary of State for Social Security, Harriet Harman, generated front-page headlines in December 1997. Alluding to the latter in his recent book, Humphrys (2001: 229) makes no apology for his interview with Harman and instead mildly rebukes listeners for failing to recognise his even-handedness: 'The audience has a pretty chivalrous streak, too. It is usually a mistake to play too rough with women politicians, even in these days of what's meant to be sexual equality.' Far from being even-handed in his attitude towards male and female interviewees, Mullany (1999: 129) found that Humphrys used *twice* as many antagonistic questions in an interview with a female politician in her corpus of interview data than was true of a separate interview with one of her male party political colleagues. Perhaps for this reason, Conservative MP Virginia

Bottomley is said to take off not only her jacket when being interviewed by Humphrys face-to-face, but also her earrings, overt signifiers of a troublesome femininity (cited in Donovan, 1997: 209).

Donovan notes that praise from politicians is almost exclusively reserved for the political interview styles of Humphrys and Naughtie, rather than MacGregor. Both are praised for their incisive questioning and their sense of humour, the only difference between them being that Humphrys is said to be the more acerbic of the two. The ex-Controller of the BBC, John Birt, is recorded as saying of Humphrys: 'You've got to be pretty good to go up against him' (cited in Donovan, 1997: 134). Significantly, however, listeners appear to be less convinced by his unrelentingly negative approach to political interviews during elections. During the 2001 election campaign, for instance, hits on the *Today* website fell from a weekly average of 200,000 to 80,000 (cited in MacGregor, 2002: 325). Even a former editor on the programme, Tony Hall, admitted to Donovan that the yah-boo style of interviewing is often a literal turn-off for listeners: 'I never enjoy it very much and the audience doesn't either' (cited in Donovan, 1997: 208). Surely the role of a political interviewer is not to portray politics as a game in which *all* the players are self-serving, but to help us to make careful and informed distinctions between the *policies* of different political parties. Humphrys' tendency to engineer on-air verbal punch-ups helps to legitimise a situation in which *political* conflict is invariably recast in terms of *personal* conflict. Yet I would argue that there is nothing inevitable about personalising the political in this way (certainly *not* the way feminists envisaged it), and that such masculinist assumptions about the conduct of political campaigns and political interviews are, in fact, open to challenge and change, by feminist listeners/viewers, media workers and media analysts.

Resistance to the masculinist genre of the broadcast political interview – a critical difference approach

Unlike white heterosexual men of Humphrys' generation, MacGregor as a white middle-class woman was placed in a self-conscious relationship to her gendered identity from the moment she attempted to carve out a career for herself in the British media. Initially, she was forced to perceive her gendered identity as a very real barrier to entry. Thus she recalls how, having been short-listed for a job as a continuity announcer on the BBC's Home Service, she was turned down on the grounds that male voices ultimately carry more authority (MacGregor, 2002: 116).

Thereafter, she came to view her gender as a potential resource, if used strategically. For instance, she took advantage of the patronising assumption that female voices offer a contrasting *texture* to those of male broadcasters to secure herself a role as a presenter on BBC Radio 4's daily news programme *The World At One*. This relatively high-profile job, together with her identity as a *female* presenter provided ideal credentials for her next job as a presenter of the long-running radio programme *Woman's Hour*, a position she occupied for fifteen years.

In her autobiography she notes, 'I . . . had found that being a woman was a positive advantage at this point in my career' (MacGregor, 2002: 183). When interviewed by me, MacGregor revealed that the experience of presenting *Woman's Hour* throughout the heady days of second wave feminism, from the early 1970s until the late 1980s, helped to politicise her in terms of gender issues (Interview with the author, 26 October 2001). This, in turn, made her acutely aware of the subtle and not-so-subtle ways in which she was marginalised when she became a full-time presenter on the *Today* programme in 1987:

> *Today* was sometimes a very macho programme to work on. It is less so than it was . . . Brian [Redhead] was a very sort of bluff, typical northern male in many ways. John is oozing testosterone. Jim's more of a new man. There are still some mornings, I guess, when I feel that I have to assert myself quietly in order to be listened to in any way.
>
> (cited in Donovan, 1997: 121)

It is obvious from this comment that MacGregor does not homogenise the identities of her male colleagues, but rather recognises that they occupy a range of gendered subject positions. It is also interesting to note that the comment about Humphrys 'oozing testosterone', although apparently intended as a criticism of his exaggerated performance of aggressive masculinity, was recontextualised in several newspaper articles as evidence of MacGregor's somewhat unlikely post-feminist credentials, especially when it appeared alongside the frivolous claim that she had agreed to take part in topless darts – on the radio.

In relation to her chosen style of political interviewing on *Today*, MacGregor appears to have adopted what I have referred to elsewhere as a 'critical difference' stance (Walsh, 2001: 7). This is a stance employed by many feminist-oriented women in public sphere roles which relies on the *selective* and *strategic* use of those norms traditionally associated with women's language that constitute a critique of, and an alternative to, dominant masculinist norms with which many women, and also some men, feel uncomfortable. I would suggest, however, that it is more difficult to provide empirical evidence for the existence of a relatively co-operative, as opposed to a combative, style of political interviewing, since it can be more readily defined by what it *omits*, such as persistent interruptions, entrapment questions, a hectoring or bad tempered tone and so on, than by what it actually includes. MacGregor certainly meets the latter criterion, since, as Donovan (1997: 92) notes, she is thought not to have lost her temper on any of the almost 3000 editions of the programme she presented. When interviewed by me, MacGregor attributed her tendency not to 'bark or shout', as she put it, not to her gendered identity, but to the intimate nature of radio as a medium. However, her recognition that not everyone is quite as comfortable with the medium, as she herself was, led her to engage routinely in pre-interview small talk with the aim of putting less experienced interviewees at their ease, something, she says, that was rarely practised by her male colleagues. This is an example of the kind of hybrid talk that Holmes and Stubbe (2003) claim is simultaneously oriented to both interpersonal *and* transactional ends and which is frequently employed by women in public sphere roles.

MacGregor's alternative approach to political interviewing is exemplified by the following comment that appeared in her recent autobiography:

> It's probably true that most women interviewers lack the more aggressive approach of their male colleagues. They possess perhaps more subtle skills: an ability to fillet the facts of a story and tease out the threads of an argument without too much obvious pushing. It's an approach that can be just as effective.
>
> (MacGregor, 2002: 234)

This more subtle, yet nonetheless incisive, approach to the genre of the political interview is illustrated by the following transcription of an interview conducted during the 2001 general election campaign with the Liberal Democrat Transport spokesperson, Don Foster (*Today*, 21 May 2001). This is the *only* major political interview conducted by MacGregor during the campaign and it is significant that it is with a spokesman from Britain's *third* political party. Foster's responses are not given in full, since the main interest lies in the way MacGregor formulates her questions:

Extract (3) BBC Radio 4, Today programme, 21 May 2001

SMG: Eh Mr Foster, you: would prefer Railtrack to be completely restructured?

DF: Yes, er I think er everybody would accept that the situation on our railways... (turn carries on for 31 seconds in all)

SMG: And what about who's responsible for em repairing and renewing the lines and that sort of [thing?

DF: [Well, that would be the responsibility of this new not for profit company...(turn carries on for 34 seconds in all)

SMG: How would you suggest affordability, as you put it, could be improved? They're not likely to slash their prices, the train operating companies, are [they?

DF: [No, but it's a ludicrous situation isn't it where...we've very recently heard that for example Virgin are putting up their fares by nine and a half per cent and look almost certain to be <u>rewarded</u> for having done [that with the franchise for the east coast main...

SMG: [Although they would say, and have said, that they've also put in lots of special offers as [well.

DF: [Oh, they have indeed but...(turn runs on for 43 seconds in all)

SMG: Do you expect (.) that Railtrack ((Foster clears his throat)) will be able to say in a couple of weeks time (0.3) 'Yes (0.2) we're back to those levels pre-Hadfield which of course were not perfect.'

DF: They certainly weren't and I mean...(turn carries on for 37 seconds in all)

SMG: .hh Don Foster, thanks very much.

The interviewer's opening gambit is obviously important for setting the tone for the interview that follows, and in this case it elicits the anticipated agreement, and therefore cooperation, from Foster. Whereas Humphrys often frames his second question as a challenge, in this instance MacGregor frames hers as a straightforward extension, signalled by her use of the conjunction 'and'. Likewise, her choice of the rather vague phrase 'and that sort of thing' cedes her right as an interviewer to control the direction of the questioning at this point, allowing Foster plenty of scope to elaborate upon policy details. Throughout the course of the interview, MacGregor permits him to do this at some length, the average length of his turns being thirty-four seconds. Her third question, however, is more challenging, containing as it does the metalinguistic gloss, 'as you put it', which has the effect of distancing her, and by implication, the overhearing audience, from Foster's use of the euphemistic nominalisation 'affordability'. This is reinforced by the sceptical tone of the tag question that follows and which subsequently leads Foster to produce the preferred negative response cued by the question.

As Bell and van Leeuwen (1994: 153) note, 'Admission must be avoided if the politician's claim to be competent in fulfilling his role is not to be weakened in the eyes of the...public', yet Foster here admits the force of MacGregor's objection. Whereas Humphrys might, or might not, of course, have achieved this admission from Foster as a result of a doggedly hectoring tone, MacGregor does so by adopting the slightly quizzical tone associated with the 'honest broker' role, rather than with the gladiatorial one. Nor is she averse to interrupting her interviewee's turn in the interest of balance, as she does with her next contribution which takes the form of a challenge, signalled by the use of the adversative conjunction 'although'. The purpose of this interruption is to put what she assumes would be Railtrack's account of its achievements thus far. This then produces another concession from Foster, although he goes on to qualify this in some detail. MacGregor's final question is a release question in that the embedded presupposition 'which of course were not perfect' is one which she could have been fairly certain Foster would have been more than happy to endorse and elaborate upon. What this extract demonstrates is that it is not necessary to employ an aggressively confrontational tone in order to encourage politicians to concede points or to hold them to account for policy detail.

Whereas MacGregor was given a virtual monopoly of 'soft news' items during the general election, there were very few examples in my corpus in which she interviewed prominent politicians, and none in which she was allocated the big political interview of the day. For instance, on a day when Humphrys conducted an extended two-way interview with the then Foreign Secretary, Robin Cook, and the then Shadow Foreign Secretary, Francis Maude, MacGregor covered a feature on spending on cosmetics and vitamins, and another on the whereabouts of the bones of the Romanov family (*Today*, 23 May 2001). This may, of course, be due in part to the perception amongst politicians that she was a less effective political interviewer than her male colleagues, but I would suggest that this judgement is itself gendered. This is implicit in Kenneth Clarke's references to her as 'waspish', 'whingey' and 'testy', adjectives that, as MacGregor herself points out, are highly unlikely to have been used to describe a male political interviewer (MacGregor, 2002: 327). Robin Cook claims that her 'relatively softer approach' is more appropriate to 'stories which perhaps lend themselves less to interruption' (cited in Donovan, 1997: 120), in other words, to 'soft news' stories.

Even praise for her style, in this instance from Humphrys, often perpetuates stereotypical assumptions about bossy, sniping woman: 'Somebody will say something thinking that Sue's a kind of a pushover and she'll snap back, and sometimes she'll do the headmistress thing and be cross with somebody' (cited in Donovan 1997: 138). However, in spite of her reputation for being less aggressive than her male colleagues, MacGregor notes that she has, nonetheless 'been criticised for being too-too aggressive and interrupting too much...now that is gendered, if you like [based on], I expect, perceptions of what women interviewers should be like' (Interview with the author, 26 October 2001). This kind of double bind for women in high-profile positions in public life has been noted by a number of feminist sociolinguists (Coates, 1995: 15; Crawford, 1995: 65). Yet, MacGregor's longevity on *Today* appears to have been due to the fact that audience research repeatedly showed that she was the most popular presenter amongst listeners. The rapport she built up with the majority of listeners enabled her to accrue what Mills (2003: 175) refers to as 'interactional power' in a community of professional practice in which she was nonetheless accorded a subordinate role.

The kind of difference a 'critical difference' stance can make is illustrated well in a two-way interview MacGregor conducted with the internationally renowned novelist Doris Lessing and the then director of the Fawcett society Mary Ann Stephenson (15 August, 2001). Lessing was invited to the programme to elaborate upon her very widely publicised claim, made at the Edinburgh Book Festival, that feminism has encouraged the 'rubbishing' of men. With an interviewer less sympathetic to feminist goals, this could have degenerated into a polarised debate between revisionist feminism and 'old style' feminism. Instead, under MacGregor's skilful questioning this kind of outright confrontation was avoided. One strategy by which she achieved this was to employ a light-hearted tone to frame a challenging question about whether Lessing believed young boys were being 'crumpled' by women, adding, by way of mitigation, 'I think you used that word.' As the following extract from the interview makes clear, MacGregor goes on to interpolate a comment that serves to strengthen Stephenson's argument against Lessing's view that things have 'swung too far' in favour of women:

Extract (4) BBC Radio 4, Today programme, 15 August 2001

MAS: Women continue to earn less than men (.) an average woman earns about a quarter of a million pounds less over her lifetime [than an average man

SMG: [We're talking about nearly thirty years after equal pay legislation.
MAS: Absolutely...

Later in the same interview, MacGregor uses her own experience as a long-standing presenter on *Today* to call into question the validity of another of Lessing's claims:

Extract (5) BBC Radio 4, Today programme, 15 August 2001

DL: Why don't you spend a day which I've recently been doing just listening to radio programmes, eh television advertisements, newspapers and just see how often men are put down and rubbished? It is quite unpleasant and quite frightening really because what is it doing to the boys? This is what we have to be concerned about.
SMG: I haven't noticed it very often on the *Today* programme, I have to say [but eh Mary Ann Stephenson
DL: [but the *Today* programme is a nice programme.
SMG: What's your view on this, that men are being put down constantly on radio programmes?
MAS: It's not (.) it's not something that I've noticed to be honest...

Rather than being a wholly impartial arbiter on this occasion, MacGregor subtly aligns herself with Stephenson to offer an alternative perspective on contemporary gender politics than the revisionist one proffered by the much more high-profile Lessing. One can imagine a very different outcome had this interview been conducted by the pugilistic and avowedly non-PC Humphrys.

Conclusion

I would challenge Humphrys' claim that 'the democratic process is at its healthiest when the argument is at its liveliest' (2001: 253), if this so-called liveliness of a political broadcast interview is to be measured in terms of how 'confrontational' it is. Robust questioning, as MacGregor demonstrates, need not be aggressive. Whereas Humphrys talks about 'long suffering interviewees' leaving the studio 'battered and bleeding' (Humphrys, 2001: 255), MacGregor's interview style makes clear that there is another, more productive, way of holding politicians to account, albeit one that is not accorded sufficient value in the male-dominated discourse of mediatised politics. As a result, as McNair (2001: 184) points out, 'The broadcasters become reviewers of political performance and rhetoric, rather than independent objective analysts and scrutinisers of policy and action.' This adversarial style that has come to assume the status of common sense is, in fact, historically contingent and is open to challenge and change. Humphrys closes his book *Devil's Advocate* with a plea for dissident voices in the media, but far from being 'dissident', his own public voice conforms all too readily to a masculinist consensual norm.

The adversarial style of interview favoured by 'big hitting' interviewers, such as Humphrys, is, I would argue, ultimately self-indulgent, leaving many listeners/voters feeling disenfranchised. This is a point also made by Bell and van Leeuwen (1994) who suggest that media commentators' view of politics as a cynical game 'encourages alienation and apathy among citizens who have little option but to become mere spectators at the circus of [mediatized] politics'. A female voice – or rather, the less confrontational style of interviewing favoured by feminist-oriented women such as MacGregor – is much more likely to encourage listeners to focus on policy issues, rather than personalities, on the substance of talk, rather than on its performance. This is an interactional style that is, of course, open to both women *and* men, but it will take a radical shift in the culture of the newsroom in order to prevent those who employ such a style from being assigned only to 'soft' news stories. A call for a less adversarial mediatised discourse does *not*, however, mean a return to old-style deference. Instead, it is a call for a style of political interviewing that will avoid leaving listeners feeling bemused and disengaged from the whole political process.

Key to transcription conventions

(0.3)	timed pause in seconds
[	
[	overlapping talk
((laugh))	paralinguistic features
he got <u>that</u> wrong	marked stress
HIS WEAKNESSES	increased volume
?	rising tone
.hh	marked intake of breath
...	omitted talk

Notes

1. Although another female *Today* presenter, Anna Ford, described the sports bulletins on the programme as particularly 'blokeish', I noted a revealing

instance in my corpus in which MacGregor and the sports presenter, Steve May, formed an apparently spontaneous cross-gender alliance with the intention of deflating what they clearly perceived to be Humphrys' over-inflated sense of his own importance as a media personality. It followed a slot in which Humphrys had held the floor for an inordinate amount of time, following an item he had just presented about a ban on ice-cream sales on Frinton beach:

Extract (6) BBC Radio 4, Today programme, 15 August 2001

SMG: Are you finished? ((said in a mock-impatient tone))
JH: Yeah. ((said in a sheepish tone))
SMG: 7.26 is the time. Steve May is here with the sport news ((laughter)).
SM: Yeah, when are they gonna give him his own series then?
SMG   ((mutual laughter))
&JH:
SM: Er morning to you. Let's get to the important part of this programme (0.2) the sport

2. Evidence to support this is provided by the fact that voter turnout at the 2001 British general election was the lowest on record, with 40 per cent of voters failing to use their vote. A survey by the Independent Television Commission revealed that 40 per cent of viewers had switched channels during the campaign in order to avoid election news and 70 per cent said that they had little or no interest in politics. In a series of public lectures broadcast on BBC Radio 4 in 2002, the philosopher Onora O'Neil referred to the widespread crisis in public trust that is prevalent in British society and that has fuelled what she terms a 'culture of suspicion'.
3. It is interesting, given the current controversy in the field of language and gender studies about women's relationship to norms of politeness (see, for instance, Holmes, 1995; Mills, 2003), that in a survey I conducted of twenty-one regular listeners of the *Today* programme, twelve of whom were male and nine female, only four respondents judged Humphrys' adherence to politeness norms as 'good' or 'very good', whereas fifteen respondents gave MacGregor a 'good' or 'very good' rating for this criterion.
4. For instance, Montague has a tendency to use the media interviewer's prerogative to manage the time allotted to a given interview to cut the interviewee off mid-sentence. Initially, I attributed this pattern of interruption to her relative inexperience on the programme, but it is, in fact, a habitual feature of her style of interviewing and one that has the effect of wrong-footing her interviewee in the closing stages of the interview, irrespective of his/her status.

References

Bell, P. and van Leeuwen, T. (1994) *Media Interview*, Kensington, N.S.W.: University of New South Wales Press.

Blumler, J. and Gurevitch, M. (1995) *Crisis of Public Communication*, London: Routledge.

Clayman, S. and Heritage, J. (2002) *The News Interview: Journalists and Public Figures on Air*, Cambridge: Cambridge University Press.

Coates, J. (1995) 'Language, gender and career', in S. Mills (ed.), *Language and Gender: Interdisciplinary Perspectives*, London: Longman, pp. 13–30.

Crawford, M. (1995) *Talking Difference: On Gender and Language*, London: Sage.

Curran, J. (1982) 'Communication, Power and Social Order', in M. Gurevitch, T. Bennett, J. Curran and J. Woolacott (eds), *Culture, Society and the Media*, London: Methuen.

Donovan, P. (1997) *All Our Todays*, London: Jonathan Cape.

Eckert, P. and McConnell-Ginet, S. (1992) 'Think practically and look locally: Language and gender as community-based practice', *Annual Review of Anthropology*, 21, pp. 461–490.

Fairclough, N. (1998) 'Political discourse in the media: An analytical framework', in A. Bell and P. Garrett (eds), *Approaches to Media Discourse*, Oxford: Blackwell, pp. 141–162.

Harris, S. (2001) 'Being politically impolite: Extending politeness theory to adversarial political discourse', *Discourse Studies*, 12 (4), pp. 451–472.

Heritage, J. and Greatbach, D. (1991) 'On the institutional character of institutional talk: The case of news interviews', in D. Boden and D. Zimmerman (eds), *Talk and Social Structure*, Cambridge: Polity Press, pp. 93–137.

Holmes, J. (1995) *Women, Men and Politeness*, Harlow: Longman.

Holmes, J. and Stubbe, M. (2003) *Power and Politeness in the Workplace*, Harlow: Longman.

Humphrys, J. (2001) *Devil's Advocate*, London: Arrow Books.

Kumar, K. (1977) 'Holding the middle ground: The BBC, the public and the professional broadcaster', in J. Curran, M. Gurevitch and J. Woolacott (eds), *Mass Communication and Society*, London: Edward Arnold.

MacGregor, S. (2002) *A Woman of Today*, London: Headline.

McNair, B. (2001) 'Public relations and Broadcast talk', in M. Bromley (ed), *No News is Bad News*, London: Methuen, pp. 175–189.

Mills, S. (2003) *Gender and Politeness*, Cambridge: Cambridge University Press.

Mullany, L. (1999) 'Linguistic politeness and sex differences in BBC Radio 4 broadcast interviews', in *Leeds Working Papers in Linguistics and Phonetics*, No. 7, pp. 119–145.

O'Neill, O. (2002) 'Spreading Suspicion' and 'A Question of Trust', @www.bbc.co.uk/radio4/reith2002/lecture1 and lecture5, broadcast April 2002.

Thornborrow, J. (2002) *Power Talk: Language and Interaction in Institutional Discourse*, Harlow: Longman.

Tolson, A. (1991) 'Television chat and the synthetic', in P. Scannell (ed), *Broadcast Talk*, London: Sage, pp. 78–200.

van Zoonen, L. (1998) 'One of the girls? The changing gender of journalism', in C. Carter, G. Branston and S. Allan (eds), *News, Gender and Power*, London: Routledge, pp. 33–46.

Walsh, C. (2001) *Gender and Discourse: Language and Power in Politics, the Church and Organisations*, Harlow: Longman.

8
Trial Discourse and Judicial Decision-Making[1]: Constraining the Boundaries of Gendered Identities

Susan Ehrlich
York University, Toronto, Canada

Introduction

Recent formulations of the relationship between language and gender, following Butler (1990), have emphasized the performative aspect of gender. Under this account, language is one important means by which gender—an ongoing social process—is enacted or constituted; gender is something individuals *do*—in part through linguistic choices—as opposed to something individuals *are* or *have* (West and Zimmerman, 1987). While the theorizing of gender as 'performative' has encouraged language and gender researchers to focus on the agency and creativity of social actors in the constitution of gender, to my mind there has been less emphasis placed on another aspect of Butler's framework—the 'rigid regulatory frame' (Butler, 1990) within which gendered identities are produced—that is, the limits and constraints on speakers' agency in constructing such identities. This emphasis on the 'performative' aspect of Butler's work, rather than on her discussions of the regulatory norms that define and police normative constructions of gender, may arise because, as Cameron (1997) suggests, philosophical accounts of Butler's 'rigid regulatory frame' often remain very abstract. For Cameron (1997: 31), too often in feminist philosophical discussions, 'gender...floats free of the social contexts and activities in which it will always be...embedded,' obscuring the fact that the routine enactment of gender is often, perhaps always, subject to what she calls the 'institutional coerciveness' of social situations. In other words, cultural norms (i.e. Butler's rigid regulatory frame) make certain performances of gender seem appropriate and intelligible; in Butler's (p. 49) words, they 'congeal over time to produce the appearance...of a natural kind of being.' These same cultural norms render other performances of gender inappropriate and unintelligible and at times subject to social and physical penalties and sanctions (e.g. homophobia, gay-bashing, the 'fixing' of intersexed infants).

By examining data from a public institution, a Canadian sexual assault trial, I demonstrate how culturally dominant notions of male and female sexuality can impose constraints on the formation of participants' gendered identities. Moreover, I show how the gendered identities ascribed and assigned to individuals can depart from the identities individuals intend to claim or adopt.

Significant to an investigation of 'talk' in trial contexts is the fact that interpretations and understandings of the talk are discernable not only in the talk's local discourse (i.e. in the trial), but also in the non-local assessments and judgments of non-speaking recipients (i.e. juries and/ or judges). Thus, while the Crown attorney (i.e. the lawyer representing the state) in the sexual assault trial 'talk' described later represented the complainant as *resisting* her perpetrator of sexual assault to the extent possible, judges at both the trial level and the appeal level represented the complainant as *participating* in consensual sex with the accused.[2] Put somewhat differently, the gendered sense-making framework, or *discourse* (see Editor's Introduction), that the judges imposed on the events in question departed quite dramatically from the gendered sense-making framework, or discourse, invoked by the Crown attorney in her questioning of the complainant. Through her questioning of the complainant, the Crown attorney allowed a feminist understanding of sexual violence to emerge: one that acknowledged the unequal power dynamics that can shape and restrict women's behavior in the face of men's sexual violence. Yet such an understanding of the complainant's behavior failed to find its way into the judicial decisions of the trial judge or the appeal judge. Indeed, the fact that it was not recognized in these judicial decisions is illustrative, I suggest, of the way that dominant, androcentric discourses (i.e. Butler's rigid regulatory frame) can render certain performances of gender as unintelligible and incoherent. Thus, this chapter considers the notion of 'the female voice' to the extent that it demonstrates the way a feminist perspective, when manifest in a public context, can be distorted or rendered invisible by the androcentric discourses that often dominate in these contexts.

The participant structure of trial discourse

In describing trial practices, Hale and Gibbons (1999: 203) make a useful distinction between 'two intersecting planes of reality' in the courtroom: the reality of the courtroom itself—what they call the 'courtroom reality'—and the reality that comprises the events under investigation in the courtroom—what they call the 'external reality.' In the court's representation of this 'external reality,' visual images (e.g. photographs, diagrams) and physical entities (e.g. weapons, clothing) are often introduced as evidence, but Hale and Gibbons (1999: 203) remark that 'by far the most common representation of this other reality [the external reality] is...through testimonial evidence which consists of descriptions of the events by witnesses—versions of the second reality presented through language.' That is, within the context of legal adjudication processes, language is the primary means by which witnesses and lawyers convey information about the events that are the subject of a court's deliberations. And, while much of the courtroom language representing this 'external reality' ostensibly occurs between lawyers and witnesses—that is, it is dyadic—the participant structure of the speech event of the trial is in fact more complex than this. Given that the primary target of courtroom interactions between lawyers and witnesses is a third-party, overhearing recipient—a judge and/or jury— trial talk is more accurately characterized as multi-party (Drew, 1985; Cotterill, 2003). One way of conceptualizing this multi-party structure is by appealing to Goffman's (1981) notion of the 'gathering.' According to Goffman (1981: 136), 'interactional facts' have to be considered in relation to 'the full physical arena in which persons present are in sight and sound of one another'—what Goffman labeled a 'gathering.' Put somewhat differently, Goffman (1981) argued that the two-person, face-to-face, speaker–hearer model is too crude a construct to account for significant aspects of talk-in-interaction given that speakers will alter how they speak and/or what they say 'by virtue of conducting their talk in visual and aural range of non-participants' (Goffman, 1981: 136). These 'non-participants,' according to Goffman, can include unratified recipients such as bystanders or eavesdroppers as well as ratified recipients. Within the courtroom context, judges and juries constitute ratified recipients, and for Levinson (1988), who elaborates on Goffman's framework, they are the 'indirect target' of trial talk.

For my purposes here, what is important is Goffman's recognition that participants who are not actively and directly participating in an interaction may nonetheless influence many of its properties. While

Goffman talks explicitly about how speakers may alter their linguistic identities under the influence of unratified indirect recipients of talk (e.g. bystanders), in this paper I am interested in how ratified indirect recipients of talk, that is judges in trial contexts, may influence and control the (gendered) meanings and interpretations assigned to speakers' linguistic identities. I shall argue that, in order to understand the complexity of gendered identities and, in particular, the way they can be constrained by cultural norms (i.e. Butler's rigid regulatory frame), we need to be attentive to the work of indirect recipients within an interaction or, in Goffman's (1981: 136) words, to 'the full physical arena in which persons present are in sight and sound of one another.'

Data

The data analyzed here come from a Canadian criminal trial involving sexual assault: Her Majesty the Queen v. Ewanchuk, 1995. The case involved a sexual assault that took place during a job interview between the accused (also referred to as the defendant) and the complainant (also referred to as the plaintiff), a 17-year-old woman who ultimately charged the man with sexual assault. The accused was a carpenter and wished to hire individuals who would sell his work for him. While the complainant suggested that her job interview be held in a mall, the accused expressed a preference for more privacy and proposed instead that the interview take place in his van. The interview was conducted in a polite, business-like fashion, according to the complainant's testimony. During the interview the complainant left the door of the van open because she was hesitant about discussing the job offer in his vehicle. After the job interview, the accused invited the complainant to see some of his work in his trailer (i.e. caravan) which was attached to the van. Again, according to the complainant's testimony, she purposely left the trailer door open out of fear of being alone with the accused in a confined space, but the accused ignored her efforts and closed and locked the door. The accused initiated a number of incidents with the complainant that involved sexual touching, with each incident becoming progressively more intimate than the previous. The complainant said that she complied with many of his requests out of fear that any resistance would prompt the accused to become more violent. However, when his touching progressed to the complainant's breast, she used her elbows to push him away and said 'no.' The accused resumed his sexual touching and began to massage the complainant's inner thigh and pelvic area, at which point the complainant again said 'no.' The accused resumed his advances by grinding his pelvis into hers, touching her vaginal area and placing his penis on the complainant's pelvic area under her shorts. He stopped after the complainant said 'no' a third time. After these incidents, the accused opened the door of the trailer at the complainant's request and the complainant left the trailer. She later charged the accused with sexual assault.

The trial judge acquitted the accused of sexual assault relying on the defense of 'implied consent' and the Alberta Court of Appeal upheld this acquittal. The Supreme Court of Canada overturned this acquittal and entered a conviction of sexual assault for the accused. In what follows, I analyze data from the 1995 trial, the 1995 decision of the trial judge and the 1998 decision of the Alberta Court of Appeal. In particular, I contrast two sets of data from this case: excerpts from direct recipients' talk, that is question–answer sequences between the Crown attorney and the complainant, *and* excerpts from indirect recipients' discourse, that is the judges' decisions. Specifically, looking beyond the face-to-face aspects of communication to the discourse of indirect recipients allows us to consider the regulatory norms—that is, Butler's rigid regulatory frame—and the constraints they can impose on identities.

Question–answer sequences in trial discourse

Like other types of institutional discourse, courtroom discourse has been the subject of much research over the past two decades—research that, among other things, has highlighted its asymmetrical character. As others have noted about courtroom discourse (e.g. Atkinson and Drew, 1979; Walker, 1987; Conley and O' Barr, 1998), differential participation rights are assigned to participants depending on their institutional roles; that is, questioners in legal contexts have the right to initiate and allocate turns by asking questions of witnesses but the reverse is not true. And, such differential participation rights, it has been argued, bestows considerable conversational power and control upon the participant who is sanctioned to ask questions (Hutchby and Wooffitt, 1998). For example, in discussing doctor–patient interaction, Drew and Heritage (1992) note that the question–answer pattern that characterizes most such interactions not only allows doctors to gather information from patients, but can also result in doctors directing and controlling talk: introducing topics, changing topics, and selectively formulating and reformulating the terms in which patients' problems are expressed. Similar claims have been made about lawyers in their role as questioners in the courtroom. However, given the *adversarial* nature of courtroom discourse within the Anglo-American common law system and the *legally sanctioned* power of lawyers to ask questions, lawyers may exercise even more conversational control than doctors in their respective institutional settings.

Adversarial dispute resolution, of which trials are a notable example, requires that two parties come together formally, usually with representation (e.g. lawyers), to present their (probably different) versions of the dispute to a third party (e.g. judge, jury, tribunal) who hears the evidence, applies the appropriate laws or regulations, and determines the guilt or innocence of the parties. Lawyers have as their task, then, convincing the adjudicating body that their (i.e. their client's) version of events is the most credible, or in Capps' and Ochs' (1995) terms, 'the official story.' Apart from making opening and closing arguments, however, lawyers do not themselves testify. Thus, through the posing of questions, lawyers must elicit from witnesses testimony that will build a credible version of events in support of their own clients' interests in addition to testimony that will challenge, weaken, and/or cast doubt on the opposing parties' version of events. Atkinson and Drew (1979: 70) note that while trial discourse is conducted predominantly through a series of question–answer sequences, other actions are accomplished in the form of such questions and answers. For example, questions may be designed to accuse witnesses, to challenge or undermine the truth of what they are saying, or, in direct examination, to presuppose the truth and adequacy of what they are saying.

Direct examination of the complainant

In contrast to the adversarial, combative nature of cross-examination, direct examination, that is the questioning of one's own witness, has been characterized by both legal practitioners and scholars as supportive and cooperative (e.g. Woodbury, 1984; Barry, 1991; Maley, 1994). According to Cotterill (2003: 129), direct examination 'represents an initial, dominant narrative statement, which is then responded to, challenged and sometimes subverted in cross-examination questioning.' Because the emphasis in direct examination is on developing new information, open-ended questions tend to be more frequent in direct examination. Moreover, Woodbury (1984: 211) suggests that open-ended questions have a strategic function as well: they allow witnesses to construct extended narratives that 'give an authentic ring to testimony' and convey to third-party recipients (e.g. judge and/or jury) that lawyers are trusting of their witnesses. Indeed, Harris (2001: 68) argues that lawyers must exercise a high degree of control over *all* witnesses, but that the strategies required to do this differ depending on whether the witness is 'friendly' or 'hostile.'

Because the varying versions of events that emerge in trial discourse are determined to a large extent by the questions that lawyers ask of witnesses (e.g. their controlling of witnesses' topics, their selective reformulations of witnesses' prior answers, etc.), Cotterill (2003: 149) argues that courtroom narratives are best characterized as 'dual-authored texts,' 'with the emphasis on the voice of the lawyer as the primary and authoritative teller.' Due to the 'dual-authored' nature of courtroom narratives, in what follows I analyze question–answer sequences between the Crown attorney and the complainant using the analytic framework of Conversation Analysis, broadly conceived. Conversation Analysis is fundamentally concerned with the sequential analysis of utterances, that is 'how utterances are designed to tie with, or 'fit' to, prior utterances and how an utterance has significant implications for what kinds of utterances should come next' (Wooffitt, 2001: 54). I adopt this approach to question–answer sequences in the direct examination of the complainant because the nature of the questions asked by the Crown attorney has significant implications for what kinds of utterances come next, specifically the kind of testimony the complainant produces and the kind of discursive identity she projects.

In the direct examination of the complainant in the Ewanchuk case, the Crown attorney typically began by asking a broad Wh-question (e.g. 'What happened then?'), that is a Wh-question that allowed the complainant to construct an extended narrative. In response to this broad Wh-question, the complainant would provide an answer that described an event or a series of events. Immediately following such an answer, the lawyer would ask a more narrow Wh-question, that is a Why-question that attempted to elicit more specific information: the plaintiff's motivation for performing a particular action that she had described. For example, in (1) below, the Crown attorney begins by asking a broad Wh-question about the events that transpired once the plaintiff reached the defendant's van. The plaintiff's answer is followed by a more narrow Wh-question—a Why-question inquiring about the plaintiff's motivation for suggesting that she and the defendant talk inside the mall, as opposed to in his van. What emerges in the answer to the Why-question is the complainant's desire to talk to the defendant in a public place.[3]

Q: Was he inside the van or trailer when you first got there?
A: I believe he was inside the van, but—he might have stepped out to meet me.

> Q: What happened once you got there?
> A: I asked him if we could go inside the mall, have a cup of coffee and talk about whatever.
> → Q: Why did you want to go inside the mall to talk?
> A: Because it was—it was a public place. I mean, we could go in and sit down somewhere and talk.

According to Woodbury (1984: 211), the narrow Wh-questions that follow broad Wh-questions in direct examination serve a narrative function. Since it is important that lawyers and witnesses co-construct 'a coherent and maximally detailed account' for the sake of third-party recipients, Woodbury maintains that narrow Wh-questions allow witnesses to elaborate on details that contribute to the coherence of the narrative. But, what is it that determines the *kind* of details that will make a narrative cohere? Why, for example, does the Crown attorney in the Ewanchuk case follow up her broad Wh-questions with Why-questions that probe the plaintiff's reasons for performing certain actions in the series of events under question?

It is my contention that the narratives elicited from the complainant through the Crown attorney's questions cohered as feminist narratives. That is, the Crown attorney allowed a feminist understanding of sexual violence to emerge in the complainant's testimony. In particular, it became clear through the question–answer sequences of the Crown attorney and the complainant that the threat of men's sexual violence can create an asymmetrical power relationship between men and women which, in turn, can shape and restrict women's efforts to resist their perpetrators. Consider examples (1)–(5) below which all come from the direct examination of the complainant (I have repeated example (1) below), and all contain a Why-question from the Crown attorney that asks why the complainant has performed a particular action. The answers elicited by these questions (italicized below) reveal the strategic nature of the complainant's actions; that is, the particular actions the Crown attorney asks about are represented by the complainant as ways she attempted to discourage the accused's sexual advances.

Example 1
Q: Was he inside the van or trailer when you first got there?
A: I believe he was inside the van, but—he might have stepped out to meet me.
Q: What happened once you got there?
A: I asked him if we could go inside the mall, have a cup of coffee and talk about whatever.

→   Q: Why did you want to go inside the mall to talk?
   A: *Because it was—it was a public place. I mean, we could go in and sit down somewhere and talk.*

Example 2
Q: What happened then?
A: He said, Why don't we just talk inside the van here. And he sat into his driver's seat, and I opened the door, and I left the door open of the passenger seat and I sat down there.
→   Q: And why did you leave the door open?
   A: *Because I was still very hesitant about talking to him.*

Example 3
Q: What happened after you agreed to see some of his work?
A: He went around to—no, first, he said, Okay, I'd like to pull the van into the shade. It was a hot day, and there was cars that were parked under the shade for an shade of a tree, I believe, and he got out, and he went and he stepped inside, and he said, Come on up and look. So I stepped up inside, took about two steps in, I didn't, like, walk around in it. And then he went to the door, closed it, and locked it.
   (some intervening turns)
Q: Had you expected him to lock the door?
A: Not at all. I left the door completely wide open when I walked in there for a reason.
→   Q: And what was that reason?
   A: *Because I felt that this was a situation that I shouldn't be in, that I—with anybody to be alone in a trailer with any guy with the door closed.*

Example 4
Q: Did you talk about other things while you were sitting in front of the van?
A: Yes. He asked—we talked a little bit more on a personal level.
Q: What do you mean by that?
A: I believe I told him that I was living on my own. Well, not totally on my own. There was about three other people living there and that I had a boyfriend.
→   Q: Why would you tell him those things?
   A: *Because I felt that he should know because I just—I felt—I felt that he might feel a little more threatened if I had said that.*

Example 5

Q: What happened after you talked about your personalities?

A: We were still mentioning a lot of personal things. Like I was still mentioning that I had a boyfriend. I believe I said his name.

Q: What was his name?

A: His name was Allan.

(some intervening turns)

→   Q: Why were you mentioning your boyfriend Allan?

A: *Because, like I said, I felt like if he ever—if—it might prevent him from going beyond any more touching.*

In example (1), when asked why she suggested going inside the mall, the complainant explains that it was a *public* place. (Presumably, sexual advances are less likely to occur in public places.) In examples (2) and (3), when asked why she left the doors open to the front of the van and the trailer, respectively, the complainant explains that she was 'hesitant' about talking to the accused alone 'with the door closed.' In examples (4) and (5), when asked why she was mentioning her boyfriend, Allan, the complainant explains that she wanted the accused to feel 'threatened' and that she wanted to 'prevent him from going beyond any more touching.' Clearly, what the Crown attorney succeeds in eliciting in asking these particular Why-questions is a sense that the complainant is not passive, but rather is actively attempting to create circumstances that will discourage the accused's sexual advances.

Examples (6)–(9) are somewhat different from (1)–(5), as the Crown attorney does not ask questions about actions intended to discourage and/or prevent the accused's sexual advances, but rather asks about actions that could be construed as preambles to consensual sex.

Example 6

Q: Did he say anything when he locked the door?

A: He didn't say anything about the door being locked, but he asked me to sit down. And he sat down cross-legged.

Q: What did you sit on?

A: Just the floor of the trailer.

→   Q: Now, why did you sit down when he asked you to sit down?

A: *Because I figured I was in this trailer, the door was locked, he was not much more than this stand is away from me here, probably only a couple of feet away from me. I felt that I was in a situation now where I just better do what I was told.*

Example 7

Q: And what happened then?

A: He told me that he felt very tense and that he would like to have a massage, and he then leaned up against me with his back towards me and told me to rub his shoulders and I did that.

Q: And up to the time he told you he was tense and wanted a massage, had the two of you talked about you giving him a massage?

A: I believe all he had said right before that is that he liked to have them, and he was tense feeling and that was all.

Q: Had you ever offered to give him a massage?

A: No.

Q: Did you want to give him a massage?

A: No.

(some intervening turns)

→ Q: If you didn't want to give him a massage at that point in time, why did you touch his shoulders?

A: *I was afraid that if I put up any more of a struggle that it would only egg him on even more, and his touching would be more forced.*

Example 8

Q: And what happened then?

A: Then he asked me to turn around the other way to face him, and he said he would like to touch my feet or he would like to massage my feet, so I did. And he was just touching my feet.

Q: Did you want him to massage your feet?

A: No.

→ Q: Why did you turn around?

A: *Because I guess I was afraid. I was frozen. I just did what he told me to do.*

Q: Did he ever ask you if you would like him to massage his feet— your feet?

A: No, he just said, Turn around I'm going to.

Q: What happened after you turned around?

A: He was massaging my feet, but he didn't stay there. He was moving up my leg more toward my inner thigh, my pelvic area, and then he'd move back again, and then he'd move back up again, and *I just sat there, and I didn't—I didn't do anything. I didn't say anything. I knew something was going to happen, and I didn't want to fight. I didn't want to struggle. I didn't want to scream, because I felt that that would just egg him on more.*

Example 9
Q: And what happened when he reached to hug you?
A: He just did, and I, at this time, I was trying really hard not to cry. I had been wiping my eyes when he was on top of me when he couldn't see me, and I just....I just responded by just lightly putting my arm on him when he hugged me because I was afraid that he would think I was really scared, and that I would leave there telling people.
→   Q: And why were you worried about him thinking that?
A: *Because I didn't think that he would stop there, that it would get worse, and it would be more brutal.*

Put somewhat differently, in examples (6)–(9), the Crown attorney asks why the complainant complies with the accused's requests: in (6), why she sits down when asked; in (7), why she begins to massage the accused when asked; in (8), why she turns around to face the accused when he asks to massage her feet; and, in (9), why her fear of the accused leads her to reciprocate his hug. In response to these questions, the complainant says a variety of things: that she was afraid; that she felt she should do what she was told; that she feared if she did not comply with the accused's requests or if she put up a struggle that she would 'egg him on even more,' 'his touching would be more forced,' and 'it would be more brutal.' Indeed, such responses reflect strategies that many victims of sexual violence employ to prevent more prolonged and extreme instances of violence. As researchers on violence against women have asserted, submitting to coerced sex or physical abuse can be 'a strategic mode of action undertaken in preservation of self' (Lempert, 1996: 281). That is, if physical resistance on the part of victims can escalate and intensify violence, as some research shows (e.g. Dobash and Dobash, 1992) and many women (are instructed to) believe, then submission to coerced sex is undoubtedly the best strategy for survival. Significant about the Crown attorney's questioning in (6)–(9) is the fact that her questions allow the complainant's actions to be revealed as strategies of resistance, rather than as precursors to consensual sex. In fact, all of the Crown's why-questions highlighted in examples (1)–(9) function to elicit responses that emphasize the complainant's active deployment of strategies meant to discourage and resist the accused's escalating sexual violence.[4] Put another way, the complainant's actions were contextualized within a framework, or discourse, that acknowledged the potential structural inequalities that characterize male–female sexual relations and the effects of such inequalities on women's strategies of resistance. We will see in the next section that, by contrast, the trial judge and the appeal judge contextualized the complainant's actions within an alternative framework or discourse—one that erased the unequal power dynamics of male–female sexual relations and, concomitantly, construed coerced sex as consensual sex.

Judges' discourse

As stated in a previous section, the trial judge's decision to acquit the accused in this case was appealed to the Alberta Court of Appeal, where the acquittal was upheld, and then to the Supreme Court of Canada, where the acquittal was overturned. In this section, I discuss both the decision of the trial judge and the Alberta Court of Appeal judge, including the defense both judges invoked in acquitting the accused—'the defense of implied consent.'

The first noteworthy aspect of both of these decisions, given that the Crown attorney and the complainant depicted the complainant as attempting to discourage and resist the accused, was the consistent representation of sexual relations between the accused and the complainant as consensual sex. Consider the following excerpt from the trial judge's decision, at a point when the judge is describing the 'facts' of the case:

Example 10
1 B [the complainant] told A [the accused] that she was an open,
2 friendly and affectionate person; and that she often liked to touch
3 people. A told B that he was an open, friendly and affectionate
4 person; and that he often liked to touch people. A and B talked.
5 They touched each other. They hugged. They were sitting on the
6 floor of the trailer and they were lying on the floor of the trailer.
7 A told B that he would like a body massage, and B gave A a body
8 massage. For the body massage, A sat in front of B so that B could
9 massage A's back. They later exchanged places so that A could give
10 B a body massage. B later lay on her back, and A gave B a foot
11 massage. After the foot massage, A massaged B's bare legs and he
12 massaged her bare inner thighs. During this period of two and one
13 half hours, A did three things which B did not like. When A was
14 giving B a body massage. his hands got close to B's breasts. B said
15 "No", and A immediately stopped. When B and A were lying on
16 the floor, A rubbed his pelvic area against B's pelvic area. B said
17 "No", and A immediately stopped. Later on A took his soft penis
18 out of his shorts and placed it on the outside of B's clothes in her
19 pelvic area. B said "No", and A immediately stopped.

20 During all of the two and one half hours that A and B were
21 together, she never told A that she wanted to leave. When B
22 finally told A that she wanted to leave, she and A simply walked
23 out of the trailer.

(from Reasons for Judgment (Moore, J., C.Q.B.A.),
November 10, 1995)

These same 'facts' are confirmed by the Alberta Court of Appeal judge in his support of the trial judge's 'doubts about consent.'

> *Example 11*
> Yet, if review of the evidence that supports the trial judge's doubts about consent in this case is called for, it may be found in the following. The advances that are now said to be criminally assaultive were preceded by *an exchange of consensual body massages, partially on the floor of the trailer, hugs and assurances of trust and restraint*....Beyond that (and somewhat inconsistent with an appellate profile of Ewanchuk as a relentless sexual predator) every advance he made to her stopped when she spoke against it.
> (from Reasons for Judgment of the Honourable
Mr. Justice McClung, February 12, 1998)

In general, these descriptions of what transpired between the accused and the complainant—with the exception of the descriptions of the three times that the complainant said 'no'—emphasize the consensual, mutual and reciprocal nature of their sexual relations. Indeed, the appeal judge states quite explicitly that the hugs and the body massages were reciprocal (i.e. 'an exchange') and 'consensual' (in italics above). Particularly striking is the fact that both judges represent as consensual and reciprocal events that the Crown attorney and the complainant depicted as coerced sex. That is, on many occasions—and this is exemplified in examples (6)–(9)—the complainant said she complied with the accused's wishes out of fear that his violence would otherwise escalate. Yet, the judges represent these events as ones that the complainant engaged in without coercion. For example, in line 5 of example (10), the trial judge states that the complainant and the accused hugged each other in a reciprocal way (i.e. 'They hugged') whereas in example (9) the complainant says that she responded to the accused's hug out of fear, that is 'because [she] was afraid that he would think [she] was really scared' which in turn would lead to even greater brutality. Likewise, in lines 7–8 of (10), the judge states simply that the complainant gave the accused a body massage in response to his request (i.e. 'A told B that he would like a body massage, and B gave A a body massage'); yet in example (7) the complainant says that she agreed to massage the accused only because she 'was afraid that if [she] put up any more of a struggle that it would only egg him on even more and his touching would be more forced.' Finally, we see that in lines 11–12 of (10), the judge states the accused massaged the complainant's bare legs and inner thighs, as if this were a consensual act (i.e. 'After the foot massage, A massaged B's bare legs and he massaged her bare inner thighs'); but in example (8) the complainant says that she complied with the accused's massages because she did not want to 'egg him on more.' In sum, despite the fact that the complainant conveyed in her direct testimony that she had little choice but to comply with the accused's sexual advances, the judges' decisions failed to qualify or modify the sexual advances in such a way. Indeed, there is a sense in both decisions that the complainant's consent was freely given. By contrast, it is noteworthy that in the decision of the Supreme Court of Canada, there are many descriptions of the 'facts' that acknowledge the coerced nature of the sexual contact between the accused and the complainant, for example 'At some point the accused said that he was feeling tense and asked the complainant to give him a massage. The complainant complied, massaging the accused's shoulders for a few minutes.' 'The complainant did not want the accused to touch her in this way, but said nothing as she was afraid that any resistance would prompt the accused to become violent.' (from 1999 decision of the Supreme Court of Canada, Her Majesty the Queen v. Ewanchuk).

In previous work on the language of Canadian sexual assault trial judgments, Coates, Bavelas, and Gibson (1994) noted that judges recognized resistance on the part of complainants only when it took the form of persistent physical struggle. Coates *et al.* (1994: 195) elaborate: 'The language of appropriate resistance seemed to us to be drawn from male–male combat between equals, where continued fighting is appropriate, rather than from asymmetrical situations . . . where physical resistance would lead to little chance of success and a high probability of further harm.' While the excerpts from the judges' decisions do not seem to deem physical struggle as the only appropriate form of resistance, they do seem to require that resistance at least take the form of verbal refusal. For example, based on lines 14–19 of example (10), it seems that verbal refusals are the only indicators or signals that the trial judge recognizes as resistance on the part of the complainant. That is, although the Crown attorney is successful in eliciting testimony (for example, (1)–(9)) that depicts the complainant as attempting to discourage and resist the accused in a variety of ways—including submitting to coerced sex, the trial judge appears to only perceive her resistance on the three occasions that she said 'no' to the accused.

The defense of implied consent

Under Canadian criminal law, an accused will be found guilty of sexual assault if the Crown attorney proves beyond a reasonable doubt that the complainant did not (or could not) consent to the acts. As stated earlier, the trial judge did not find the accused guilty of sexual assault, but rather acquitted the accused, relying on the defense of 'implied consent.' The Alberta Court of Appeal upheld this acquittal and the defense. For both of these judges, then, the complainant was considered to have *implied* consent; moreover, the Alberta Court of Appeal judge defined implied consent as 'consent by conduct.' One of the questions that arises from these judgements concerns the kind of 'conduct' that these judges deemed as signaling consent. Both the trial judge and the Court of Appeal judge found that the complainant was a 'credible witness' (from the trial judge, Moore) and that she was genuinely afraid of the accused: 'Certainly the complainant was afraid of Ewanchuk as the trial judge found' (from the Court of Appeal judge, McClung). However, both judges also commented in their decisions that she did not communicate her fear to the accused. Consider the follow excerpt from the trial judge's decision:

> *Example 12*
> All of B's [the complainant's] thoughts, emotions and speculations were very real for her. However, she successfully kept all her thoughts, emotions, and speculations deep within herself. She did not communicate most of her thoughts, emotions and speculations.... Like a good actor, she projected an outer image that did not reflect her inner self. B did not communicate to A by words, gestures, or facial expressions *that she was 'frozen' by a fear of force*. B did not communicate that *she was frozen to the spot*, and that fear prevented her from getting up off the floor and walking out of the trailer.

The picture that emerges from this description of the complainant is that she was 'frozen to the spot' and 'that she was "frozen" by a fear of force' (italicized above), yet she kept her emotions and feelings hidden from the accused. And, on the basis of this type of 'conduct,' the trial judge acquitted the accused, suggesting that the complainant's conduct *implied* consent. Given that the accused would have to draw inferences in order to understand the complainant as 'implying' consent, one wonders what kind of cultural background knowledge these inferences would rely upon. In other words, what kind of cultural assumptions might give rise to the inference that concealing emotions and being frozen to the spot conveys consent? What becomes clear from questions such as these is the ideological nature of the cultural assumptions that the accused is understood to rely upon in drawing such an inference. That is, by ruling that a woman who is emotionless and frozen to the spot *is implying* consent, the judges are invoking assumptions about women's lack of agency and passivity in the course of 'normal' hetero-sexual sex. As Cameron and Kulick (2003: 36) remark about such societal assumptions, 'the denial of sexual agency to women means that saying "yes" to sex (or initiating it) is disapproved of. Nice girls should demur coyly in order to demonstrate that they are not sluts or nymphomaniacs, but this is a ritual, formulaic gesture and men should not be deterred.' Clearly, the accused in Her Majesty the Queen v. Ewanchuk was not deterred by the complainant's emotionless and frozen demeanor (indeed, not even by her three verbal refusals); and, such behavior was authorized by the trial judge and the Alberta Court of Appeal judge presumably because of the weight of cultural beliefs that equate a woman's sexual passivity with consent.

Conclusion

Recent approaches to language and gender, while emphasizing the agency and creativity of speakers in constructing gendered identities, have paid less attention to the normative discourses (i.e. Butler's rigid regulatory frame) that police and regulate the intelligibility of such identities. In this paper, I have suggested, following Goffman (1981), that a full understanding of identity construction requires looking beyond the face-to-face aspects of interaction to what Goffman calls the 'gathering.' Put somewhat differently, I have used a sexual assault trial to demonstrate how participants who are not directly and actively involved in an interaction can nonetheless influence the meanings and understandings that are assigned to that interaction. More specifically, I have attempted to show how the identity *imposed* upon the complainant in this sexual assault case—as a participant in consensual sex—departed quite dramatically from her identity—as a victim of coerced sex—as it was co-constructed in her direct testimony.

Capps and Ochs (1995: 21) argue that adjudicators in legal cases never determine the truth of a case; rather, 'on the basis of divergent versions of events, jury members [and adjudicators] construct a narrative that is plausible and coherent in their eyes.... In this sense rendering a verdict is analogous not to ascertaining the facts of a case but to determining an official story.' While there are undoubtedly many factors contributing to the determination of an 'official story,' I am suggesting here that a crucial determining factor, especially in the context of a sexual assault trial, is the intelligibility—or lack thereof—of participants' 'performances' of gender. Indeed, in the judicial decisions analyzed so far, the version of events endorsed by the trial judge and the Court of Appeal judge relied upon a very particular understanding of gender and sexuality—one that viewed women's verbal refusals as necessary to resistance and equated women's lack of physical responsiveness with consent. As demonstrated before, the Crown attorney and complainant invoked an alternative, feminist sense-making framework in this trial—one that viewed submission to coerced sex as a way for the complainant to resist more extreme and prolonged instances of violence. Yet, this alternative way of assigning meaning to the events in question did not seem to resonate with the sense-making frameworks of the trial judge and the Alberta Court of Appeal judge. McConnell-Ginet (1988, 1989) has argued that counter-hegemonic viewpoints or discourses may encounter difficulty functioning as background knowledge in linguistic exchanges that do not take place among familiars (McConnell-Ginet, 1988: 92). In other words, because the Crown attorney's discursive strategy involved a feminist understanding of sexual assault, it had difficulty surviving as a contextualizing framework within a public institution, such as a trial. Rather, this trial—or at least crucial and defining aspects of it—relied on dominant, androcentric background assumptions (i.e. Butler's rigid regulatory frame) to inform and constrain its interpretation of events.

Notes

1. I thank Judith Baxter for valuable comments on a previous version of this paper. The research for this article was funded, in part, by a Regular Research Grant from the Social Sciences and Humanities Research Council of Canada, grant # 410–2000–1330.
2. Within the Canadian criminal justice system, Crown attorneys represent the state and complainants assume the role of witnesses for the state. That is, complainants are not *directly* represented by Crown attorneys.
3. The arrows within the transcripts point to narrow Wh-questions asked by the Crown attorney.
4. In previous work on the language of sexual assault trials (Ehrlich, 2001), I have argued that defense lawyers strategically invoke the 'utmost resistance

standard' in trial discourse as a way of undermining the credibility of complainants. Until the 1950s and 1960s in the United States, the statutory requirement of utmost resistance was a necessary criterion for the crime of rape (Estrich, 1987); that is, if a woman did not resist a man's sexual advances to the utmost then the rape was said not to have occurred. While the 'utmost resistance standard' is no longer encoded in legal statutes in the United States or Canada, the adjudication of sexual assault cases often relies on such a principle. Moreover, given that this standard has found its way into trial discourse, it is possible that the Crown attorney's questioning of the complainant in the Ewanchuk case anticipated, and was designed to counteract, such a strategy on the part of Ewanchuk's lawyer.

References

Atkinson, J. M. and Drew, P. (1979) *Order in Court*. London: Macmillan Press.
Barry, A. (1991) 'Narrative style and witness testimony', *Journal of Narrative and Life History*, 1: 281–293.
Butler, J. (1990) *Gender Trouble: Feminism and the Subversion of Identity*. London: Routledge.
Cameron, D. (1997) 'Theoretical debates in feminist linguistics: Questions of sex and gender', in R. Wodak (ed.), *Gender and Discourse*, pp. 21–36. London: Sage.
Cameron, D. and Kulick, D. (2003) *Language and Sexuality*. Cambridge: Cambridge University Press.
Capps, L. and Ochs, E. (1995) *Constructing Panic: The Discourse of Agoraphobia*. Cambridge, Massachusetts: Harvard University Press.
Coates, L., Bavelas, J., and Gibson J. (1994) 'Anomalous language in sexual assault trial judgements', *Discourse & Society*, 5: 189–206.
Conley, J. and O'Barr, W. (1998) *Just Words: Law, Language and Power*. Chicago: University of Chicago Press.
Cotterill, J. (2003) *Language and Power in Court: A Linguistic Analysis of the O.J. Simpson Trial*. London: Palgrave Macmillan.
Dobash, R. E. and Dobash, R. P. (1992) *Women, Violence and Social Change*. London: Routledge.
Drew, P. (1985) 'Analyzing the use of language in courtroom interaction', in T. A. van Dijk (ed.), *Handbook of Discourse Analysis* (Volume 3), pp. 133–147. New York: Academic Press.
Drew, P. and Heritage, J. (1992) 'Analyzing talk at work: An Introduction', in P. Drew and J. Heritage (eds), *Talk at Work: Interaction in Institutional Settings*, pp. 3–65. Cambridge: Cambridge University Press.
Ehrlich, S. (2001) *Representing Rape: Language and Sexual Consent*. London: Routledge.
Estrich, S. (1987) *Real Rape*. Cambridge, Massachusetts: Harvard University Press.
Goffman, E. (1981) *Forms of Talk*. Philadelphia: University of Pennsylvania Press.
Hale, S. and Gibbons, J. (1999) 'Varying realities: Patterned changes in the interpreter's representation of courtroom and external realities', *Applied Linguistics*, 20: 203–220.
Harris, S. (2001) 'Fragmented narratives and multiple tellers: Witness and defendant accounts in trials', *Discourse Studies*, 3: 53–74.
Hutchby, I. and Wooffitt, R. (1998) *Conversation Analysis*. Oxford: Polity Press.

Lempert, L. (1996) 'Women's strategies for survival: Developing agency in abusive relationships', *Journal of Family Violence*, 11: 269–289.

Levinson, S. C. (1988) 'Putting linguistics on a proper footing: Explorations in Goffman's concepts of participation', in P. Drew and A. Wooton (eds), *Erving Goffman: Explorations in the Interactional Order*, pp. 161–228. Oxford: Polity Press.

Maley, Y. (1994) 'The language of the law', in J. Gibbons (ed.), *Language and the Law*, pp. 11–50. London: Longman.

McConnell-Ginet, S. (1988) 'Language and gender', in F. Newmeyer (ed.), *Linguistics: The Cambridge Survey*, Volume IV, pp. 75–99. Cambridge: Cambridge University Press.

McConnell-Ginet, S. (1989) 'The sexual (re)production of meaning: A discourse-based theory', in F. Frank and P. A. Treichler (eds), *Language, Gender, and Professional Writing*, pp. 35–50. New York: Modern Language Association of America.

Reasons for Judgment (Moore, J., C.Q.B.A.), November 10, 1995, Queen v. Ewanchuk.

Reasons for Judgment of the Honourable Mr. Justice McClung, February 12, 1998, Queen v. Ewanchuk.

Walker, A. G. (1987) 'Linguistic manipulation, power and the legal setting', in L. Kedar (ed.), *Power through Discourse*, pp. 57–80. Norwood, New Jersey: Ablex.

West, C. and Zimmerman, D. (1987) 'Doing gender', *Gender and Society*, 1: 25–51.

Woodbury, H. (1984) 'The strategic use of questions in court', *Semiotica*, 48: 197–228.

Wooffitt, R. (2001) 'Conversation analysis', in M. Wetherell, S. Taylor and S. Yates (eds), *Discourse as Data*, pp. 49–92. London: Sage Publications.

9
'Do We Have to Agree with Her?' How High School Girls Negotiate Leadership in Public Contexts

Judith Baxter
University of Reading, UK

Introduction

The facility to speak authoritatively in public—with its power to influence personal opinions as well as to change social and professional practices—is usually an important qualification for career success and, ultimately, leadership, in most professional and business contexts. In Britain at least, there is still a distinct minority of women in leadership positions, despite almost 30 years of equal opportunities and educational reforms. In the business world, for example, women occupy just 10 per cent of all non-executive positions and 3 per cent of executive directorships (Aurora, 2002). At the time of this survey, there was just one female CEO in the UK, one female chairman and one female joint Managing Director working within FTSE 100 companies. This chapter seeks to contribute an *educational* perspective to the much wider discussion about why Britain lacks women in senior management (e.g. Singh, Vinnicombe and Johnson, 2001), by considering the relationship between gender and students' use of authoritative talk in the classroom. This area of investigation is supported by recent studies on gender and leadership (e.g. Tannen, 1995; Singh, Kumra and Vinnicombe, 2002). These have shown that females often avoid adopting authoritative positions as speakers, which may be detrimental to their credibility in senior professional posts.

In this chapter, I will specifically consider the issue from an *educational* perspective by exploring why female students in a British secondary (high) school are less inclined to take up leadership positions through their talk than their male counterparts. Drawing on an ethnographic research study I conducted into the classroom talk of 24 Year 10 (14–15-year-old) students, I will investigate the particular ways in which girls, through discussion work for an oral examination, construct their identities as authoritative speakers (Baxter, 2003). I will consider one particularly powerful explanation for girls' apparent *avoidance* of overtly authoritative subject positions, by examining the spoken interactions of same-sex discussion groups.

Language and gender literature has posited that the ways in which girls or boys interact in same-sex groups are likely to have a powerful effect upon their identities and future interactions as adults (e.g. Maltz and Borker, 1982; Eckert, 1990). Taking a sub-cultural perspective on gender difference, Maltz and Borker (1982) argued that girls in same-sex peer groups develop relationships involving intimacy, mutual commitment and loyalty. The idea of a 'best friend' is central for girls, who often interact together in pairs or small groups. What girls learn to do with speech, the authors suggest, is cope with 'the contradiction created by an ideology of equality and co-operation, and a social reality that includes difference and conflict' (p. 205). They learn to create and maintain relationships of closeness and equality, to criticise each other in acceptable ways and to interpret accurately the speech of other girls. This 'world of girls' contrasts significantly with the 'world of boys' who are said to associate in larger, more hierarchically organised groups where leaders are accepted, and relatively fluctuating status positions are taken as a norm. Within all-male peer groups, boys learn to assert their position of dominance, attract and maintain an audience, and assert themselves when other speakers 'have the floor'.

Drawing on social constructionist theory a decade later, Eckert (1990) recognises that *both* sexes are prepared to compete for 'personal mainstream success' in terms of the status or opportunities offered by contexts such as school or a job. The difference between the biological sexes, she argues, is in terms of 'symbolic capital'—the careful development of an image of the whole self as worthy of authority (Bourdieu, 1977). So, while boys compete openly with each other for individual accomplishments, possessions or individual status, girls must justify theirs on the basis of 'their overall character and the kinds of relations they can maintain with others' (Eckert, 1990: 93). In other words, girls are expected to compete with each other without obviously appearing to. Above all, they need to show other girls that they are still likeable. However, Eckert's interpretation of 'symbolic capital' was based on the increasingly outdated assumption in the western world that 'the domestication of labour involves a strict division of roles, with men engaged in the public marketplace and women's activities restricted to the private, domestic sphere' (p. 93). With ever-growing numbers of women taking up paid employment and pursuing professional and business careers, it is difficult to see that a woman's worth today is primarily defined by her ability to control the domestic realm. Yet, as we shall see, gendered discourses continue to define and determine the range of speech and behaviour available to both males and females.

In this chapter, I will investigate how, in all-female groups, girls who explicitly adopt leadership positions over other girls are simultaneously subject to a discourse of gender differentiation, which exposes them to censure and possible exclusion by their female peers. In contrast, in all-male groups, this same discourse locates boys as strongly instrumental in the construction of leadership positions of their more dominant male peers. In other words, boys support other boys who demonstrate leadership qualities, while girls tend to undermine other girls who attempt to do so. However, this is not to presume a sub-cultural 'gender difference' stance in seeking possible explanations; rather, I will employ a feminist post-structuralist approach to analyse the way in which discourses of gender compete or conspire with other powerful, institutionalised discourses to position female speakers in persistently disadvantaged ways.

The subject of authoritative talk is of particular pertinence within secondary school education given the recent generation of British GCSE examination syllabuses (EDEXCEL, 1998). This has placed a stronger emphasis than before upon the importance of authoritative talk within its 'discuss, argue, persuade' category. For a top A* grade, students are expected to be able to 'use language in a dynamic and influential way' as well as to 'make thought-provoking contributions through powerful expression and command of the situation'. From a liberal-humanist perspective it might be argued that this is potentially an empowering voice for both girls and boys in their personal, social and, later, professional lives. However, from a feminist standpoint, it could be argued that the examination syllabuses are merely reproducing the normative male voice of authority, confidence and success, thus alienating scores of future female speakers (Baxter, 1999). This paper seeks to explore some of the possibilities, contradictions and challenges currently experienced by female secondary school students as they aim to demonstrate leadership qualities as speakers for assessment purposes.

Feminist post-structuralist discourse analysis

Feminist post-structuralism (e.g. Butler, 1990; Weedon, 1997; Baxter, 2003) takes issue with the traditional feminist view that, for example, female students are uniformly disempowered. It prefers instead to promote an understanding of the complex and often ambiguous ways in which girls/women are simultaneously positioned as relatively powerless within certain discourses, but as relatively powerful within alternative and competing discourses. This ceaseless shape-shifting that speakers experience between different subject positions can occur within a single speech event such as a class discussion, or across a range of speech events and contexts. The key point is girls/women are not permanently trapped into silence, disadvantage or victimhood by dominant discursive practices; rather there are moments within competing discourses when females can potentially convert acts of resistance into 'new', if intertextualised forms of expression.

In this chapter, I will argue that, according to a feminist post-structuralist approach to discourse analysis or FPDA (Baxter, 2003), sometimes known as positioning theory, speakers are constantly negotiating for positions of power, determined by the range of discourses to which they have access, or within which they find themselves positioned. Thus, a student's 'ability' to adopt authoritative speaker positions is continuously mediated by his/her subject positions within a number of competing discourses operating in the secondary English classroom. As a consequence of several months' observation within this context, I gradually became aware of the interaction of three interwoven 'discourses' on students' talk repeatedly observed in their conversation and behaviour. Drawing on Foucauldian definitions (1972; 1984), I took 'discourses' to be different sets of language/texts patterns that appear to constitute the subject positions of the students as speakers.

The first 'discourse' was *approval* constituted differently by teachers and students. In terms of the students, *peer* approval denotes the ways in which students' relations with each other are organised and expressed in terms of notions of popularity, personal confidence, physical attractiveness, sexual reputation, friendship patterns, sporting prowess and so on. *Teacher* approval was the extent to which a teacher appeared to favour or privilege one student over another, considered a mixed blessing by students themselves. The second discourse I noted was that of *gender differentiation* (Davies and Banks, 1992; Francis, 1998) which not only appeared to inform common-sense thinking and day-to-day conversation but was also deeply embedded within the structures of classroom discursive practice. The third discourse was that of *a model of collaborative talk*: that is, sets of expectations from the teacher and the students themselves that all assessable talk should be co-operative, facilitative and supportive (e.g. Wilkinson, Davies and Berrill, 1990). All these discourses appeared to operate in an 'intertextualised' way: that is, each discourse is permeated with cross-currents of the others. The feminist post-structuralist approach in this chapter aims to show how students' efforts to demonstrate their abilities as authoritative speakers in class discussions are *mediated* by their subject positions within these three intertextualised yet competing discourses.

My analysis first considers the spoken interactions of an all-female group in close detail, then goes on to make a comparative examination of the interactions of an all-male group. There are two types of analysis. The first is a *denotative* analysis: a description of what is going on in each extract in turn by making close and detailed reference to the verbal and non-verbal interactions of the key speakers. The second is a *connotative* analysis, which adds a more general, explicitly interpretative commentary on the ways in which the three identified discourses position the speakers in competing ways. An FPDA approach should also give space to the multiple voices and perspectives of an event in order to create multi-faceted, multi-layered insights into the case. My own commentary is juxtaposed and interwoven with the accounts of the key participants in the study: that is, student self-evaluations, follow-up interviews with the two student groups, their class teacher and a team of teacher assessors.

The following analysis is taken from a larger research study, which is described fully in Baxter (2003).[1] The students were taking part in a series of formally assessed oral activities for the GCSE exam, and, for the task that follows, had been split into three groups of eight. My analysis is based on the interactions of *two* of the three groups—a self-selected all-female group and a self-selected all-male group.

How girls negotiate leadership

Within a classroom setting, definitions of what constitutes a 'public' context are always likely to be debatable. The discussion activity below could be regarded as operating in a public context *first* because the students were working in groups of 8 (groups of 3–5 were the norm in this class for less formal, small-group work), and *secondly* because the whole exercise was being filmed by a television crew for research and assessment purposes. In other words, both groups were aware that they were required to perform before a multiple audience: their peers, the class teacher, their assessors, the researcher and a film crew.

Only three (Sophie, Charlotte and Gina) of the eight students in the female group speak in the first extract below. Before arriving in the room, each member of the class has individually rank ordered a list of 15 items such as water, a compass, first-aid kit and sunglasses, in terms of their relative importance to human survival, in the imaginary circumstance that they have crash-landed in a desert. The discussion task is to agree on a team consensus about this rank order. Members of the group were not assigned any particular roles (such as 'chair person' or 'group leader'), nor were they advised about any specific discussion strategies to follow in order to reach their team consensus. The group is therefore free to discuss the issues and reach a decision in whatever ways in which it sees fit, within a given time limit of 30 minutes. The following extract[2] is taken from the discussion when it is in 'full flow'.

Extract A

1   SOPHIE: Wouldn't you need the sunglasses?
2   CHARLOTTE: Yeah, that's what I think.
3   SOPHIE: Because it would be really hot..... (OVERLAPS OF 'I PUT
4   THAT', FROM THE OTHERS) and protect yourself from the sun......and
5   you'd be able to see more.
6   GINA: Yeah, but if you're trying to *live*, does it matter whether you
7   can see?
8   CHARLOTTE: (INTERRUPTS GINA FROM 'WHETHER') You can go *blind*
9   (DOES ACTIONS).
10 GINA: Exactly, but if you're trying to survive, does it really matter?
11 CHARLOTTE: (SOUNDING IRRITATED AND BOLSHY. SHE IS STABBING
12 HER PEN INTO THE DESK) *I* wouldn't want to go *blind*.
13 SOPHIE: (OVERLAPPING WITH CHARLOTTE FROM 'WANT') It does,
14 because if you were blind you wouldn't be able to see what you were
15 doing and you would end up dying anyway. You'd have less chance of
16 surviving anyway. (GENERAL LAUGHTER IN SUPPORT OF SOPHIE, HEAD
17 NODDINGS, AND CRIES OF 'YES' AND 'EXACTLY' FROM THE GROUP)
18 GINA: Yeah, but you're not likely to go blind unless you're looking
19 right up into the sun.
20 CHARLOTTE: (INTERRUPTING GINA FROM 'LOOKING') Yeah, but there
21 are some people who........(.)
22 SOPHIE: (INTERRUPTING CHARLOTTE FROM 'WHO') Yeah, but there's
23 also the sand.....and the sand could blow into your eyes as well.
24 CHARLOTTE: I think that's essential.

Denotative analysis

It is clear in the group discussion as a whole that some speakers are more voluble than others. Sophie, Charlotte and Gina are by far the three most talkative members of the group as represented in this extract. Of the three, Sophie in particular takes on a double role as a questioner to promote discussion and as a participant within the discussion. She makes more extended contributions (e.g. lines 13–16) compared to the one-liners from other group members, putting forward her case and supporting this with reasons. This extract represents a moment midway through the exercise, when Sophie is one of the most voluble speakers, and appears to be playing a leading part in the discussion. This is indicated in a number of ways. First, she appears to have gained the support of other members of the group who endorse her views through head noddings, minimal responses and supportive laughter as she talks (e.g. lines 16–17), and who also applaud and 'egg on' her attempts to put down the persistently challenging comments of Gina (e.g. lines 18–19). Secondly and more specifically, Sophie seems to have won the backing of Charlotte who not only echoes and forcefully agrees with her case for the sunglasses (line 2 and 8), but also 'takes on' Gina, apparently on Sophie's behalf. Sophie freely overlaps and interrupts Charlotte's contributions (lines 13 and 22), perhaps indicating her assumed greater prerogative to speak in relation to her supporter.

Charlotte herself defends Sophie's point of view quite forcefully. This is signified by the ways she appears to 'protect' Sophie by warding off Gina's threat to the group consensus. She does this not so much by systematic case-making as by resisting and attacking Gina's argument: that is, through the use of antagonistic 'displacement gestures' (lines 11–12), 'an irritated and bolshy' tone of voice (line 11), interruptions (lines 8 and 20), unsubstantiated assertions (line 8) and emphatic 'blocking' statements (line 12). Sophie and Charlotte as a pair develop a kind of 'collaborative duet' as they argue against Gina with Sophie in particular overlapping, reinforcing and building on the assertions made by Charlotte.

Connotative analysis

Particularly powerful in the setting of the female group is the discourse of *peer approval* that defines and, in my view, potentially limits the possibilities for students to use authoritative speech (as defined by GCSE criteria) in public contexts. My description of Sophie and Charlotte's linguistic interactions indicate that Sophie has negotiated a leadership position for herself within the group, which is actively constructed by the support she receives both from Charlotte as a 'side-kick', and from the rest of the group, especially when challenged by Gina. Sophie's preferential access to speech in this public context appears to be guaranteed by her dominant subject position within the discourse of peer approval as someone who is 'popular' enough to earn the support of almost all the other group members. In contrast, Gina emerges as someone who is rather less popular and therefore has to fight for access to 'the floor'. Gina's role in the group appears to be that of a self-appointed 'agent provocateur'. While her challenge to the group consensus is eventually 'seen off' by the Sophie–Charlotte partnership, it is interesting to note that her determination to make a reasonable counter-argument without *any* obvious backing from the other group members succeeds in granting her a number of extended turns which ultimately appear to produce a more widely ranging and probing discussion.

However, drawing upon the supplementary data of my student interviews with the all-girls group, a surprisingly resistant reading of the group's interactions emerges. By chance, Sophie was unable to attend the student interviews. The girls' recalled version of the group discussion differed somewhat from my own analysis above, particularly in their representation of Sophie's role, *not* as a leading speaker by popular choice, but as a 'pushy' power-seeker:

> **Charlotte:** I didn't agree with anything Sophie was saying. She wanted to be the leader. To be in charge. I felt a bit uncomfortable with that.
> **Helen/Gina:** (TOGETHER) Yes, so did I.
> **Helen:** Because she was the one who was, like, organising it and it was supposed to be a group.
> **Charlotte:** And she went around going, 'What about you? What about you?' I couldn't do my opinions very well because she was going, 'No, no.'
>
> (Student interviews; female group)

This collective reconstruction of Sophie's status in the group can be understood in terms of the competing ways in which these students are positioned both within and across different classroom discourses. For example, during this interview, Sophie was continuously 'positioned' by the three girls as someone who was not particularly popular in class, and therefore did not qualify for peer approval in terms of her leading contribution to the discussion. And yet, while Charlotte seemed concerned to 'rubbish' Sophie's position in the group discussion, there were competing hints that Charlotte herself felt 'miffed' that she had not gained *Sophie's* approval during this activity:

> **Charlotte:** I'm not being horrible but I was really worked up because of Sophie because she took my answers and she put them down. She wouldn't take them into consideration or anything, so I was getting a bit angry. I was *trying my best to get her to notice me* (my italics), but she wasn't having any of it.
>
> (Student interviews; female group)

This extract gives sub-textual hints that if Sophie's good opinion was being sought, she was perhaps more 'popular' than these girls were giving her credit. But it may be the case that constructions of female popularity are overshadowed by other issues. For example, Sophie's assumption of the group leadership position not only may have transgressed the norms of peer approval discourse according to these girls, but also may have challenged the norms of a *model of collaborative talk* in English. In both the interview extracts above, Sophie's discursive actions are perceived to be inconsistent with the 'rules' of co-operative talk in a group as understood by these girls, such as taking too many turns, taking over, interrupting and controlling others, and speaking at too great a length. Interestingly, Gina's role as 'agent provocateur' and Charlotte's apparent resistance to this were not remarked upon during this interview. This was possibly because, as Gina was present, the other girls were sensitive to Gina's 'face-needs' (Coates, 1993), and, while apparently quite unconcerned about criticising Sophie 'behind her back', were not prepared to do so 'to some-one's face'. Indeed, by the same token, I could have asked Charlotte directly about her resistant behaviour towards Gina during the group discussion but, as I had been alerted by the class teacher to the quite delicate relationship between this group of girls, I also opted to observe their 'face-wants'.

There is some evidence to suggest that the girls' acknowledged resistance to Sophie's leadership role was also positioned by a discourse of *gender differentiation*. It is possible to argue from a 'difference as strength' school of feminist socio-linguistics (e.g. Holmes, 1992, 1995; Tannen, 1992, 1995; Coates, 1993) that girls tend to prefer a more co-operative style of linguistic interaction, so that when a particular member of a female group threatens to usurp this unspoken code by 'doing power', this may cause ill-feeling and antagonism. However, the two extracts analysed above cannot be said to exemplify the characteristics of co-operative styles of speech attributed to females by the 'difference as strength' school. Indeed, Charlotte's talk contains a number of features more associated with competitive 'styles' of interaction—such as her use of assertive disagreements, challenging utterances, blocking statements and interruptions. Rather this signifies an alternative reading: that the girls demonstrate that they can flexibly utilise different speaking 'styles', and are quite capable of adopting either co-operative or competitive strategies according to the shifting subject positions of power they negotiate for themselves. This point was illustrated quite well when I asked Charlotte, Gina and Helen how well the group worked together:

> **Gina:** Quite good. Girls work well together. They co-operate.
> **Charlotte:** No. Not really, because we argued loads. I didn't agree with anything Sophie was saying.
> **Helen:** I agree that we were quite argumentative but I think that was a good thing, because we got different views from different people.
>
> (Student interviews; female group)

However, the resentment expressed here against Sophie may none-theless be 'read' according to the girls' position within a discourse of gender differentiation. When I asked the three girls what some of the disadvantages were of working in an all-female group, they replied in this way:

> **Charlotte:** Bitchiness, like trying to win over people, like God, we've got to listen to her, do we have to agree with her!
> **Me:** Do you think having boys in the group changes things?
> **Helen:** Yes. Boys aren't as bitchy as girls. And girls aren't as bitchy towards blokes.
>
> (Student interviews; female group)

Aside from noting the girls' use of semantically derogated and yet re-appropriated terms in order to construct their own experiences, this exchange raises a number of speculations, rather than providing answers at this stage. Might these girls find the dominant speaking role assumed by Sophie to be offensive because any form of female leadership is still a highly contestable construct in our patriarchal society? If this theory is the case, then it may partially explain why Helen says that 'girls aren't as bitchy towards blokes'. Arguably, females are positioned by a traditional discourse of gender differentiation to compete with each other, often quite viciously or disloyally, for the attentions of males (hence the pejorated term 'bitchy'). So, even if there is a conventionalised, if resentful, acceptance of female competitiveness with each other *for* the attention of males, there is possibly far less acceptance of inter-female competitiveness for positions of power, in a world where male leadership is still regarded as a cultural norm. If this is the case, it follows that a classroom discourse of gender differentiation may position female students to feel that it is quite acceptable for *male* students to be dominant speakers in public settings, but for *females* to do so may still be perceived to threaten or transgress codes of gender-appropriate behaviour. In the class teacher interview, these girls were all judged to be capable of speaking confidently in a group situation and indeed all three showed some self-awareness about this. Indeed, Gina commented in the student interview that 'I'm usually a leader in my group but I don't think I was as much because I was with people who talk a lot.' So they may have positioned the absent Sophie as a 'scapegoat' for so obviously occupying the space of dominant speaker and leader of the group, which consequently appeared to marginalise their own contributions. The class teacher described this issue of contestation over the leadership position in the female group in this way:

> [Sophie's leadership] was not accepted by the group. You could see the resentment bubbling up and the way in which they interrupted and challenged [her] for the sake of it rather than in order to make a particular point. I think that's a shame. I don't think the fault lay in the way Sophie conducted herself.
>
> [Class teacher interview]

In summary, such an analysis shows that complex issues about the extent to which authoritative speech is considered appropriate for female students in this classroom setting are closely tied up with other discourses, such as that of collaborative talk in secondary English, and further complicated by the social discourse of class popularity and peer approval. Thus, playing a dominant role as a public speaker is associated with 'doing power', and this in turn is construed at a highly personal level by these girls: struggles for power are seemingly reconstructed as nakedly personal, as was indicated when I asked a mixed observer group from the class (Kate, Robert, Simon and Cathy) to comment on how the *female* group would have managed the group discussion task:

Kate: Sophie would have been the leader and Charlotte would have been arguing.

Me: But how would it have been different from the boys' group?

Simon: It would turn into a scrap. Whereas the boys could laugh about it afterwards, the girls would still be sat hating each other afterwards.

Kate: Yes, that's right. They would take it really personally.

The girls would be seething for a couple of weeks afterwards. Giving looks of hate across the classroom.

(Student interviews; observer group)

How boys negotiate leadership

Mirroring the pattern of my discourse analysis of the female group, I shall first carry out a denotative analysis of the extract below, followed by a connotative commentary. Here, only four boys (Charlie, Tom, Hassan and Matt) out of the group of eight elect to speak. This echoes the female group where certain individuals proved more voluble as speakers than others. As with the female group, individuals were not assigned any particular roles such as 'chair person' or 'group leader', nor were they advised about any specific discussion strategies to follow in order to reach their team consensus. Again this extract is taken at a mid-point in the discussion.

Extract B

```
1   (CHARLIE DIRECTS THE FOLLOWING SEQUENCE BY POINTING HIS PEN AT
2   EACH SPEAKER) Right. What did you put?
3   MATT: Compass.
4   CHARLIE: What did you put?
5   TOM: I put sunglasses.
6   CHARLIE: Right, I put the parachute so that it could like shelter
7   from the wind at night, and it would give you something to shelter
8   under, so the heat wouldn't get to you, and the red and white.
9   Also if planes fly over, they'd see this big red and white para-
10  chute patch on the floor. They'd see where you'd crashed or
11  whatever. (THROUGH THIS OTHER VOICES ARE SAYING, 'YEAH, YEAH' AND
12  NODDING IN AGREEMENT)
13  OTHER VOICES: Mirror, mirror.........the torch
14  CHARLIE: And you could use a gun, couldn't you? You could
15  shoot....
```

16 HASSAN: You could shoot the pilot.
17 CHARLIE: Right. So has anyone changed their mind? What do
18 you think?
19 (POINTING AT HASSAN)
20 HASSAN: I say compass
21 TOM: I think sunglasses are quite important because you have to be
22 able to see what it says on the compass for a start (LAUGHTER FROM
23 THE GROUP)
24 HASSAN: You could just go like that (MIMES SHADING EYES); shut
25 your eyes for a moment
26 CHARLIE: Right. You go (POINTING AT HASSAN). Say why you thought
27 the first aid kit.

In this extract, Charlie appears to direct the agenda of the group discussion
through his use of features associated with 'chairing' such as nominating
and authorising people to speak (lines 1–2, 4), use of commands or directives
(line 27), decision markers (lines 2, 6, 17, 26), canvassing opinion (lines
4, 18), and helping people to develop their point of view (lines 26–27).

However, he does not simply use the discursive practices associated
with chairing. He also acts as an active participant in the discussion,
able to develop a point of view with a range of supporting reasons
(lines 7–11). That he appears to want to be taken seriously as a persuasive
case-maker who is having an impact on group opinion is evident
when he asks shortly after his quite lengthy contribution (lines 6–11),
'So, has anyone changed their mind?' (line 17), and this is even more
demonstrable later in the discussion when he asks the group, 'Have
I persuaded you all to put "parachute?"'. In unison, they all reply,
'parachute'.

In this extract, there is no sign of any opposition to his leadership
position, and indeed, he appears to have something of a 'support
group'—other members of the group who willingly echo or endorse his
view. For example, no one tries to interrupt Charlie when he speaks at
length (lines 6–11). On the contrary, they express their support of his
viewpoint as he speaks, through minimal responses and head nodding.
Other speakers add to his point about the gun (line 16) and, later on in
the discussion, the parachute rather than challenging or contradicting
his comments.

Tom, a dominant speaker in the class, keeps a 'low profile' during this
sequence as he does throughout the activity. Here, he appears not to

be overly swayed by the case Charlie is making, making flippant comments and low-key jokes or bantering casually with Hassan (line 21).

Connotative analysis

There is evidence from this extract to indicate that Charlie occupies an authoritative position as a speaker and leader of the group, and that to a large extent this is largely being produced through a discourse of peer approval. Charlie seems to be 'popular' with his peers, and this extract provides some insights into how that 'popularity' or approval is discursively constructed and reinforced. After a slight interjection from Hassan (line 9), Charlie assumes almost instant control over the group from the start of the discussion as the following extract, from an earlier stage in the discussion, shows:

Extract C

1 (AS THE BOYS ENTER THE ROOM, CHARLIE IMMEDIATELY HEADS FOR THE
2 CENTRAL, MOST VISIBLE POSITION ON THE TABLE, HAVING ASKED ME (AS
3 THE RESEARCHER) WHETHER THE MICROPHONE IS 'ON'. HE LEANS
4 FORWARD AND SAYS, 'TESTING, TESTING'. THERE IS GENERAL LAUGHTER
5 AND DELIBERATELY DIRECTED FACE-PULLING AT THE CAMERA. CHARLIE
6 THEN BLOWS AT THE 'MIKE' AND THERE IS MORE LAUGHTER FROM THE
7 OTHERS.)
8 CHARLIE: Alright, let's get on with it, then.
9 HASSAN: For a start, what does everyone think is the most
10 important?
11 ALL: (IN UNISON) Water, water, water......
12 CHARLIE: Right, let's go round one at a time. Matt?

Charlie's easy assumption of control from the start is gained here by playing to an audience (both his peers and the camera crew) through his use of clowning and humour which seems to lighten the way for his later use of authoritative commands. In both extracts, there is little evidence of *negotiation* with his peers about his position of authority, or any direct challenge from them. This lack of self-doubt about his 'right' to assume the leadership position was so much the case that, in his written self-evaluation, he seems entirely unaware that this *might* have been an issue for contestation by the other boys:

I think I worked quite well with my group and listened to everyone's point of view. I tried to be as fair to everyone as possible and to give everyone an equal chance to express their views. I tried to be positive to everyone but I always wanted to be right. I enjoyed this talk.

When I raised the question of Charlie's role in my follow-up interviews with the male group, it was again clear that there had been no issue among them about his assumption of authority, unlike the case with the female group.

> **Me:** What role do you think you played in the group? Charlie?
> **Charlie:** I thought I was like the chair (EVERYONE LAUGHS). I was sitting in the middle of the table and pointing at everyone saying, 'What do you think and why?' I think I contributed less than normal in this group.
> **Tom:** He's always like that. (EVERYONE LAUGHS)
>
> (Student interviews; male group)

The class teacher also did not seem surprised that Charlie had assumed the leadership role in the discussion, or that the group had accepted this with good humour:

> **Class teacher:** Charlie is......a very assertive and dominant personality in the class in oral work in particular and he always feels that he has to make himself heard. Although he was quite brisk and domineering in the [group of eight], they did actually respond to that and he did manage to control the discussion......I felt that he was quite aggressive in the way that he pushed the discussion along and directed the others with 'you...you...you.'
> **Me:** Was that tolerated by the others?
> **Class teacher:** I think it was, yes. They all responded to it. They felt fine that he had adopted this role.
>
> (Class teacher interview)

In this interview extract, the teacher constructs Charlie's powerful position in the discussion and influence over others as being a function of his 'assertive and dominant personality', a perspective which seems unsurprising in the light of Charlie's own apparent lack of insight about the possibility that such a speaking role might be contestable, as it was in the female group. But the construct of a 'personality' assumes an essentialist stance of a unique and unitary individual, statically defined, rather than the post-structuralist stance that subjects are discursively produced through their actions. Charlie constructs his influence over others by persuading his peers to *accept* his leadership, and to support his point of view. One example of this is the way in which he appears able to orchestrate the voices of different members of the group not only through a convincing argument supported by reasons, but also by his non-verbal use of direct gaze and finger-pointing to allocate speaking turns, so that they speak in unison with him, as illustrated in this later extract:

Extract D

1 CHARLIE: So we said 'shelter' (LOOKS TO TOM AND HASSAN WHO ARE
2 PROMPTING HIM DURING THIS SEQUENCE; OTHER VOICES JOIN IN AS HE
3 SPEAKS ECHOING) 'protect from the sun' and 'distractions' (sic), that's
4 three. Have I persuaded you all to put parachute?
5 GROUP: (CHARLIE POINTS TO EACH ONE IN TURN AND THEY ALL SPEAK IN
6 UNISON) Parachute.

However, Charlie's predominant position here is not solely a result of his persuasive actions or 'skill' in deploying particular discursive strategies. His position as a 'cool and popular' member of the group, as he is described by the class teacher, is multiply constructed and maintained by the discursive actions of *all* its members, and this is largely the result of an implicit collusion between those students who support Charlie and therefore wish to endorse what he says.

Particularly instrumental in this respect is Tom, who has been represented so far in this chapter as a rather silent and perhaps 'ineffective' speaker in comparison to Charlie. Yet, Tom's class teacher suggested in her interview that his speech behaviour in this setting was quite uncharacteristic:

Tom was much quieter than I would have expected in that situation. Usually Tom and Charlie are a bit of a twosome. Most of the time, Tom is the dominant one, actually. That emerged in the class discussion. I was happy that Tom appeared completely happy in the role and didn't feel any need to compete with it and in fact supported a lot of what Charlie was saying.

(Class teacher interview)

Indeed, it emerged from my interviews with the class teacher and the student groups that Tom is also regarded as 'cool and popular' and probably more so than Charlie. (As the class teacher said, 'Charlie doesn't have quite the same popularity outside the classroom as Tom does.') Therefore, Tom's decision, whether conscious or otherwise, to remain relatively silent in the small group discussion may have been quite instrumental in providing Charlie with a mandate to speak without fear of competition. Furthermore, there is evidence in the transcript that Tom actively provides Charlie with a 'platform' to speak by performing the role of 'right-hand man' or 'sidekick':

Extract E

1 CHARLIE: If we, if we . . . . . (TRIES TO INTERRUPT HASSAN)
2 TOM: I think Charlie wants to say something . . . .
3 CHARLIE: If we, say, are travelling by night, we could use all
4 the day to try to distract (sic) people with all the . . . parachute,
5 mirror . . .
6 TOM: (ECHOES) Parachute . . . mirror . . . and you could start a fire using
7 the vodka . . . .
8 MATT: And the mirror . . . .
9 TOM: We could set fire to Charlie . . . . (LAUGHTER FROM THE GROUP)

By 'clearing the speech channel' for Charlie (line 2), by echoing and reinforcing his message (line 6), and finally by making him the 'butt' of some light, subversive humour (line 9), Tom first legitimises, and also proscribes the limits to Charlie's position as dominant speaker in the group. Charlie is allowed to *be* the group leader but only at the 'say so' of Tom and the others.

But the construction of Charlie's leadership position in the group is not just a case of subject positioning by a discourse of peer approval. Following my argument about how the discourse of *gender differentiation* positions a powerful *female* speaker as less 'popular' or culturally acceptable than a powerful male one, I would suggest that the discourse of peer approval is interwoven with that of gender differentiation to produce boys as more willing to accept the concept of hierarchical leadership and the support structure this necessarily entails. More colloquially, these boys were more accustomed to accept one of their number in the role of leader because, unlike girls, they do not take the leadership issue personally. As Kate from the observer group said, 'that's blokes for you'.

Conclusion

In the film *Mean Girls* (Paramount Pictures, 2004), the leading character played by Lindsay Lahon arrives as an ex-patriot fresh from Africa to enter the strange, turbulent and manipulative world of female friendships at a Californian high school. She learns that girls do operate in hierarchies, that the most beautiful, rich and popular girls vie for position as 'Queen Bee', but that, once achieved, a girl must be careful of flaunting her superior position too brazenly, or she will be brought down by her so-called 'friends'. In a climactic scene towards the end of the film, a feminist teacher encourages a large group of girls to 'talk out' their long-suppressed animosities, rivalries and jealousies.

This chapter has argued that girls who blatantly adopt leadership positions over other girls are subject to a discourse of gender differentiation which exposes them to censure and possible exclusion. In contrast, this same discourse of differentiation works to boys' advantage by locating them as strongly supporting 'popular' male peers who establish leadership positions in public contexts. The female tendency to censure their own sex for 'standing out' is proposed as one reason why females sometimes find it hard to adopt authoritative or leadership positions in later life. Yet, from a post-structuralist perspective, this is not being viewed as a deficiency in the female character, or even as the effect of complex male/female socialisation into different sub-cultures. Rather, socio-cultural and educational discourses combine to position females in such a way that they are less likely to adopt authoritative positions as speakers than males. Socio-cultural discourses routinely position girls as non-competitive friends and equals, and educational discourses position girls as *responsible for* taking the collaborative role in discussions (Jenkins and Cheshire, 1990; Swann and Graddol, 1995). The recent examination requirement (e.g. EDEXCEL, 1998) that girls should openly compete to adopt commanding positions as speakers suddenly makes visible any latent competition and conflicts between them. Arguably, for women to become confident and accepted leaders in the public sphere—with other females as well as males—they must first be taught *how* to deconstruct the gendered power relationships assumed within many social and educational discourses. In short, girls will need to learn *how* to talk their way to the top.

Notes

1. The research findings were drawn from an ethnographic case study of a single Year 10 class (aged 14–15 years, 24 pupils, 22 white, 1 Asian, 1 Chinese)

within a co-educational, comprehensive school, whose oral work I observed over a period of three months. The class was broadly grouped for the subject of English within the middle to upper ability range (that is, students were predicted grades A–D).

Data were drawn from observing and video-recording a series of lessons during two terms that were leading to the assessment of oral work for GCSE. There are two reasons why I have chosen here to highlight the analysis I conducted of one particular oral activity 'The Desert Survival Situation' (Lafferty and Pond, 1989) involving a simulation of an air crash in a desert. First, the activity was especially tailored by the English staff to provide focused opportunities for students to speak and listen in public contexts. Second, the activity provided multiple accounts and perspectives of the oral activity—from the class teacher, the students themselves and other assessors. Both the class teacher and the small groups of students were separately inter- viewed for their impressions of the activity, and a cross-moderation meeting of nine assessors was video-recorded in which the performances of all the students were discussed.

2. In terms of transcript conventions, a simple method of presentation is used that would depict 'the whole picture' as well as capture the nuances and detail of non-verbal and verbal interaction. I have used a 'standard lay-out' (Swann, 1993: 41–42), which is set out rather like a dialogue for a play, with speaking turns shown as following one another in sequence. Where there are instances of overlapping speech and interruptions, I have indicated exactly where they occur by the use of 'stage directions' (in brackets and caps).

As little punctuation as possible is used in order to capture the greater fluidity and spontaneity of speech compared to writing. The use of 'paralan- guage' (such as intonation, volume, stress, pitch, etc.) is also described, where it appears significant, in the 'stage directions', but pauses have been indicated by the standard convention (.) within the body of the text. I have incorpo- rated descriptions of non-verbal communication within the 'stage directions' as they occur within the body of the transcript.

References

Aurora (2002) *Managing Gender Capital*. Internal Document, British American Tobacco.

Baxter, J. (1999) 'Teaching girls to speak out: The female voice in public contexts', *Language and Education*, 13 (2), pp. 81–98.

Baxter, J. (2003), *Positioning Gender in Discourse: A Feminist Methodology*. Basingstoke: Palgrave Macmillan.

Bourdieu, P. (1977) *Outline of a Theory of Practice*. Cambridge: Cambridge University Press.

Butler, J. (1990) *Gender Trouble: Feminism and the Subversion of Identity*. New York: Routledge.

Coates, J. (1993) *Women, Men and Language*. London: Longman.

Davies, B. and Banks, C. (1992) 'The gender trap: A feminist post-structuralist analysis of primary school children's talk about gender', *Curriculum Studies*, 24 (1), pp. 1–25.

Eckert, P. (1990) 'Co-operative competition in adolescent "girl-talk" ', *Discourse Processes*, 13, pp. 91–122.

EDEXCEL (1998) *GCSE Syllabus 1999: English*. London: EDEXCEL Foundation.

Fey, T. (2004) *Mean Girls*. California: Paramount Pictures.

Foucault, M. (1972) *The Archaeology of Knowledge and the Discourse on Language*. New York: Pantheon.

Foucault, M. (1984) 'What is enlightenment?', in Rabinow, P. (ed.), *The Foucault Reader*. London: Penguin.

Francis, B. (1998) *Power Plays: Children's Constructions of Gender, Power and Adult Work*. Stoke-on-Trent: Trentham Books.

Jenkins, N. and Cheshire, J. (1990) 'Gender issues in the GCSE oral examination: Part 1', *Language and Education*, 4 (4), pp. 261–292.

Holmes, J. (1992) 'Women's talk in public contexts', *Discourse & Society*, 3 (2), pp. 131–150.

Holmes, J. (1995) *Women, Men and Politeness*. London: Longman

Lafferty, J. C. and Pond, A. (1989) *The Desert Survival Situation*. 4th edn. Hampshire: Human Synergistics-Verax.

Maltz, D. N. and Borker, R. A. (1982) 'A cultural approach to male-female miscommunication', in J. Gumperz (ed.), *Language and Social Identity*. Cambridge: Cambridge University Press, pp. 196–215.

Singh, V., Vinnicombe, S. and Johnson, P. (2001) 'Women directors on top UK boards', *Corporate Governance: An International Review*, 9 (3), pp. 206–216.

Singh, V., Kumra, S. and Vinnicombe, S. (2002) 'Gender and impression management: Playing the promotion game', *Journal of Business Ethics*, 37, pp. 77–89.

Swann, J. (1993) *Girls, Boys and Language*. Oxford: Blackwell.

Swann, J. and Graddol, D. (1995) 'Feminising classroom talk?', in S. Mills (ed.), *Language and Gender*. London: Longman.

Tannen, D. (1992) *You Just Don't Understand!* London: Virago.

Tannen, D. (1995) *Talking from 9 to 5: Women and Men at Work: Language, Sex and Power*. London: Longman.

Weedon, C. (1997) *Feminist Practice and Post-structuralist Theory*. 2nd edn. Oxford: Blackwell.

Wilkinson, A., Davies, A. and Berrill, D. (1990) *Spoken English Illustrated*. Milton Keynes: Open University Press.

10
Positioning the Female Voice within Work and Family

Shari Kendall
Texas A & M University

Introduction

Although social talk in the workplace is commonly dismissed by people at work as gaps between more serious and important 'institutional' discourse, scholars have identified many important functions served by social talk. In her analysis of talk in several large corporations, Tannen (1994a, pp. 64–65) finds that social talk provides 'the grease that keeps the gears running in an office'. It establishes a friendly working environment, opens the lines of communication for working relations, and is part of the 'friendly loop' through which information circulates through the office. It has also been found to be a necessary element for institutional success at any level (Tracy and Naughton, 2000). In fact, even for individuals with intellectual disabilities, their 'social and interpersonal skills' are a more significant predictor of workplace success than their actual ability to perform work tasks (Holmes, 2003, p. 68). Social talk is also one of the means by which women's and men's identities within public and workplace contexts are expressed, realized, and negotiated.

In this chapter, I examine the social talk of a woman and a man about family at work as part of my ongoing research on the challenges faced by dual-income parents with young children. I examine an extended example of social talk about family that takes place between the study participant, Elaine, and her male colleague, Richard, using a positioning approach (Davies and Harré, 1990; van Langenhove and Harré, 1999) and the methods of interactional sociolinguistics (Gumperz, 1982; Tannen, 1989; Schiffrin, 1994). The study participant, Elaine, tape-recorded herself at work and at home for a week in the first of two research projects examining how dual-income couples with children linguistically create their parental and professional identities at work and at home.[1]

I consider social talk about family in the workplace as a nexus between public and private, a means through which the family sphere interpenetrates the work sphere. As such, social talk about family is relevant to issues of women in public contexts because it brings to bear the weight of beliefs and expectations about mothers' competence and commitment to work. In a review of research and US case law, Williams and Segal (2003, p. 90) found that when a woman becomes pregnant or has a child, she 'may begin to be perceived as a low-competence caregiver rather than as a high-competence business woman'. These assessments are made by superiors and co-workers alike, and they persist even when the woman's job performance remains unchanged (Fiske *et al.*, 2002). Thus, social talk about family may impact these assessments because it makes employees' identities as parents salient in the workplace; and, as research suggests, a woman's identity as a mother may be more salient in the workplace than a man's identity as a father (e.g. Hochschild, 1989; Maddock and Parkin, 1994).

I begin by describing how social talk about family in the workplace creates a site in which individuals' 'private' identities are integrated with their 'public' identities in relation to sociolinguistic work based on 'institutional' and 'ordinary' language. In the following section, I outline the discursive means through which individuals create gendered identities through positioning, and describe a caregiver archetype which serves as a touchstone for positioning in talk about family. I then present illustrative examples showing how the study participants position themselves in relation to this archetype, thus creating gendered caregiving identities through social talk about family at work. Following the analysis, I suggest that the individuals' discursively produced identities reflect changes motivated by second-wave feminism, but continue to be gendered, albeit in more subtle ways. Finally, I consider how these parental identities may be salient to the participants' professional identities at work.

Social talk as a nexus between public and private

Traditionally, researchers of language in the workplace have distinguished between 'institutional' and 'ordinary' language. 'Institutional' language has been characterized as having an orientation to a goal or task, and as entailing an identity associated with an institution. Linguistically, it is characterized by restrictions on what participants can relevantly say and restrictions on turn-taking; the use of specialized vocabularies; asymmetrical question–answer sequences; and special opening and closing sequences (Goodwin and Heritage, 1990; Drew and Heritage, 1992). This contrasts with 'ordinary' language that is characterized by casual conversation between peers (Drew and Heritage, 1992). Levinson (1983, p. 284) defines 'ordinary' talk as 'that familiar predominant kind of talk in which two or more participants freely alternate in speaking which generally occurs outside specific institutional settings like religious services, law courts, classrooms and the like'. However, McElhinny (1997, p. 108) problematizes the dichotomy of 'ordinary' and 'institutional' language used in sociolinguistic research by linking it with ideologies of public and private, arguing that, among other problems, it emphasizes 'the separation rather than the interpenetration of spheres'. Through a review of studies of 'institutional' talk in welfare, legal, and medical contexts, McElhinny demonstrates that the distinction between ordinary and institutional language 'obscures the fact that the possibility of insisting on such a difference is a privilege associated with one's economic and social status within a society'. People who must rely on state aid are 'forced to open themselves up to state scrutiny in ways that collapse this distinction'.

Social talk in the workplace also brings this distinction into question because it does not fit comfortably in either institutional or ordinary language as so defined. Although 'ordinary' talk is characterized as lacking an orientation to a goal or task, many managers consider talk about employees' lives as a way to get employees to do their best work. For example, Tannen (1990, p. 118) describes a successful director of a counseling center who fostered social talk to contribute to 'a sense of rapport that makes the women on her staff happy in their jobs and lays a foundation for the working relationship that enables them to conduct business so efficiently'. In Kendall (2004), I demonstrate that the female technical director of a national radio news and talk program engages a nervous soundboard operator in social talk to help him relax and thereby perform his demanding work error-free.

In addition, social talk is not exempt from the institutional roles of the participants. As with many other linguistic options, people who engage in social talk simultaneously create rapport and negotiate status. Tannen (1994b, 1999) demonstrates that status relations in the workplace influence when social talk occurs and how it progresses. For example, a higher-ranking woman, who shifted from telling a story to complimenting a lower-ranking woman's clothing, creates rapport by including the lower-ranking woman in social talk and by complimenting her, but she sustains the hierarchical relationship because she, as the highest status person, controls the framing of the interaction. Similarly, many studies find that it is the higher-ranking person who generally brings workplace social talk to a close (Clyne, 1994; Tannen, 1994b; Holmes, 2003).

The importance of social talk when considering women in public contexts is that talk about 'private' contexts is not separate from the active creation and portrayal of 'public' professional identities. I suggest that the parental identities women and men create through social talk about family may influence how they are perceived in the workplace, particularly talk about family that characterizes speakers' orientations to their children in terms of the types of tasks and activities they identify themselves as doing and the degree of parental involvement they divulge.

Framing, positioning, and gendering identities

Davies and Harré (1990, p. 47) describe positioning as the interactional process through which individuals produce 'a diversity of selves'. At each moment in an encounter, participants take up, resist, and assign positions by locating self and other in relation to values or character-istics (e.g. definitive or tentative); types of people in 'social category formations' (e.g. father/daughter); and discourses, ways of speaking and behaving that occur at 'the disciplinary, the political, the cultural and the social group level', and/or 'develop around a specific topic, such as gender or class'. For example, a discourse of paternalism has the associ-ated positions of 'independent powerful man' and 'dependent helpless woman' (van Langenhove and Harré, 1999, p. 45). Individuals create identities by discursively taking up, contesting, or countering the positions that discourses, and other participants, make available (see Editor's Introduction).

The archetype of the caregiver is a gendered position within a discourse of gender relations. It is constituted by sociocultural beliefs and expectations for women with young children, and involves being the child's primary caregiver; performing the kinds of tasks that female caregivers have traditionally performed; and having ultimate responsibility for managing the logistics of caregiving, such as making sure the child has a gift for an upcoming birthday party, making dentist appointments, and so on. The archetype is based on non-factual ideals (Coontz, 2000), but reflects some persistent patterns in the distribution of caregiving and domestic work as well. For example, these tasks correspond to the three types of caregiver involvement that women are more likely to perform cross-culturally: accessibility, direct care, and overall responsibility (Lamb, 1987). Among dual-income couples with children, the sex-based division of labor persists in childcare and domestic work. In 1989, Hochschild found that women worked roughly fifteen hours longer each week than men—an extra month of twenty-four-hour days a year. She concluded that 'Most women work one shift at the office or factory and a "second shift" at home' (p. 4). Research continues to show that women still do at least twice as much housework and childcare as their partners, even when both parents work full time (Robinson and Godbey, 1999; Bianchi, 2000; Bianchi *et al.*, 2000; Buunk *et al.*, 2000; Coltrane, 2000). The division of tasks continues to be gendered as well: In caring for children, women spend more time on caregiving tasks, such as feeding and bathing children, whereas men spend more time playing with children, taking them on enjoyable outings, such as going to the park or the movies. In terms of domestic work, women tend to wash clothes, clean, cook, shop for food, pay the bills, take children to appointments, and arrange for childcare. Men tend to mow lawns or shovel snow, make minor household repairs, and take out the trash (Deane, 1998; Morin and Rosenfeld, 1998).

After introducing the participants and describing the methodology, I present one extended conversation between the study participant, Elaine, and her co-worker, Richard, in which she and her co-worker create relatively traditional parental identities as caregiver and breadwinner, respectively. Elaine indexes gender by positioning herself as a mother who has primary responsibility for her daughter, and who accomplishes the types of caregiving tasks associated with this role. Richard, on the other hand, avoids taking up the parental positions she provides, and constructs his identity as a breadwinner rather than as a caregiver. In this way, Elaine and Richard create gendered parental identities—that is, 'mother' and 'father'. Following the analysis, I consider the relevance of the positionings the participants take up in relation to a caregiver archetype and discuss the work identities the participants create, and how these identities may be relevant to their professional identities.

Topical classification of social talk in the workplace

The linguistic definition of topic is, perhaps, necessarily vague. Wardhaugh (2002, p. 300) defines it as 'the thing that is talked about'. Brown and

Yule (1983, pp. 89–90) describe it as 'What we're talking about' and, for each speaker, 'what I think we're talking about'. To analyze the topics of social talk, I first identified the linguistic moves that had an impact on the direction of the talk. Blum-Kulka (1997, p. 57) refers to these moves as topical actions, following Bublitz (1988, p. 40), who defines them as actions participants use 'to intervene in the development and the course of the [discourse] topic, and thus to contribute to a topical thread'. I then identified the domain of each topic: work, family, home, or personal (i.e. a non-work-related focus that is not associated with home or family). In this chapter, I focus on social talk that concerns family and/or home.

The basic topic domain categories are helpful for analyzing social talk, but it is not sufficient to identify, simply, who talks with whom about family because not all references to family equally influence the identities the speakers create, or the nature of those identities. There are three components of social talk about family that must be considered. First is the degree of relevance of family/home to the topic. For example, if an individual mentions a family member when telling a co-worker about going out of town the past weekend to visit friends, the reference to family does not necessarily position the speaker as a parent if that speaker could relate the story in the same way if he or she went out of town alone. I refer to topics that are connected with family in this way as 'family-linked'. These instances contrast with those in which family/home is to some extent part of the topical thread; I refer to these topics as 'family-related'. Individuals take up parental positions through family-related but not family-linked topics.

Second, individuals jointly negotiate the nature of the parental identities they display through the positionings they take up. I identify two discourse features that are fundamental to this negotiation: individualization and generalization. Conversational participants take up parental positions by talking about their family members in particular ('individualized'), or avoid taking up these positions by referring to how people are, or the way the world is, in general ('generalized'). Two ways speakers individualize talk about family are specific references (e.g. using a child's name) and constructed dialogue (Tannen, 1989). When individuals 'quote' themselves through constructed dialogue, they cast themselves speaking from the perspective of a family identity (e.g. 'mother', 'father') and thus, in a sense, embody that social identity. In contrast, individuals generalize talk about family by avoiding mention of their own children, using generic 'you', mass generic terms such as 'children' and 'kids', and mass quantifiers such as 'every' and 'all'. Speakers take up parental positions by individualizing their references to family; and if family does become a part of the topical thread (family-related), they avoid taking up parental positions by generalizing their references to family members.

Third, when conversational participants take up parental positions, they characterize themselves as parents by positioning themselves in relation to a caregiver archetype. In the conversation presented in this analysis, the speakers position themselves as primary caregivers by using singular 'I' and 'me' but distance themselves from this archetype by talking about themselves as part of a parenting team through the use of plural 'we' and 'us'.

A second way in which speakers position themselves in relation to a caregiver archetype is by identifying the activities they perform as parents. They do so by positioning themselves on a continuum of caregiving and breadwinning tasks, presented in Figure 10.1. These tasks range from those activities most closely associated with traditional caregiving (caregiver positioning) to those involved in traditional breadwinning (breadwinner positioning).

The ordering of activities in Figure 10.1 is based, first, on a continuum of private through public, moving from those activities that tend to occur in the home ('bathe', 'feed', and 'stay home with sick child'), to those occurring in a private space within a public setting, that is a car ('drive to/from school'), and finally to activities that occur between parents and institutional entities ('arrange schooling' and 'pay for school'). Second, the continuum reflects the physical contact between caregiver and child, from direct feeding and bathing of infants, to co-presence with the child ('stay home with sick child' and 'drive to/from school'), to activities that do not require co-presence ('arrange schooling' and 'pay for school'). Third, the continuum

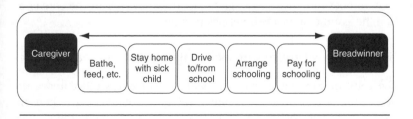

Figure 10.1   Parental involvement continuum: Caregivers and breadwinners

reflects, to some extent, the growing independence of the child, from complete dependence as a baby ('bathe, feed') through higher education when children may not live at home ('pay for school'). Speakers position themselves in relation to a caregiver archetype through the location of the tasks and activities they perform on this continuum.

The participants

The analysis is based on data from the first of two research projects examining how dual-income, heterosexual couples with children linguistically create their parental and professional identities at work and at home, conducted in the greater Washington DC area in the US in 1997 and 2000, respectively. In this chapter, I consider the participant from the initial study, Elaine, and her equal ranking colleague, Richard. (All names are pseudonyms.) The participant, Elaine, was instructed to tape-record herself for a week from the time she woke up until after she and her family had eaten dinner, cleaned up, and moved on to other activities. The tape-recordings were transcribed in their entirety by transcribers I trained. Both Elaine and Richard are white, middle class, in their mid-forties, and live in the greater DC area. Both work in managerial positions within a national organization. Elaine and her husband have a ten-year-old daughter. Richard and his wife have three children, the oldest being twelve, two years older than Elaine's daughter.

In the following analysis, I demonstrate that Elaine frames her social talk with Richard as a reciprocal exchange of information about family from the perspective of a parent by engaging in individualized family-related talk, but Richard does not take up the position her frame provides. Through her talk about family, Elaine creates a traditional caregiver identity as the primary caregiver who performs traditional, gendered caregiving, and domestic tasks and activities. In contrast, Richard does not create a caregiver identity and, later in the conversation, he assumes a breadwinner positioning.

Gendered positionings in social talk about family at work

The conversation begins when Richard enters Elaine's office and overhears another co-worker ask Elaine if she wants a guinea pig. When the co-worker leaves, Richard initiates talk, in 1, by asking Elaine if she's going to get one, framing the encounter as social talk. Elaine tells

Richard that she is not, but that she has a note to ask Beth about it. When she asks if he is going to take a guinea pig, he says *no* because, he adds, his *chameleons had babies:*[2]

(1) *Richard*: So, you don't want any guinea pigs?
     Elaine: No. I have a- we-
                 I have a note there to ask. Beth,
                 but I'm gonna say no.
                 Want one?
                 Are you gonna take any?
     Richard: Absolutely not..
                 Our- my chameleons had babies.

By mentioning Beth's name, Elaine introduces family into the social talk, creating a link which opens up the possibility of talk about family. Since the topic of conversation is Elaine's daughter, it concerns Elaine in particular, making it individualized as well. In his response, Richard does not pursue the family-link. He does not identify the chameleons as belonging to one of the children (e.g. *Tom's chameleons*) or to the family (e.g. *our chameleons*), but identifies them as his own: *my chameleons*. His false start, *our- my chameleons*, highlights his disassociation of the topic and family, shifting from the family domain.

After Elaine and Richard discuss Richard's options about what he can do with the baby chameleons, he says that he does not want any more pets. Elaine tells him that Beth, her daughter, wants a dog, again linking the topic to family. Richard responds by transforming Elaine's reference to her child in particular to a reference to kids in general:

(2) *Elaine*:   Beth just really wants a dog, but uh
     Richard: Oh yeah?
     Elaine: Yeah.
     Richard: Every kid does, I think.
                 Most of them.

By referring to *every kid* rather than his own children, Richard generalizes the topic that Elaine has individualized: *Beth just really wants a dog*. Consequently, Elaine assumes a parental position, but Richard does not. He could have responded in the same way if he was not a parent himself.

Elaine does not accept the generalized response to her statement about Beth wanting a dog; she asks a question to elicit information about Richard's family:

(3)   *Elaine*:   And you've said no, didn't you say no.
       Richard: Yeah, to dogs and cats, yeah.

By asking Richard what he said to his own children, Elaine reframes the conversation as a symmetrical exchange of information about the participants' families. Her question provides Richard with the opportunity to repair the symmetry of this conversational frame, encouraging him to mirror her personal experiences with his (Tannen, 1990; Coates, 1996). Richard provides the required information, but he does not match Elaine's experience by elaborating on what happened when he told his children they could not have a dog or cat.

In 4, Elaine explains that she does not get Beth a dog because she and Mark, her husband, take care of the guinea pig that Beth already has. Her move shifts the topic closer to both the family and home domains because she refers to a domestic task that she performs as a mother, and she mentions Mark as well. However, she maintains some distance from a traditional caregiver positioning by presenting the accomplishment of this domestic task as joint parenting:

(4)   *Elaine*:   Maybe if she gets a little older and she would clean up.
                   But you know she doesn't take care of that guinea pig.
                   Shit, I take care of it.
       Richard: Surprise, surprise. [<*facetiously*> Really?>]=
       Elaine: [And Mark takes care of it.]
       Richard: =Do you.

Richard does not respond by identifying a similar problem, or by relating the topic to his or Elaine's families. He responds facetiously, communicating that it does not surprise him that Elaine takes care of her daughter's pet. He says, *Surprise, surprise. Really?> Do you*, in a way that conveys the message, 'of course you do'. By responding in this way, Richard does not provide a matching experience, although he does convey understanding based, perhaps, on personal experience. However, someone who does not have children could reply in precisely the same way Richard does. In other words, this statement does not position him as a parent, but as someone who knows about children in general.

In Elaine's subsequent turn, she again attempts to repair the symmetry of the conversational frame by asking Richard a question that invites him to relate the topic to his family:

(5) *Elaine*: Don't you take care of all of your pets?
    Richard: Damn right.
    Elaine: <laughs>
    <*laughing*> That's right.>
    I said Beth—
    You know, she can be sitting right there next to that thing and it'd start squealing for food, she just tunes it out..
    It could be on its last legs, I don't think <*laughing*> she'd even notice>.
    I'm serious. Isn't that sad?
    Richard: I think that's the way kids are, at that age.

Elaine's question indicates that she expects Richard to provide a parallel problem. She even suggests what type of trouble that might be in her question, *Don't you take care of all of your pets?* Then, having received an albeit minimal response, *Damn right*, Elaine elaborates on the topic, maintaining her parental positioning. However, in his response, Richard refers to *the way kids are* instead of referring to his own children, generalizing his response and, thus, avoiding a parental positioning. It is doubtful that Richard takes up an authoritative stance based on greater parental experience because his oldest child, a twelve-year-old boy, is only two years older than Beth.

In the subsequent talk about chores, Elaine displays her expectation that Richard will volunteer information about his family from the perspective of his role as a father. This begins in 6 when Elaine, for the third time, asks a question which invites Richard to particularize the topic to his family:

(6) *Elaine*: Don't your kids do chores?
    Richard: <chuckles>
    Elaine: <chuckles>
    Do they do chores, [or not?]
    Richard: [Nah.]
    Elaine: None at all?

> *Richard*: Not structured, no.
>   I mean we have some help from time to time.
> *Elaine*: Do they make their beds every day?
> *Richard*: Um, periodically.

After Elaine asks Richard if his kids do chores, he chuckles and Elaine mirrors his response by chuckling herself. However, apparently lacking an adequate response, Elaine asks the question again. When he gives only a one-word response, *Nah*, she rephrases the question once again, attempting to elicit more information: *None at all?* Richard responds by elaborating somewhat: *Not structured, no. I mean we have some help from time to time*. However, he does not mention his children, and he only refers to his spouse through the use of the first person plural 'we'. Richard does not actually state that it is his children who *help from time to time*; this interpretation must be inferred. It could actually refer to hired help as well. Thus, again, Elaine attempts to elicit specific information about Richard's family by providing a specific example: *Do they make their beds every day?* After he gives a one-word response, *periodically*, Elaine waits. One second, two seconds, three seconds. Richard doesn't say anything else. Throughout the conversation, Elaine attempts to frame the conversation as a symmetrical exchange of family experiences by assuming a parental position within talk about her family, but Richard does not take up the reciprocal position Elaine's frame provides. Although he does refer to his spouse by saying 'we', which links his topic to family, he positions himself as a joint, rather than a primary, parent regarding domestic work.

Subsequently, Elaine continues to talk about her daughter's chores and, through this dialogue, reveals her level and type of parental involvement. In 7, Elaine continues the discussion by describing the difficulties she has getting Beth to do chores, but Richard does not respond by volunteering similar information. Instead he generalizes his responses:

(7) *Elaine*:   Oh God, it's hard though.
               It's hard to keep it going.
               Beth makes her bed every day, that's it.
               She'll set the table most nights.
               And then anything else, you know if we ask her.
     Richard: That's good.
     Elaine: Yeah.
     Richard: That's good.

Elaine: I have to ask her, I have to tell her, 'please set the table'.
          She doesn't just do it.
          But she'll make her bed. [She does do that.]
Richard: [I think that's normal.]
Elaine: [How come?]
Richard: [I: don't] think that's- that's abnormal
Elaine: And if I put her clothes in on her bed, she will put them
          away, now.
          And when we go on trips I m- make her do her own
          packing, so she'll know how to pack her own clothes.
Richard: Well, that's good.
          You're doing the right things.
Elaine: Try to teach her, you know?
Richard: Yeah.
Elaine: And she'll- she'll do it, she likes doing it, she likes laying
          it all out and then having me come in and see if she got
          the right stuff out.
          She loves to do that stuff, so.
Richard: Yeah, but, yeah, it's normal.
          That's normal.
          That's how I was.

Elaine speaks from the perspective of a mother who is, to some extent, solely responsible for her child's everyday activities. She begins by referring jointly to herself and her husband by using 'we' when describing her efforts to get Beth to do her chores: *And then anything else, you know if we ask her*. However, she then shifts to the first-person singular 'I' and uses constructed dialogue to embody herself speaking to her daughter, revealing that she alone directs Beth in this regard: *I have to ask her, I have to tell her, 'please set the table'*. In terms of domestic tasks, we discover that she does the laundry (*And if I put her clothes in on her bed, she will put them away, now*), and she monitors Beth's packing (*And when we go on trips I m- make her do her own packing*). Richard, on the other hand, does not take up the position of a parent, but responds in generalized terms about the nature of children: *I think that's normal*. What is crucial here is that, again, he could respond in the same way if he were not a parent himself.

At this point in the conversation, Richard shifts the topic to work: *So we're meeting this Wednesday, huh?* When he asks this question, he maintains the social talk frame of the encounter but shifts to work-related matters: the new educational requirements that will affect their advancement; the job that he applied for within the organization, but did not get; the people they know who have been promoted—a list of topics that bears an uncanny resemblance to Tannen's (1990, p. 101) finding that when men engage in social talk they tend to talk about 'political rather than personal relationships', such as 'institutional power, advancement and decline, a proposal that may or may not get through the committee, a plan for making money'.

During this social talk about work, Richard makes one notable reference to family. Elaine asks Richard if he is going to return to school in order to meet the new educational requirements necessary to advance at work. He says that he does not particularly want to pursue this path, but (in 8) he says that one reason he needs to advance is to pay for his children's higher education (*college tuition*):

> (8)   *Richard*: Oh, yeah, I- I'll—
>   If it were just us, you know,
>   retiring · is- is not an issue.
>   It- it's- it's- it's the college tuition thing,
>   if we're going to be paying for those.

In this reference to his children, Richard does not actually mention them, but omits them altogether with the nominalization, *the college tuition thing*. In this way he weakens his association with a parental position, as he does in the conversation about children's chores. Furthermore, he refers to them in the context of paying for their higher education. This reference, paying for schooling, falls within the realm of the breadwinner, not the caregiver position that is still associated more strongly with women.

Throughout the stretch of conversation in which Elaine and Richard talk about children, Richard avoids taking up a parental position by generalizing his references to children. Elaine, in contrast, speaks from the perspective of a parent and creates a parental identity by discussing Beth in particular. She aligns herself with a caregiver archetype by referring to herself as the primary caregiver, identifying tasks that a female caregiver performs, and presenting herself as the parent who manages the logistics of caregiving. It is these family-related positions that Richard avoids.

Discussion: Negotiating identities at work

Second-wave feminists[3] emphasized the need to integrate women into the public sphere without delay, to bring them 'into full participation in the mainstream of American society now, assuming all the privilege and responsibilities thereof in truly equal partnership with men' (Thornham, 2000, p. 30). Subsequently, the number of working mothers in the US increased dramatically during the past forty years. Whereas one quarter of children in two-parent families had a mother who worked full time in the early 1960s, about half did by 1997 (Waite and Nielsen, 2001). For children aged six and over, this figure reached 69 percent by 2002 (Clark, 2002). The rise of the dual-income family has been called the 'most dramatic, far-reaching change affecting women, men, and families' in the latter half of the twentieth century (Waite and Nielsen, 2001, p. 35).

In this chapter, I have considered the relation between gender and speech in public settings by considering how one woman and one man create gendered identities through social talk about home and family. This type of social talk constitutes one way in which private and public spheres interpenetrate. In the workplace, people do not exist in a single dimension, but bring the complexity of their lives, and their array of possible identities, with them. Social talk is one means through which these identities become salient at work. As co-workers engage in social talk, they talk about the roles and relationships that constitute their lives outside work, foregrounding and backgrounding the social identities associated with these roles and relationships. Hamilton (1996, pp. 65–66) notes that a goal in the study of language and identity is to 'understand more fully how an individual makes salient [the participants'] varied social identities throughout a given conversation, as well as which of these identities are ratified or denied by which conversational partners'. The analysis described in this chapter shows that a primary means through which participants make their identities as parents salient is by talking about tasks and activities from the perspective of a parent.

Although it is accurate to say that both of the conversational participants, Elaine and Richard, talk about family at work and create parental identities, there are systematic differences in the types of parental identities they create: Elaine creates a more traditional caregiver identity as a mother who accomplishes caregiving and domestic tasks primarily without assistance, whereas Richard avoids such a positioning and creates the parental identity of a breadwinner. In their conversation, we discover that Elaine takes care of her daughter's guinea pig, cooks, does the laundry, helps Beth pack, is responsible for setting the table, and expends a great deal of effort to ensure that Beth does her chores. The chores that she monitors are everyday jobs at home: setting the table, making beds, putting clothes away. We also learn that Elaine is preparing Beth for the future: She says she tries *to teach her, you know?*, and she monitors her progress by checking to *see if she got the right stuff out*. Furthermore, the tasks that Elaine describes are among those tasks that women tend to do more than men: cooking, washing clothes, setting the table. Finally, the tasks she describes indicate a high degree of involvement in her child's care. In this way, Elaine creates and displays her identity as a mother, an identity that includes the responsibilities for home and child that she describes. In contrast, we do not know anything about Richard's activities and responsibilities as a father based on the same conversation. The types of tasks that Elaine identifies in her talk about family, and the level of involvement entailed by these tasks, index women's traditional role since women have traditionally been responsible for these tasks. In contrast, when Richard makes his one reference to family in the conversation with Elaine, *the college tuition thing*, he takes up the position of the traditional, breadwinning father.

The two positionings that Elaine and Richard take up in relation to 'domesticity' (Williams, 2000) have different implications for the work identities they create. Taking up the position of breadwinner, as Richard does, enhances a work identity because it evokes a greater commitment to work. In the early 1900s, men were paid more than women based on the perception that they needed more money in order to support a family. Notably, Richard mentions his children's college tuition when talking about pursuing advancement at work. In contrast, Elaine takes up the position of a traditional mother by aligning herself with a caregiver archetype. Unfortunately, this position evokes the possibility of conflict between work and family in terms of time and commitment. Glass and Camarigg (1992) find that men are preferred for positions that provide greater autonomy, such as managerial positions, precisely because they are not expected to have family competition for their time and energy.

In conclusion, I suggest that the two study participants, Elaine and Richard, create gendered identities that are significant to their work-related identities through the family-related positions they take up as they talk about family at work. As people talk about family, they create gendered identities through the topics they choose and how they frame these topics. The positions that conversational participants take up in relation to the domestic sphere create gender-related identities that are relevant to the workplace because they index sex-based patterns of housework, childcare, and parental responsibility. In this way, individuals create and reproduce gendered identities through the language they use to create and maintain friendly relations at work.

Shari Kendall 195

Notes

1. Elaine was the participant in the first project, a study of one woman at work and at home, which I conducted myself with support from a grant to Deborah Tannen from the Alfred P. Sloan Foundation. This study provided the basis for my dissertation (Kendall, 1999). It also served as a pilot for a second, larger study of both the women and the men in four couples, conducted by Deborah Tannen and myself, based on a grant from the Alfred P. Sloan Foundation to Tannen and myself (Kendall, Tannen, and Gordon, 2005). I am deeply grateful to Deborah Tannen for her continuing support for my work, and to the Sloan Foundation. I am also grateful to the families in both research projects for their time and generosity in allowing us to enter their lives.

2.

text—	Dashes indicate an abandoned or incomplete utterance, for example a 'false start'.
text-	Hyphens indicate breaks in utterances which are subsequently completed, for example 'He went- I went to the store'.
[text]	Square brackets enclose simultaneous talk.
text=	Equal signs indicate that the speaker's turn continues to the next line without interruption, even if another person's talk intervenes.
((comment))	Double parentheses contain researcher's comments, for example ((door closes)).
<*manner*> text >	Angle brackets contain italicized descriptions of the manner in which the subsequent text is spoken, for example '<*softly*> He went home>'.
<vocal noise>	Angle brackets without italics contain descriptions of vocal noises produced by the speaker, for example <coughs>.
text · text	Dots with a space before and after indicate a perceptible pause of approximately one second per dot.
(text)	Parentheses enclose unsure transcription.
( )	Empty parentheses indicate unintelligible text.

3. Contemporary feminist writers generally recognize three waves of feminism in the US. The 'first wave' was defined by the suffragist movement and ended when this goal was achieved in 1920. The 'second wave' emerged in the post WWII era and extended into the 1990s, and was defined primarily in the 1960s and 1970s (see Thornham, 2000; Lotz, 2003). The 'third wave' began in the 1990s (Shugart, 2001). However, Baxter (2003) points out that these different stages of feminism actually represent different strands of feminist thought that have co-existed throughout these periods.

References

Baxter, J. *Positioning Gender in Discourse: A Feminist Methodology* (Basingstoke: Palgrave MacMillan, 2003).
Bianchi, S. M. 'Maternal Employment and Time with Children: Dramatic Change or Surprising Continuity?', *Demography*, 37 (2000), 401–414.

Bianchi, S. M., Milkie, M. A., Sayer, L. C., and Robinson, J. P. 'Is Anyone Doing the Housework?: Trends in the Gender Division of Household Labor', *Social Forces*, 79 (2000), 191–228.

Blum-Kulka, S. *Dinner Talk: Cultural Patterns of Sociability and Socialization in Family Discourse* (Mahwah, NJ: Lawrence Erlbaum Associates, 1997).

Brown, G. and Yule, G. *Discourse Analysis* (Cambridge: Cambridge University Press, 1983).

Bublitz, W. *Supportive Fellow-Speakers and Cooperative Conversations* (Amsterdam: John Benjamins, 1988).

Buunk, B. P., Kluwer, E. S., Schuurman, M. K., and Siero, F. W. 'The Division of Labor Among Egalitarian and Traditional Women: Differences in Discontent, Social Comparison, and False Consensus', *Journal of Applied Social Psychology*, 30 (2000), 759–779.

Clark, K. 'Mommy's Home: More Parents Choose to Quit Work to Raise Their Kids'. *U.S. News & World Report*, 32–33, 36, 38 (25 November 2002).

Clyne, M. *Inter-cultural Communication at Work* (Cambridge: Cambridge University Press, 1994).

Coates, J. *Women Talk: Conversations Between Women Friends* (Oxford: Blackwell, 1996).

Coltrane, S. 'Research on Household Labor: Modeling and Measuring the Social Embeddedness of Routine Family Work', *Journal of Marriage and the Family*, 62 (2000), 1208–1233.

Coontz, S. (2000) *The Way We Never Were: American Families and the Nostalgia Trap*. (NewYork: Basic Books, 2000).

Davies, B. and Harré, R. 'Positioning: Conversation and the Production of Selves', *Journal for the Theory of Social Behavior*, 20 (1990), 43–63.

Deane, C. 'Husband and Wives. Reality Check: The Gender Revolution Series', *The Washington Post*, A14 (25 March, 1998).

Drew, P. and Heritage, J. (eds), *Talk at Work: Interaction in Institutional Settings* (Cambridge: Cambridge University Press, 1992).

Fiske, S. T., Cuddy, A. J. C., Glick, P., and Xu, J. 'A Model of (Often Mixed) Stereotype Content: Competence and Warmth Respectively Follow from Perceived Status and Competition' *Journal of Personality and Social Psychology*, 82(6) (2002), 878–902.

Glass, J. and Camarigg, V. 'Gender, Parenthood, and Job-Family Compatibility', *American Journal of Sociology*, 98 (1992), 131–151.

Goodwin, C. and Heritage, J. 'Conversation Analysis', *Annual Review of Anthropology*, 19 (1990), 283–307.

Gumperz, J. J. *Discourse Strategies* (Cambridge: Cambridge University Press, 1982).

Hamilton, H. E. 'Intratextuality, Intertextuality, and the Construction of Identity as Patient in Alzheimer's Disease', *Text*, 16 (1996), 61–90.

Hochschild, A. and Machung, A. *The Second Shift: Working Parents and the Revolution at Home* (New York: Avon Books, 1989).

Holmes, J. 'Small Talk at Work: Potential Problems for Workers with an Intellectual Disability', *Research in Language and Social Interaction*, 36 (2003), 65–84.

Kendall, S. *The Interpenetration of (Gendered) Spheres: An Interactional Sociolinguistic Analysis of a Mother at Work and at Home* (Unpublished Dissertation, Washington DC: Georgetown University, 1999).

Kendall, S. 'Framing Authority: Gender, Face, and Mitigation at a Radio Network', *Discourse and Society*, 15 (2004), 55–79.

Kendall, S., Tannen, D. and Gordon, C. (eds), *Family Discourse* (New York: Oxford University Press, 2005).

Lamb, M. E. 'Introduction: The Emergent American Father'. In M. E. Lamb (ed.), *The Father's Role: Cross-Cultural Perspectives*, 3–25 (Hillsdale, NJ: Lawrence Erlbaum, 1987).

Levinson, S. C. *Pragmatics* (Cambridge: Cambridge University Press, 1983).

Lotz, A. D. 'Communicating Third-Wave Feminism and New Social Movements: Challenges for the Next Century of Feminist Endeavor', *Women and Language*, 26 (2003), 2–9.

Maddock, S. and Parkin, D. 'Gender Cultures: How They Affect Men and Women at Work'. In M. J. Davidson and R. J. Burke (eds), *Women in Management: Current Research Issues*, 29–40 (London: Paul Chapman, 1994).

McElhinny, B. 'Ideologies of Public and Private Language in Sociolinguistics'. In R. Wodak (ed.), *Gender and Discourse*, 106–139 (London, Thousand Oaks and New Delhi: Sage, 1997).

Morin, R. and Rosenfeld, M. 'With More Equity, More Sweat: Poll Shows Sexes Agree on Pros and Cons of New Roles. Reality Check: The Gender Revolution Series'. *The Washington Post*, A1 and A17 (22 March, 1998).

Robinson, J. P. and Godbey, G. *Time for Life: The Surprising Ways Americans Use Their Time* (University Park, PA: Pennsylvania State University Press, 1999).

Schiffrin, D. *Approaches to Discourse* (Malden, MA and Oxford: Blackwell, 1994).

Shugart, H. A. 'Isn't It Ironic: The Intersection of Third-Wave Feminism and Generation X', *Women's Studies in Communication*, 24 (2001), 131–168.

Tannen, D. *Talking Voices: Repetition, Dialogue, and Imagery in Conversational Discourse* (Cambridge: Cambridge University Press, 1989).

Tannen, D. *You Just Don't Understand: Women and Men in Conversation* (New York: William Morrow, 1990).

Tannen, D. *Talking from 9 to 5: Women and Men in the Workplace: Language, Sex and Power* (New York: Avon Books, 1994a).

Tannen, D. 'The Sex-Class Linked Framing of Talk at Work', *Gender and Discourse*, 195–221 (New York: Oxford University Press, 1994b).

Tannen, D. 'The Display of (Gendered) Identities in Talk at Work'. In M. Bucholtz, A. C. Liang and L. A. Sutton (eds), *Reinventing Identities: The Gendered Self in Discourse*, 221–240 (New York: Oxford University Press, 1999).

Thornham, S. 'Second-Wave Feminism'. In S. Gamble (ed.), *The Routledge Critical Dictionary of Feminism and Postfeminism*, 29–42 (New York: Routledge, 2000).

Tracy, K. and Naughton, J. M. 'Institutional Identity-Work: A Better Lens'. In J. Coupland (ed.), *Small Talk*, 62–83 (Harlow: Pearson, 2000).

van Langenhove, L. and Harré, R. (eds) 'Introducing Positioning Theory', *Positioning Theory*, 14–31 (Oxford: Blackwell, 1999).

Waite, L. J. and Nielsen, M. R. 'The Rise of the Dual Career Family: 1963–1997'. In R. Hertz and N. L. Marshall (eds), *Working Families: The Transformation of the American Home*, 23–41 (Berkeley: University of California Press, 2001).

Wardhaugh, R. *An Introduction to Sociolinguistics*, 4th edn (Malden, MA: Blackwell, 2002).

Williams, J. *Unbending Gender: Why Work and Family Conflict and What to Do About It* (New York: Oxford University Press, 2000).

Williams, J. C. and Segal, N. 'Beyond the Maternal Wall: Relief for Family Caregivers Who Are Discriminated Against on the Job', *Harvard Women's Law Journal*, 26 (2003), 77–162.

11
Culture, Voice and the Public Sphere: A Critical Analysis of the Female Voices on Sexuality in Indigenous South African Society

Puleng Hanong
The University of Witwatersrand, South Africa

Introduction

Despite the escalation of domestic violence, sexual abuse against females, and the prevalence of HIV/Aids in South Africa, *women* – usually the most affected group – often seem reluctant to enter into public discussions on matters pertaining to sexuality (including sex crimes). Central to this problem is the culture of secrecy that surrounds sexuality in many African communities, and, in particular, cultural constraints on women's speech behaviour that weaken or 'silence' their voices. Furthermore, virtually no research has been done on discourse and gender in South Africa, let alone on the notion of voices and silence.

This gender-based study, theoretically underpinned by poststructuralism and critical discourse analysis (CDA), analyses the subject of female voices (or lack thereof) in South African indigenous communities with a special focus on sexuality discourses. Through this analysis of talk-in-interaction, the paper explores the dialectal tension between the apparent transformation in the changing African socio-political public sphere, on the one hand, and the cultural institutions that construct and mediate social interaction, on the other. I argue for the analysis of the female voice (including silence) as a gender-variable mediated through the context of the patriarchal ideologies and practices of South African indigenous cultures.

Background to the study

One of the highlights of democracy in post-apartheid South Africa was its constitution (i.e. adopted in 1996 and came into operation in 1997) in which the international Bill of Rights as well as many individual and social freedoms are enshrined. Section 9 of the Constitution declares that no person shall be unfairly discriminated against on the grounds of 'race, gender, sex, pregnancy, marital status, ethnic or social origin, colour, sexual orientation, age, disability, religion, conscience, belief, culture, language and birth'. This constitution has since been used by the South African government as a guide to the establishment and implementation of its social equality agenda. First, the Commission on Gender Equality (CGE) was established through an Act of Parliament in 1996, and given the mandate to monitor and evaluate all policies and practices of state organs, public organizations, and the private sector to ensure their adoption of gender-sensitive policies and practices. Secondly, the government took decisive steps to promote gender equality by, among other things, encouraging and supporting female participation in politics, and ensuring significant representation of women in national parliament and provincial legislatures. As a result, many crucial government departments (e.g. Foreign Affairs, Education, Justice and Constitutional Affairs, Energy and Mining, Home Affairs, Land Affairs, Housing, etc.) are now led by women ministers. It is this gender-driven agenda that has influenced the formation of gender-based and women's organizations that campaign for the eradication of gender discrimination and all forms of violence against women.

Despite such positive strides, cultural institutions (e.g. family, marriage, religion, etc.) seem to have failed to locate the gender equality pulse of the 'new' South Africa. An important question to be asked, therefore, is why cultural institutions have behaved differently from other social institutions with regard to gender transformation? The answer to this question might be found in the interrogation of the androcentric ideologies of these institutions, their roles in the mediation of social practices (e.g. gender, power, identity, etc.), and the discourses that give them meaning. South Africa boasts diverse cultural, ethnic and linguistic indigenous communities, most of which were founded on patriarchal ideologies and value systems. This character of African communities has been fairly documented in several studies on the dynamics of gender and power politics in Africa. Maitse's (2000) study of gender violence, for example, observes that in post-apartheid South Africa 'men of all ages are socialized to define their power in terms of their capacity to effect their will, especially over women' (Maitse, 2000: 200). This problem is said to be further compounded by the ineffectiveness of the South African legal system to protect women against all forms of abuse (e.g. Mbete-Kgositsile, 1995); this point is also made in a couple of studies on discursive constructions of asymmetrical gender and power relations in rape trials in South African courts (e.g. Bronstein, 1994; Hanong Thetela, 2002). Hanong Thetela (2002), in particular, illustrates how the linguistic repertoire of *hlonipha* – the language of respect for women (e.g. Finlayson, 1995; Moeketsi, 1999) constrains female voices in court trials, and thus disempowers women before the law.

Discourse, gendered voice and cultural dynamics

The post-structuralist discourse analytical approach to gender that guides the present study sees gender as a discursive phenomenon not inherent in individuals, but negotiated through social meanings such as in talk (e.g. Edley and Wetherell, 1997; Stokoe and Smithson, 2001; Baxter, 2002a). Taking this social constructionist view of gender, I analyse the notion of voice against the background of a specific discursive social space (i.e. the South African socio-cultural public sphere) through which various kinds of social meanings (e.g. gender identities and subject positions) are constructed (e.g. Laclau, 1993; Edley, 2001). In addition, I look at the role of the cultural context in the construction of gendered talk, drawing on the discursive psychology thinking that 'recogni[ses] culture as supplying a whole range of ways of talking about or constructing an object or event' (Edley, 2001: 190). The social constructionist approach used in this paper makes possible the examination of 'the rhetorical organization of the linguistic and cultural repertoires, made up of the figures of speech, recurrent descriptions and metaphors, by which we construct specific accounts of ourselves and the world' (Barker and Galasiński, 2001: 35). Hence my argument is that the analysis of female voices requires a full understanding of the linguistic resources for communicating culturally constructed definitions of gender (e.g. Gumperz and Cook-Gumperz, 1982; Ochs, 1996).

Any critical analysis of discourse and gender cannot be complete without lending itself to the power dynamics of social interaction. In many studies of male and female speech patterns, in particular, powerful speech has been traditionally associated with masculinity and powerless speech with femininity (e.g. Spender, 1980; Lakoff, 1995). This view of male domination of speech in public contexts (e.g. media, politics, religion, etc.) is supported by recent studies in Britain. For instance, such studies point to a lack of strong female voices in the media where, despite attempts to include some women's stories, setting the media agenda (e.g. news or story selection, angle of reporting stories, etc.) remain almost exclusively the domain of men – the result is either the trivialization, or the absence of female voices in the media (e.g. Macdonald, 1998). Moreover, research on gender and voice in classroom discussions in British schools (e.g. Sunderland, 1995; Baxter, 2002a, 2002b) shows that boys dominate girls in the area of public speaking. Baxter (2002a, 2002b), in particular, expresses concern that despite girls' ever improving performance in, for example, GCSE examinations, they still lag behind boys in the area of public speaking. A similar study at the University of Natal by Ige and de Kadt (2002) finds that Zulu males dominate public discussions.

So far I have alluded to the notion of 'voice' without providing either a definition of the way the term is used in this study. The two notions – 'voice' and 'silence' – are used as metaphors following from studies of feminist gender research 'to figure all the ways in which women are denied the right or the opportunity to express themselves freely' (Cameron, 1998: 3). Thus the claim 'that women are "silent" or "silenced" cannot mean that they are always and everywhere *literally* silent, nor that they lack the capacity to use language, which is the inalienable birthright of every human being' (Cameron, 1998: 3). Instead the term is used to point to the fact that women's speech is often relegated to non-prestigious genres (e.g. gossiping, etc.) most of which occur in the private sphere (e.g. the family), while in the public domain, 'and especially the domain of official culture...the genres associated with women have little currency' (Cameron, 1998: 3). Thus the analysis of female voices is situated within a broader framework of the African socio-cultural public sphere in which women are either given or denied a voice.

Discourse and cultural scripts

The South African indigenous communities almost invariably regard silence by women as a virtue rather than a flaw. This can be seen in a variety of ways through which female voices are regulated and policed – the gender-exclusive discursive spaces and cultural practices. The Sesotho *kgotla* or Zulu *inkundla* (i.e. men's court) is an example of a social domain in which only masculine-specific issues (e.g. animal pastures, initiation, etc.) are discussed (Sekese, 1999). Another example is that of initiation where boys undergo circumcision as well as rigorous training of the rites of passage from boyhood to manhood. All discourses surrounding initiation are strictly confidential – only referred to as **koma** (i.e. a secret), which are the exclusive domain of the initiated men.

The gendered social spaces are also found in an array of rich linguistic repertoires and cultural scripts (songs, poetry, proverbs, oral narratives, rituals, etc.) in which gender hierarchies are constructed and where gendered power relations are played out. Here female voices are excluded through derogatory references to talkative women – for example, **ndabazabantu** (news of other people) in Zulu or **mmaditaba** (mother of news) in Sesotho. Sekese (1999: 62–67), for example, provides a detailed narration of girls' socialization into womanhood in which the value of silence is emphasized through cultural and linguistic repertoires. These serve as a deterrent against, among other things, gossiping, swearing, spreading lies, and taking part in controversial conversational spaces.

Applying the above framework of cultural scripts wholesale to the analysis of female voice might be an oversimplification of discursive constructions of gender in South Africa. I refer to the socialization of women using the past tense to acknowledge societal and cultural transformation that has taken place since 1994. For, indeed, men (or women) may belong to different social categories depending on the discursive contexts in which they may from time to time find themselves.

Research data and methodology

The study uses only a small part of the data of a much bigger research project on gender-based issues (e.g. domestic violence, women's rights, etc.) collected over three years (2001–2004). For the present study, I use focus group discussions and interview sessions over a period of eight months (November 2003–June 2004). The focus group consisted of 75 postgraduate students (aged between 23 and 35) from three academic institutions (i.e. 25 from each institution) – the University of the Free State (UFS), Vista University (VU) and the University of the Witwatersrand (WITS). All students were mother tongue (MT) speakers of at least one indigenous South African language. In the first two institutions, 90 per cent of the participants were MT speakers of Sesotho, while at WITS, the language profiles of participants were evenly distributed across Zulu, Xhosa, Setswana, Sesotho, Sepedi, and TshiVenda.

The focus groups were given different tasks based on a given set of data. The UFS and VU groups, on the one hand, were given four cuttings of news stories and two video recordings (7 and 5 minutes, respectively) of television news items on domestic violence, specifically the issue of marital rape. Participants were asked to read the news stories, watch the video recordings, and then discuss the issues raised, and express their own opinions. They were also provided with a set of questions to use as a guide to the discussions (e.g. whether or not women should report rape). Three members of the research team sat throughout the sessions to observe and record the discussions, and to intervene where necessary (e.g. clarify given tasks, solve conflicts, etc.). While same tasks were given to the WITS group (but using different but similarly themed stories), this group was given an additional task of listening to excerpts of audio recordings from the first two groups in order to evaluate the issues raised therein as well as to express their opinions.

Another set of data came from interview sessions with two groups of people in the Johannesburg area – 11 professionals (2 public health nurses, 2 doctors, 3 social workers, 2 rape counselors, and 2 gender research specialists) and 7 women at a 'women's centre for survivors of violence'. While interviews for professionals centred on experiences and challenges of working with victims of abuse, those for the victims were based on their level of awareness of issues of violence, legal recourse, as well as various intervention services (e.g. counseling). For ethical reasons, pseudonyms have been used to protect the identities of individuals and their organizations.

Language choice played a pivotal role in the research. For example, despite repeated calls by the research team for the use of African languages in the discussions, the majority of participants opted for English, and even those who used African languages employed a great deal of code switching and mixing. This situation posed a great challenge for transcription – as a result, some data were transcribed in their original mediums (e.g. Sesotho or mixed code) to highlight unique cultural meanings (e.g. Extracts 1, 2, and 3), while others were transcribed through the medium of English.

Data analysis

I adopt a two-pronged analysis. First, I focus on linguistic gender-indexing resources; indexicality here is used in the sense of Ochs' (1996) point that many of the features of language do not always presuppose either male or female, but that within the context of the conversational event, these features are seen to be used by one more than the other sex. I illustrate how specific discourse choices construct and categorize participants as belonging to a specific gender grouping and not the other, and hence the discursive construction of gender identity and subject positions (e.g. Edley, 2001). Secondly, I investigate how these choices are located in the wider context of androcentric ideologies, cultural repertoires and scripts, which shapes and are in turn shaped by the nature of the interaction itself. It is from this viewpoint that I look at silence as an implicit gender-indexing feature, and suggest that its systematic recurrences within the context of gendered talk could be interpreted as a gender-indexing resource (e.g. Nwoye, 1985).

Cultural gender roles and subject positions

The focus group sessions were, more often than not, dominated by the participants' digression from the content of the news reports to arguments involving gender bias in the reports, to the extent that many comments became very personal and often degenerated into very gender polarized positions. While male participants complained that the stories were biased in favour of women, and that women often falsely accuse men of rape, many females were of the view that men who rape their wives deserved to be put behind bars for life. It was through such discourses of blame and counter-blame that gender identities and subject positions were constructed.

The first UFS session started with a newspaper story about a man alleged to have raped his pregnant wife, and causing the latter's miscarriage. This was followed by two video recordings (i.e. 5 minutes and 7 minutes long, respectively) from a television news bulletin and a talk show, respectively, on issues of sexual violence. Extract 1 is a verbal exchange involving two males, Joe and Sipho, and two females, Thato and Palesa. The focus is on whether marital rape exists, and whether it is a criminal offence.[1]

Extract 1: Bloem2.3/1

1 Joe: .hh uhm na <u>monna</u> ya nyetseng a ka beta <u>mosadi wa hae</u>? (.)
   JWANG ? (1.0)
   .hh uhm can a married man rape his wife? (.) HOW? (1.0)
2   monna o na le TOKELO ya **ho robala mosadi** <u>ha feela a rata</u> (0.2)
   haeba ke phoso uh uh
   *a man has the RIGHT **to sleep his wife** <u>whenever he wants</u> (0.2) if I
   am wrong uh uh*
3   le tla nthiba, ja? (.) that is why lenyalong conjugal rights e leng
   ntho ya bohlokwa
   *you will stop me, yeah? (.) that is why in marriage conjugal rights is an
   important issue*
4   hantle conjugal rights tsa monna ke right tsa hae to sexual intercourse
   in fact a man's conjugal rights are his right to sexual intercourse

5   (0.5)
6   Jwale mpolelle (.) haeba mosadi a hana ho phetha MOLAO le
       MOETLO
       So tell me (.) if the wife disobeys the LAW and the CULTURE
7   ((simultaneous noisy talk))
8   E::, E::, [ke hlile ke cho jwalo (.) mpolelle hore na uhm ha a
       mo] hanela =
       Ye::s, Ye::s, [I mean exactly that (.) tell me when uhm she denies him =

9: Thato: [Modimo (.) o bua **jwaloka ka monna wa Mosotho
              hantle!**]
              [*God, You are speaking **exactly like a Mosotho man** !*]

10 Joe   = ka ditokelo tsa hae (.) o lebeletse hore **monna yeo wa
          Modimo** [a phele jwang?
          *= his rights (.) how does she expect **this man of God** [to live?*
11 Thato: [athe mosadi yena ha se wa Modimo?
                [*is the woman not of God? -*
12 Sipho: Arabang potso ya **Bra Joe** (.) monna a lebe kae ha mosadi wa
          hae **a mo hana** ?
          *Answer **Bra Joe**'s question (.) where should the husband go if his
          wife refuses him?*

13:      **Moholwane** o a bona hore jwale BEIJI::NG e re baketse mathata?
         *My brother do you realise that now BEIJI::NG has caused us
         problems?*
14   jwale uhm (.) basadi ba se ba re behela **di-sanction**
        now uhm (.) women are imposing sanctions on us
15   ((murmuring and laughter))
16   (3.0)
17 Palesa: Ka mantswe a mang molao ha o re letho ka ditokelo tsa basadi?
          In other words the law says nothing about the rights of women?
18   haeba monna uhm (.) .hh **a batla dikobo** mosadi wa hae a sa
        [batle uh uh] -
        *if the man uhm (.) .hh **wants blankets** but his wife does not
        [want uh uh]-*
19 Sipho: [a ka hana jwang] (.)
         [*how can she refuse*] (.)
20   **mosadi A NTSHEDITSWE DIKGOMO?** (0.4)
        a wife FOR WHOM CATTLE HAVE BEEN PAID? (0.4)
21   ntle le haeba **e se le yena hlooho** ka tlung
        *except if **it is she who is now the head** in the house*

The verbal exchange above illustrates a blurring of boundaries between sex and gender through repeated associations of the biological man or woman with the social man or woman. Since the male speakers skilfully claimed (and maintained) most of the speaking turns, most gender identities were constructed from their own perspectives and through their own voices. For example, in Joe's initial turn unit in lines 1–8 (see McLaughlin, 1984), **monna** (used for both man and husband) and **mosadi** (used for both woman and wife) represents a very masculine gendered position constructed through his question–answer rhetorical style – a combination of questions (e.g. 'HOW' in line 1), tags such as **'ja'** (i.e. the Afrikaans equivalent of 'yeah') in line 3, as well as other linguistic strategies. In his speech, Joe appears to rally male support behind his position that a man is entitled to unrestricted sex with his wife (i.e. 'whenever he wants' in line 2), and that any refusal to sex by the wife amounts to a breach of **molao** (law) and **moetlo** (culture/tradition), both of which protect the husband's demand of conjugal rights (i.e. line 3). Another interesting linguistic feature of Joe's speech is the grammatical choice, **ho robala mosadi** (literally translated as **to sleep a wife**) in line 2, in which the verb **robala** (sleep) is used transitively to position the husband in agency position in the grammar of the clause, while the wife is in the 'beneficiary' position (see, for example, Halliday, 1994 on transitivity roles). This transitive use of verbs of sexual acts common across most South African languages can be interpreted as constructions of the dominant role that a man plays in a sexual relationship as opposed to the woman's subservient one. The dominant–subservient relationship between husbands and wives in African families is symbolically realized through the institution of **lobola** (bride price), the point brought up in Sipho's reference to **dikgomo** (cattle) – the traditional currency of African marriage transactions (line 20). Sipho's reference to lobola, therefore, constructs the gender hierarchical relationship in the African family – the wife for whom lobola has been paid has no right to deny her husband sex, thus she cannot make any claims to rape, and by implication her voice is silenced. The point for **lobola** as a symbolic construction of women's powerlessness has been made in several cultural studies on African cultures (e.g. Chigwedre, 1982; Cooper, 1982).

Masculine subject positions in the data were also seen in the blurring of discursive boundaries between the 'man as subject in the topic' and the 'man as a speaker in the interaction', exclusive to the speech of male participants. This was realized in the use of first-person plural pronoun 'we' to refer to 'the men in the topic'. In Extract 1, for instance, Sipho blames **Beijing** (i.e. reference to the 1995 United Nations Fourth World Congress on Women) for women's allegations of marital rape (lines 13–14). Beijing is said to cause problems for 'us' (line 13); and a woman's rebuttal of her husband's sexual demands is referred to as the imposition of **sanctions** on 'us' (line 14). In addition, 'the man in the topic' is referred to in endearment terms as **this man of God**; while fellow male interactants are addressed in kinship terms – **Bra Joe** ('Bra' refers to 'brother') in line 12 and **moholwane** (older brother) in line 13. It is through such strategies that male bonding, solidarity, and the collective masculine position are discursively constructed.

By contrast, female contributions were few and far apart, and most blamed men for sexual violence and for excessive use of swear words. Moreover, female speech was marked by protest discourses: men were accused of gender intolerance, disrespectfulness, and outright arrogance, with many female speakers frequently threatening to withdraw from the discussions. Thato's interruption of Joe (line 11) to express her objection to the latter's derogatory remarks (e.g. **'when she refuses him'** in line 12) is a good example – refusing a husband (i.e. denying him sex) is a cultural expression used by older community members to express disapproval at a young wife's refusal to perform her sexual duties. Female speech was at times very conciliatory, often intended to call for calmness during controversial moments. In line 11, for example, Thato appeals to Joe to extend the use of endearment terms (e.g. 'this man of God' in line 10) to refer to women. This conciliatory stance and other peacemaking strategies appeared to weaken and silence female voices in the face of confrontation and dominance by their male colleagues.

The notion of weak (and silent) female voices is also discursively constructed through the gendered speech style from the subsystem of respect language, known as *hlonipha* in Southern African languages (e.g. Finlayson, 1995). Although *hlonipha* is not necessarily gender-exclusive, sociolinguistic evidence has shown that in South African languages, it is often reserved for women (e.g. Finlayson, 1995). Many features of this repertoire are found in euphemisms and vague expressions used with reference to sexuality (Hanong Thetela, 2002). Palesa's reference to a man's demand for sex (in line 18) as **ho batla dikobo** (to demand blankets), for example, is an illustration of this repertoire. This repertoire was also common in interview sessions with professional women. In one interview, for example, a Zulu rape counsellor referred to a condom as **ijazi likamkhwenyana** (the son-in-law's jacket) and to sexual intercourse as **ukuya ocansini** ('to go to the mat'), the latter probably originating from grass mats used as beds in African rural communities.

Cultural gender stereotypes

Another interesting feature emerging from the data was the construction of gender stereotypes, and, in particular, the stereotypical image of the 'ideal' African woman. This was done, among other things, through the construction of the ideal African woman as opposed to the modern (and thus western) one. Extract 2 below illustrates this point. The participants are one female, Missy, and two males, Monty and Baba. The discussion focuses on the role of women's organizations in South Africa. Baba's question (line 1) questions an earlier suggestion by a female speaker that women should be encouraged to report marital rape.

Extract 2: VIST37

1	Baba:	Are you saying women should publicly humiliate their
2		husbands?
3	Missy:	No, she is not saying that [but...
4	Monty:	[but what?] basadi ba kajeno
5		ba se ba lahlile **moetlo le maseko** a bona haholo bana ba
6		reng ba rutehile
7		[but what] *women these days*
8		*have lost their **culture and traditions** especially those who*
9		*claim to be educated*
10	Missy:	The issue is whether or not it is right for a man to rape his wife.
11	Baba:	You know what my sister, marital rape is a new concept in
12		our society. Our mothers never accused our fathers of rape.
13		Are you saying that today's husbands are rapists? These
14		women's organizations are not fair. Am afraid this so-called
15		gender madness is a new kind of cultural colonialism.
16		African women now behave like whites. They treat their
17		husbands like kids.
18	Missy:	Excuse me, are you saying that it is good for husbands to
19		rape their wives?
20	Baba:	No, I am saying allegations of marital rape show loss of
21		African values.
22		((noise and murmuring))
23	Baba:	Oa bona basadi ba se ba apere **mabrukgwe** mo malapeng?
24		*Are you aware that women are now wearing **trousers** in the*
25		*home.*

It is interesting how participants' gender stereotypes are realized through constructions of 'Otherness' – specifically through Foucault's (1971) notion of exclusion. Otherness here is constructed through 'Us'-versus-'Them' binary opposition. It is this opposition that in turn defines the ideal African identity (and stereotypes) through 'Us' (e.g. Africans) as the in-group and 'Them' (Whites or Westerners) as the 'out group' (see, for example, Van Dijk, 1998, on group identity). In the Extract 2 above, male speakers take it upon themselves to define the 'ideal African woman' from their own viewpoint. They employ exclusion discourses – the use of 'exclusion' follows Foucault's (1971) theory defined in terms of 'what is usual, habitual and expected as opposed to what constitutes a deviation, an exception' (Rojo, 1995: 51). In this extract, Baba's emotional outburst about the modern (i.e. westernized) African woman – the one who publicly voices her opposition to marital rape – is a good example of exclusion and, by implication, a rejection of the modern woman seen as an embodiment of undesirable western values foreign to the African culture. It is such women who 'have lost their culture and traditions' (lines 5 and 8) and 'behave like whites' (line 16). The 'white' values are in turn rejected through verbal processes such as 'claiming to be educated' (line 6), 'humiliating' husbands in public (line 1) and 'accusing' husbands of rape (line 13), an indication of 'loss of African values' (line 21). This 'Otherness' is constructed with the ideal epitomized by '*our* mothers' who 'never accused *our* fathers of rape' (line 12).

It is worth noting the value of 'voice' in the discursive constructions of African-versus-Western morality realized in the verbs of saying. For example, women who 'claim to be educated' (line 9) are derogatively associated with 'the gender thing', which is, in turn, rejected as 'a new form of cultural colonialism' (line 15). In short the typical African woman is associated with respect for her husband – she does not treat her husband like a kid (line 17), she does not 'publicly humiliate' her husband (line 1) and does not engage in 'the so-called gender madness' (line 15). Most importantly the African woman does not usurp the power and authority of her husband, the deviant value constructed through the metaphorical notion of **mabrukgwe** (trousers). In South African indigenous culture, 'wearing trousers' symbolizes manhood and male authority and the notion of women wearing trousers implies the usurpation of masculine authority, a threat to the societal moral order.

Silence and gendered African morality

As I have already argued, morality in African society seems gendered. Women are obliged to adhere to strict moral codes while men are under no such obligation. Maitse (2000), for example, rightly points out that in post-apartheid South Africa, many women support the very cultural institutions that oppress them (e.g. lobola), and she observes that such institutions 'compel women to collude with men owing to fear of individual reprisals and breaking up of community cohesiveness' (Maitse, 2000: 206).

Extract 3 is a discussion involving three males, Vuyo, Shuz, and Meshu, and two females, Thuli and Tshidi. The argument follows a confrontation between Thuli and Meshu on the former's claim that a black man (referred to as **darkie** by Vuyo in 1) rapes his wife/partner at least once a year.

Extract 3: WITS15

1	Vuyo:	O kenyeletsa le wa hao (.) ke **darkie** le yena
		Are you including yours (.) he is also a black man
2		.hhh ((laughs)) ke hore **Sware** le yena **o o robala** ka kgang
3		(3.0)
		*.hhh ((laughs)) that means **Brother in Law** also sleeps you by force* (3.0)
4		ha ke re?
5		*isn't it?*
6		((Thuli does not respond))
7		(2.0)
8	Vuyo:	Ha o arabe keng? (.) e re feela E kapa E-E
9		*Why don't you respond? (.) Just say YES or NO*
		((Thuli doesn't respond))
10		(3.0)
11	Tshidi:	Na ke potso yeo **motho wa mme** [a ka e arabang]=
		*Is that a question that **a person who is a mother** [can answer]=*
12	Shuz:	[Why a sa arabele], a re
13		fe evidence
		[*Why can't she respond and give us evidence*]
14		((Thuli doesn't respond))

I use the above interaction to comment on two 'patterns' of silence observed – first, the silence that occurs across the turn boundaries, and secondly that which occurs either intra-sententially (e.g. following the *uh*) or within the same turn unit. I look at the duration of the conversational gap, and then its gender-indexing value. First, Thuli's non-response occurrences (lines 6, 9, and 14) can be seen to exemplify the first type. I look at these occurrences from the perspective of preference organization (e.g. Pomerantz, 1984) – a characterization of the ways in which 'second actions' (e.g. accepting an invitation) are routinely accomplished. Thus according to recurrent features and sequential structure of turns we could see Vuyo's repeated questions to Thuli, such as 'isn't it?' in which Vuyo uses a tag to get confirmation to his question, and to which Thuli does not respond. This question–silence pattern continues despite various attempts by Vuyo to elicit a response from Thuli. Thuli's silence causes intervention by Shuz. Thuli's non-cooperation results in long conversational lapses, causing various attempts by other speakers to salvage the discussions and to move the interaction forward (e.g. Vuyo's demand for a 'yes' or 'no' option in line 8). Tshidi attempts to defend Thuli's action through self-selection (line 11). Interestingly, she attributes the latter's silence to her being **a mother**. This term **mother** has the underlying notion of the metaphorical reference to **motherhood**, the identity assumed by all young brides – they do not only adopt their husbands' surnames, but are also given new names, marked by the nominal prefix **mma-** (mother of) first in anticipation of her impending fertility as well as for her role as an embodiment of African feminine morality. It is against this background that Thuli's non-response to the demand for information relating to her sexual relationship with her husband could be interpreted as her adherence to the values of motherhood referred by Tshidi in line 11. It is in this way Thuli's silence can be seen as a virtue and not a flaw – the construction of desirable feminine values.

The relationship between silence and morality was also significant in interview sessions with victims of abuse. Almost all the women I spoke to concurred that sexuality (including sexual crimes) is a very difficult topic for African women to discuss not only in public domains but also in the private spaces such as in the home with their own children. In Extract 4, for example, the respondent explains why she waited for over two years to report her husband's violence.

Extract 4: RV09

A: Because he was my husband. You know we have three children, and my eldest son is now 15 years old. I was worried that if I reported this matter, my son would be affected by it as well as my husband's

family. I also did not want my family to be the talk of the neighbour-
hood. Remember that my husband was respected by the people.

The response above points to an important issue – women choose not
to disclose abuse for fear of bringing shame on the family. The
respondent had to keep her silence for the sake of her children, and, in
particular, her 15-year-old son. It is interesting to note that for the duration
of the abuse, she remained silent for the sake of her son, her husband's
family as well as the neighbours. Similar stories were found among
women. One HIV positive woman told me how her boyfriend refused to
use condoms and also prevented her from using contraceptives, and yet
the woman could not argue with him; there were also stories of women
being abused by husbands, ex-husbands, and boyfriends, and a widow
repeatedly raped by her brother-in-law. In all these stories, these women
opted for silence for a variety of reasons – among others, financial
dependence on men, fear of physical violence, and fear of a scandal
that would bring shame to the family. This behaviour corroborates
Gilligan's (1998) view of women's conception of their moral values as
based primarily on what society defines as good or bad.

The analysis of silence above seems to suggest a two-way relationship
between men silencing women and women colluding with men in
order to construct their own African gender identity – silence as indexical
of dignity, femininity, and respect for family values. In this way women
can be seen both as victims of silencing and agents of silencing.

The female voice: Implications for social transformation

The discussion has focused on serious problems with very far-reaching
consequences for social programmes to inform, educate the public, as
well as challenge the cultural gender hegemony through empowerment
programmes in a country with an escalating rate of sexual violence and
HIV/Aids infections. It is important to acknowledge significant efforts
by government, NGOs, and media institutions – for their campaigns to
educate the public on issues such as safe sex, abstinence, empowerment
of women, and many others.

Despite these important steps, there are still genuine concerns that
these messages do not reach the public, especially in the rural areas
where patriarchal ideologies and cultural practices are still entrenched.
Interviews with professionals, for example, raise similar issues brought
up in focus group discussions. For instance, professionals pointed to
many socio-cultural obstacles to implementing gender equity
programmes as well as combating abuse of women – most importantly,

that of women's seeming reluctance to speak about sex and abuse. A good example is that of Extract 5 below.

Extract 5: Prof 2: Rape Counsellor on women's reluctance to report abuse

When it comes to rape and domestic abuse, Africans are generally very secretive. You can understand why talking to strangers like myself can be extremely challenging. Family problems such as the husband's infidelity, physical violence, rape, and other forms of domestic violence are not easy topics for women to deal with. I have a recent case where a recently widowed woman was raped by her husband's younger brother several times within the space of eight months. Just the day before the case could go to court, she phoned to say she was withdrawing the charges. No explanation, nothing. How do you like that? Professionals argue that the implementation of a gender-friendly social agenda needs a collective effort by the government, the judicial system, civil society, gender-based organizations, and many others bodies. These professionals call for education programmes aimed at raising public awareness, especially men, on gender related issues. As one gender specialist puts it, "It is not enough to educate women on gender and violence when perpetrators are left roaming the streets of Johannesburg looking for their next victims. There is an urgent need for changes of attitudes in South Africa".

Concluding remarks

The study has attempted an analysis of a complex array of gender issues in the post-apartheid South African indigenous society, with a view to highlighting issues related to the notions of voice and silence. The study has illustrated the domination of male voices over female ones in specific social contexts in the public domain. I have used focus group discussions and interview data to interrogate the metaphorical notions of voice and silence. The study has also illustrated that culture is a core ingredient in the discursive constructions of gender identity, subject positions, and power relations, regardless of whether it is masculinity or femininity; and also how this impacts on the female voice within the context of South Africa.

In the study, on the one hand, I have attempted the analysis of the aspects of the socio-cultural context and how this contributes to the discursive constructions of gender and voice. On the other, I have analysed aspects of talk-in-interaction that systematically express or signal gender identity, and consequently evoke dominant patriarchal ideologies.

The study was, however, limited to the analysis of gendered discourses linguistically constructed through lexico-semantic choices and other forms of cultural repertoires in South African indigenous sexuality discourses. This is just one of the ways in which many other aspects of gender constructions could be teased out. It is also worth mentioning that the analysis of gender identity from the socio-cultural context may often be misconstrued as rooted in variationist models of gender. This might partly be true in that within most androcentric societies, a culturally constructed definition of gender is based on dichotomous differences rather than over-lapping categories (e.g. Basso, 1990). Although I have attempted to use the micro-level analysis of approach to interrogate macro-level social phenomena (e.g. power relations and patriarchal ideologies), the purpose of my analysis was to ask how and when the participants in the talk draw inferences and interpretative repertoires from the cultural context to construct gender identities – how these empower or disempower women and thus affect their voices in the public domain.

Despite concentrating on constructions of 'male as positive and powerful' as opposed to 'female as negative and subservient' identities by male participants, female participant talk was significant in that despite the establishment of the African female as polite, dignified and moral, their contributions did not challenge the dominant androcentric hegemony. By adhering to the *hlonipha* code which constrains them from expressing themselves effectively, they effectively collude in the gender hegemony of male domination in public discourses of sexuality.

As I have said, there is very little research on discourse and gender in South Africa, let alone that on the notion of voices and silence. Thus, to understand how cultural gender is constructed, and consequently how voices are assigned, negotiated, and mediated, there is a need for a full understanding of the discursive ideologies at play. Having a deeper insight into how power is mediated through choices of cultural and linguistic repertoires, for instance, we can begin to look at the ways and means by which patriarchal cultural ideologies and practices might be challenged with a view to bringing about meaningful gender equality in South Africa.

Notes

1. *Transcription Notation (modified from Jefferson 1984)*

Underlining: stress placed on a word
Capital letter (e.g. CAT): loudness placed on a word
Bold type: culture-specific expressions
Italics: English translation of mother tongue
Bold italics: English translation of culture-specific expressions

.hh: audible intake of breath
One or more colons (::): the previous sound extended
Numbers in parenthesis (0.2): pauses measured in tenths of a second
(.): a minor pause
Double parenthesis: Transcriber's descriptions
Equal sign (=): the absence of a discernible gap between the end of one utterance of one speaker's utterance and the beginning of another's utterance
Square brackets [ ]: overlapping speech

References

Barker, C. and Galasiński, D. (2001) *Cultural Studies and Discourse Analysis*. London: Sage.
Basso, Keith H. (1990) 'To give upon word': Silence in Western Apache culture' in D. Carbaugh (ed.), *Cultural Communication and Intercultural Communication*, pp. 303–320, Hillsdale, NJ: Lawrence Erlbaum Associates.
Baxter, J. (2002a) 'Competing discourses in the classroom: A post-structuralist discourse analysis of girls' and boys' speech in public contexts', *Discourse & Society*, 13(6): 827–842.
Baxter, J. (2002b) 'Jokers in the pack: Why boys are more adept than girls at speaking in public settings', *Language and Education*, 16(2): 81–96.
Bronstein, V. (1994) 'The rape complainant in court: An analysis of legal discourse', in C. Murray (ed.), *Gender and the New South African Legal Order*. Kenwyn: Juta & Co.
Cameron, D. (1998) 'Introduction: Why is language a feminist issue', in D. Cameron (ed.), *The Feminist Critique of Language*, pp. 1–30, London: Routledge.
Chigwedre, A. (1982) *Lobela: Pros and Cons*. Harare: Books for Africa.
Cooper, A. (1982) *Wives for Cattle: Bride Wealth and Marriage Payments in Southern Africa*. London: Routledge.
Edley, N. (2001) 'Analysing masculinity: Interpretative repertoires, ideological dilemmas and subject positions', in M. Wetherell, S. Taylor and S. J. Yates (eds), *Discourse as Data: A Guide for Analysis*, pp. 189–228, London: Sage (in Association with the Open University).
Edley, N. and Wetherell, M. (1997) 'Jockeying for positions: The construction of masculine identities', *Discourse & Society*, 8(2): 203–217.
Finlayson, R. (1995) 'Women's language of respect: Isihlonipho sabafazi', in R. Mesthrie (ed.), *Language and Social History: Studies in South African Sociolinguistics*, pp.141–153, Cape Town: David Philip.
Foucault, M. (1971) *L'ordre du discours*. Paris: Gallimard.
Gilligan, C. (1998) 'In a different voice: Women's conceptions of self and morality', in B. McVicker Clinchy and J. K. Norem (eds), *The Gender and Psychology Reader*, pp. 347–382, New York: New York University Press.
Gumperz, J. and Cook-Gumperz, J. (1982) 'Introduction: Language and the communication of social identity', in J. Gumperz (ed.), *Language and Social Identity*, pp. 1–21, Cambridge: Cambridge University Press.

Halliday, M. A. K. (1994) *Introduction to Functional Grammar*, 2nd edn, London: Edward Arnold.

Hanong Thetela, P. (2002) 'Sex discourses and gender constructions in Southern Sotho: A case study of police interviews of rape/sexual assault victims', *Southern African Linguistics and Applied Language Studies*, 20: 177–189.

Ige, B. and de Kadt, E. (2002) 'Gendering politeness: Zulu-speaker identities at the University of Natal, Durban', *Southern African Linguistics and Applied Language Studies*, 20: 147–161.

Jefferson, G. (1984) 'Transcription notation', in J. M. Atkinson and J. Heritage (eds), *Structures of Social Action: Studies in Conversation Analysis*. Cambridge: Cambridge University Press.

Laclau, E. (1993) 'Politics and the limits of modernity', in T. Docherty (ed.), *Postmodernism: A Reader*, pp. 329–344, London: Harvester Wheatsheaf.

Lakoff, R. T. (1995) 'Cries and whispers: The shattering of silence', in K. Hall and M. Bucholtz (eds), *Gender Articulated: Language and the Socially Constructed Self*, pp. 25–50, New York: Routledge.

Macdonald, M. (1998) 'Politicizing the personal: Women's voices in British Television documentaries', in C. Carter, G. Branston and S. Allan (eds), *News, Gender and Power*, pp. 105–120, London: Routledge.

Maitse, T. (2000) 'Revealing silence: Voices from South Africa', in S. Jacobs, R. Jacobson and J. Marchbank (eds), *States of Conflict: Gender, Violence and Resistance*, pp. 199–214, London: Zed Books.

Mbete-Kgositsile, B. (1995) 'National machinery for promoting the status of Women', in S. Liebenberg (ed.), *The Constitution of South Africa from a Gender Perspective*, pp. 23–27, Cape Town: David Philip.

McLaughlin, M. L. (1984) *Conversation: How Talk is Organised*. Beverly Hills: Sage.

Moeketsi, R. (1999). *Discourse in a Multilingual and Multicultural Courtroom: A Court Interpreter's Guide*. Pretoria: J.L. van Schaik.

Nwoye, G. (1985) 'Eloquent silence among the Igbo of Nigeria', in D. Tannen and M. Saville-Troike (eds), *Perspectives on Silence*, pp. 185–191, Norwood, NJ: Ablex.

Ochs, E. (1996) 'Linguistic resources for socializing humanity', in J. J. Gumperz and S. Levinson (eds), *Rethinking Linguistic Relativity*, pp. 407–437, Cambridge: Cambridge University Press.

Pomerantz, A. M. (1984) 'Agreeing and disagreeing with assessments: Some features of preferred/dispreffered turn shapes', in J. M. Atkinson and J. C. Heritage (eds), *Structures of Social Action: Studies in Conversation Analysis*, pp. 57–101, Cambridge: Cambridge University Press.

Rojo, L. M. (1995) 'Division and rejection: From the personification of the Gulf conflict to the demonization of Saddam Hussein', *Discourse & Society*, 6(1): 49–80.

Sekese, A. (1999) *Mekhoa le Maele a Basotho*. Maseru: Morija Sesuto Book Depot.

Spender, D. (1980) *Man Made Language*. London: Routledge and Kegan Paul.

Stokoe, E. H. and Smithson, J. (2001) 'Making gender relevant: Conversation analysis and gender categories in interaction', *Discourse & Society*, 12(2): 217–244.

Sunderland, J. (1995) 'We're boys, miss: Finding gendered identities and looking for gendering identities in the foreign language classroom', in S. Mills (ed.), *Language and Gender: Interdisciplinary Perspectives*, pp. 160–178, London: Longman.

Van Dijk, T. A (1998) *Ideology: A Multidisciplinary Approach*. London: Sage.

12
"They Say It's a Man's World, but You Can't Prove that by Me": African American Comediennes' Construction of Voice in Public Space

Denise Troutman
Michigan State University, US

Although the "Godfather of Soul," James Brown, asserted in 1966, "It's a Man's, Man's World," in seemingly call and response fashion in 1967, Aretha Franklin retorted:

> Yeah-yeah they say that it's a man's world.
> But you can't prove that by me.
> And as long as we're together baby,
> Show some respect for me.

In her mezza-soprano voice, Franklin counters the point that this is a man's world. In fact, she uses a number of linguistic practices available to Black women in the U.S. Most notably, Franklin signifies, talks smart, reads dialect, and uses a culturally toned diminutive to carry her message. (See the linguistic strategies discussed later in this chapter.) As well, she uses two other social strategies available to a broader cross-section of the Black community, direct address and loud talking (which are not discussed in this chapter).

Based upon their research, African American women scholars, in particular, have described a variety of linguistic strategies, which are reflective of the language patterns of their African American women subjects, as well as strategies that are reflective of a cross-section of African American women within the U.S.[1] These features, which I have schematized under the umbrella label "talking that talk" (Troutman, 2001; see schema below), include use of reading dialect (Morgan, 1996), culturally toned diminutives (Troutman, 1996), signifying (Mitchell-Kernan, 1972), and smart talk (Abrahams, 1975; Houston Stanback, 1982). In the schema, I have placed two additional strategies that my preliminary work suggests are permissible within the repertoire of linguistic strategies for African American women (AAWL): "bawdy language" (Troutman 1995, 2004) and "playing the dozens" (Brown, 1972). Each strategy receives some discussion in later sections.

As in earlier publications (e.g. 1996, 2001), I do not claim that the working list of features given in the schema below represents language used by all African American women. As the semanticist S. I. Hayakawa phrased this condition, "we cannot say all about everything" (1964). Indeed, as an African American woman who has grown up in Black neighborhoods, I do not use all of the strategies. They are, though, available within African American women's speech community(ies) and the broader African American speech community (AASC) for self-selection. Certainly, a number of factors bear upon the selection or non-selection of the strategies for African American women, such as belief systems, identity (self- and cultural), age (though less determinative than the other factors), permissibility rights, and social expectations (especially intragroup). As will be observed, the schema varies from one that may be diagrammatically framed for the nebulous construct "women's language" or for language patterns representative of European American women's speech/talk (EAWL). In this context, variation occurs between AAWL and EAWL, among a number of social factors, owing to social constructions of race, reality, and gender.[2]

In this chapter, I discuss some of the salient features of Black women's talk and analyze one representation of this talk. Specifically, I examine four African American comediennes' speaking in public contexts, as a microcosm of some instances of Black women speaking in such contexts. One segment of each comedienne's monologue receives analysis and placement within the linguistic resources framework. The paper contents are divided into three main sections: (1) Some Linguistic Resources for AAWL; (2) Textual Analysis of transcripts; and (3) Discussion of AAWL and "bawdy language."

Some linguistic resources for AAWL

For this section, I present a schema and discussion on some linguistic resources within AAWL (Figure 12.1). Note that the strategies are randomly ordered.

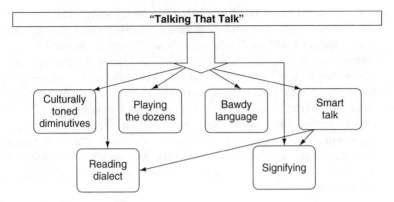

Figure 12.1 Working schema of some linguistic strategies within the speech community of African American women

Culturally toned diminutives

One common feature of African American women's language that I have coined and described previously (Troutman, 1996) is "culturally toned diminutives," or CTDs. Each term in this phrase contributes to the meaning of the feature. Diminutives are words that express small size, familiarity, or lovability, even contemptibility, and may appear in languages as suffixes, prefixes, words, or names. In English, the suffix -ette (as in dinette), the word *sonny*, and the names Charlie, Mikey, Susie, and Bobbie are diminutives. Among African American women, diminutives are culturally intoned in terms of both their derivation by the community of speakers and the prosody accompanying their production. Diminutives for African American women occur at the word level, as I discuss them here; thus, words such as *sugar, honey, baby, precious, muh'dear* ("mother dear" yet not "father dear"), *sister/sister friend, Auntie, girl,* and others appear as diminutives. As a whole, CTDs express solidarity for its female users within Black America.

African American women may refer to each other by the diminutive, "sister," which has a long-standing tradition of usage within the AASC. Both women and men in many community situations use "sister"; it is socially situated and indexed as referring to females only. There are at least two instances of the occurrence of this diminutive:

1. Within African American families throughout the U.S., many African American females, at very young ages, are called "sister" instead of their given names. Maya Angelou was called "Sister" by her grandmother, not Marguerite, her given name.

2. "Sister" occurs in a second usage that is a metaphorical extension of the broader reference term "sister, female, blood-related sibling." For many speakers within the AASC, African American women are all "sisters" because of the similar oppressive and racist experiences they encounter in the human lifeworld and because of the supportive bonds they establish, regardless of blood-relatedness, in order to overcome negativisms and to enjoy positive circumstances. Collins (1991) writes, "all African-American women share the common experience of being Black women in a society that denigrates women of African descent" (22). Thus, African American women are "sisters" because of shared experiences and bonds of support, unity, and love.

For generations, African American women have used the CTD "girl." As a socially meaningful locution within African American women's speech community(ies), "girl" is heavily imbued with the ideological stance of solidarity, occurring in both public and private contexts. If African American women see themselves as peers, especially sharing experiential, gendered, and cultural/racial living conditions, they can and, with great probability, will use "girl."

European American feminists in the U.S., historically, have rejected the referent "girl" as a result of inequitable and demeaning treatment within the patriarchically dominant social system. Thus, they consciously avoid referring to other women as "girl." African American women's speech community permits and encourages "girl" usage unobtrusively. Its usage, in fact, is devoid of belittling or degrading denotations or connotations. African American women obviously do not see themselves diminished in any way through the use of this term, especially since its usage is recurrent and historical. Within my grandmother's, mother's, and my generation, "girl" usage has been prominent. Now the baton has been passed on to my daughter's generation.

Playing the dozens

Morgan (2002) has argued that African American women are the main conveyors of language to children, female and male, for the early formative years. On this basis, I consider that African American women seem to influence and impact the language of females and males so intrinsically that it carries over into adulthood. Thus, I take the position that African American females and males learn basic and fundamental linguistic skills that carry over into the rest of their lives from mothers or mother figures or, more generally, women. I assert furthermore that African American children learn to use African American rhetorical patterns and learn elements of "talking that talk" (TTT), as well as gendered kinesics from mothers/women in their lives. Some evidence of this principle is found in African American men's imitations of Black women, especially their language patterns. Flip Wilson, Tyler Perry, Eddie Murphy, and other male comedians/actors have presented realistic images of African American women in comedic form.[3] In order to execute portrayals that are convincing for Black audiences, it is not unreasonable to suggest that these Black men, with great probability, received first-hand exposure to the social, particularly linguistic, practices of Black women in socially real contexts, beginning in homes and expanding to public contexts, including public schools (particularly in contexts where there is a significant population of African Americans) and in Black churches. This social practice can be extrapolated to a larger cross-section of Black men growing up in Black America.

Men/fathers/males figure significantly within the Black family, as well, yet here my aim is to dissect the contribution of women/mothers. The role of mothers within the family is so essential that a game of verbal wit emerged centered on them, namely playing the dozens[4] or "yo momma" jokes.

H. Rap Brown (1972) gained a highly esteemed reputation for his ability to "talk the talk." Below, he gives a personal accounting of "playing the dozens":

> The street is where young bloods get their education. I learned how to talk in the street, not from reading about Dick and Jane going to the zoo and all that simple sh--. The teacher would test our vocabulary each week, but we knew the vocabulary we needed. They'd give us arithmetic to exercise our minds. Hell, we exercised our minds by playing the dozens.... We played the dozens for recreation, like white folks play Scrabble.... In many ways, though, the dozens is a mean game because what you try to do is totally destroy somebody else with words.... There'd be sometimes forty or fifty dudes standing around and the winner was determined by the way they responded to what you said. If you [they?] fell all over each other laughing, then you knew you'd scored. It was a bad scene for the dude that was getting humiliated. I seldom was. That's why they call me Rap, 'cause I could rap.... The real aim of the dozens was to get a dude so mad that he'd cry or get mad enough to fight. You'd say sh-- like, 'Man, tell your mama to stop coming around my house all the time. I'm tired of fucking her and I think you should know that it ain't no accident you look like me.' And it could go on for hours sometimes.
>
> (205–206)

One of the most revealing statements from this pre-eminent, antiquarian rapper relates aptly to my contention about women and playing the dozens. Brown asserts that "some of the best dozens players were girls" (206). Although the hard evidence has not been collected in this domain of AAWL, it is forthcoming. Several informants have shared that they or their female relatives/associates play the dozens, although the standard scholarship characterizes such usage as male.

Folb (1980) writes about the speech of Black teenagers between the ages of fifteen and twenty, who lived in the inner city of South Central Los Angeles. Focusing on the lexicon, specifically, Folb collected data in the field for nine years, developing close, personal relationships with the teenagers. In the chapter, "Talkin' My Talk," Folb records: "Whether lack of accessibility, lack of interest, or other factors have intervened, the fact is that the black female's expressive behavior has gone undocumented and is assumed to be limited by some" (194). Folb makes the point clear that community expectations (parents, relatives, adults, male peers, even female peers in male company) dictate that females do not use "cuss words or fight words or sex words or low-rider words or junkie words or hooker words or getting-on-your-case words—'else they ain't actin' like nice young ladies'" (195; see Houston Stanback, 1982). In all-female contexts, Folb reports that the females paid "lip service" to "acting like a nice young lady." "When I was privy to all-female conversations, I found that the quantity of talk, joking, boasting, argument, cursing, and even shooting [playing] the dozens rivaled male expressive behavior. . . . Indeed, some of the most original and graphic dozens I've heard were shot back and forth between females" (196). One of Folb's examples follows:

A: Hey, girl, wha' chu got on yo' hair? You smell like a skunk in a shit house! Cain't get no funkier.
B: Well, bitch, leas' I got hair. You hair so short cooties on yo' haid be starvin' to death.

Bawdy language

As I have coined this linguistic strategy, "bawdy language" refers to ribald language usage. Women, for the present circumstances, who use bawdy language speak frankly, humorously, and directly; by some outsider standards, these women speak crudely, offensively, indecently, brashly. In general, these women do not "blush at vulgarity" (Maria Stewart quoted in Giddings, 1984: 51). I discuss this linguistic resource in a later section in the analysis, as it pertains to the "Queens" and the broader AAWL speech community.

Talking smart

Based upon reported materials (e.g. anecdotal data collected from men in Ulf Hannerz' *Soulside* and narratives by Black women, including Zora Neale Hurston and Katherine L. Morgan), Abrahams (1975) claims that Black women, ideally, have the ability to "*talk smart or cold* with anyone who might threaten [their] self-image" (62). Although there are limitations in his work on Black women's presentational devices, Abrahams accurately describes talking smart as "just one of a number of black types of speaking which involve an agonistic motive and the use of cleverness. Smartness may be found in the repertoires of men, women, and children, but it does seem to be especially important in women's talk both with each other and with men" (76).

Based upon my participant observation among friends and family members, as well as observations of women in public spaces, I have found that African American women engage in regular occurrences of smart talk in informal settings, particularly under conditions of familiarity or defensibility.

During a recent class discussion on Affirmative Action[5] in the U.S., one African American female student engaged in smart talk. The conversation among students, who had interacted with each other for two months on topics dealing with race and racism, vacillated between support and non-support for the program. Most students of color rallied around the flag of support for Affirmative Action, articulating rationales for doing so. As the socio-political and historical state of affairs currently in the U.S. has constructed it, the non-supporters were all European Americans, though some European American students also supported Affirmative Action, primarily outside of educational arenas. The latter group of students did not think that Affirmative Action is fair in college and university settings.

Near the end of the conversation, one African American woman, a first-year student, created an analogy for non-supporters to consider. She did not quiver in her articulation of the point,[6] nor did she aim to mitigate the content or the illocutionary force. She stated,

> For those of you who don't agree with Affirmative Action because you feel that you are being cheated, now [points finger] you know how people of color feel everyday. People of color have been cheated out of so many things because of skin color. But, you know what, now you get to feel what it's like. You may not [rising intonation contour begins here] like it, but it's the real world. [Snaps fingers.] Welcome to reality!

The African American woman's commentary invoked silence in most non-supporters, yet one European American male challenged her stance through an ameliorated query, meant to diffuse her point and probably to enrage her, "So what are you saying?" The majority of those present got the message clearly.

This real-time example suggests that the African American woman[7] deemed it appropriate to use smart talk under adversarial conditions in a public context. Other factors may have influenced the student's use of smart talk. Her personality throughout the semester has reflected a high level of conscientiousness and seriousness about her class performance, studiousness, and excellence. She has been one of the top achievers in the course. From the first day of the course, she has expressed her point of view openly and straightforwardly, when others have not spoken. Thus, this student's personality seems to have played a part in her speech action. As well, grooming within the AASC seems apparent. Disregarding, momentarily, stereotypical media images (especially television and movies), within the real lives of girls and women (typically younger women) in the AASC, finger snapping and rhythmic head movement, used to embellish communication of points, hold social reality. Some members of the AASC feel that these non-verbal gestures are belittling, reactions that may reflect some residual elements of nineteenth-century African American women's club members, whose aim was to show that Black women were "true" women. There are many other Black women, who do not find these non-verbal gestures embarrassing, yet accept them as markers of cultural self-pride and positive self-identity. Rickford and Rickford (2000) and Nehusi (2001) report on a continuum in the usage of one type of non-verbal communication, specifically "cut-eye and suck teeth."[8] John and Angela Rickford conducted a study in the U.S., finding that the Africans and African Americans that they surveyed had heard of or were familiar with "cut eye and suck teeth," whereas the European Americans included did not know nor could demonstrate the appropriate non-verbal behavior. The longevity of this paralinguistic behavior speaks partially to an assignment of a [+ positive] value to finger snapping and rhythmic head movement, as well as "cut-eye and suck teeth."

The fact that the Black female student used those non-verbal mechanisms when communicating her position suggests that she has emerged from a setting that promotes and endorses their usage, in all probability, a predominantly Black setting (home, school, church, and/or social venues). Personal communication with the student revealed that this scenario holds true for her. She attended a predominantly African American school and has lived with one parent in a Black metropolis and with another parent in a suburb outside of the Black metropolis, enabling her to participate in different speech communities.

Smart talk marks the above instances of speech. The contributions are quick, amusing or witty (in the sense of engaging mental acuity), confrontational (not necessarily intended or received negatively), and apposite.

Signifying, a form of smart talk, is commonly defined as a verbal game of wit and indirection (Smitherman, 1977; Morgan, 2002). Mitchell-Kernan (1972a, cited in Rickford and Rickford, 2000) explains:

> The black concept of *signifying* incorporates essentially a folk notion that dictionary entries for words are not always sufficient for interpreting meaning and messages, or that meaning goes beyond such interpretations. Complimentary remarks may be received in a left-handed fashion. A particular utterance may be an insult in one context and not in another. What pretends to be informative may intend to be persuasive. Superficially, self-abasing remarks are frequently self-praise. The hearer is thus constrained to attend to all potential meaning carrying symbolic systems in speech events—the total universe of discourse.

Reading dialect, as created and conceptualized by Morgan (2002), is another linguistic strategy that I place under talking smart. This practice stems from the broader social practice, labeled "reading." Within the Black community, one speaker may "read" another interactant. Morgan (2002) explains:

> This form of interaction occurs whenever a speaker denigrates another to his face in an unsubtle and unambiguous manner.... When a target gets read, he or she is verbally attacked for inappropriate or offensive statements or what is perceived, by the reader, as the speaker's false representation of his or her beliefs, personal values, etc.
>
> (53)

Reading dialect, then, builds upon "reading." Speakers can "read" others by markedly highlighting one dialect over another. "When speakers employ dialect reading in interactions, they immediately signal to members that some indirect form of communication where the varieties are contrasted is in play" (Morgan, 2002: 74).

One example of reading dialect is through the use of the African American expression, "Miss Thang." Female and male speakers may use the expression to refer to a female whom they believe has displayed inappropriate behavior. In order to read dialect, one speaker may begin an utterance using General English (GE; or the dialect of wider communication) and at a salient point switch to Ebonics (or African American English): "Some people, like Miss Thang, think they know everything!" The Ebonics influence and the reading become marked as a result of the pronunciation of "thing." "Thang" reflects a common practice among African Americans of changing the [ɪ] sound to [æ], for greater effect. Thus, "sing" becomes "sang"; "ring" becomes "rang"; and "thing" becomes "thang." Additionally, the vowel may become elongated, tha-a-ang, thus compounding the force of the reading dialect event. Finally, the denigrating force embedded in "thang" is realized within the purview of Black culture. A "thing" is an object, typically impersonal in nature. By association, the receiver is the same.

Textual analyses of transcripts

The following transcripts stem from a live performance of four African American comediennes onstage in Memphis, Tennessee, at the Orpheum Theater in 2001. The stand-up concert toured U.S. cities, being filmed on location in Memphis with a live audience. Produced, according to some accounts, in response to Spike Lee's "The Original Kings of Comedy (2000)," the film is interspersed with footage of the "Queens" interacting with local people in the community prior to the show; as well, each "Queen" presents a monologue, in the following order: Miss Laura (also serves as the emcee), Adele, Sommore, and Mo'Nique. The local footage shows the "Queens" engaged in spontaneous banter or playful joking with each other in public spaces while some local African Americans watch or minimally participate. The spontaneous scenes capture displays of wit from the "Queens," as well as some contestations. Here are portions of their monologues:

Queen #1

Miss Laura

Ooh hold up wait a minute . . . Hey is the security still out there? The two by the door? OK
Cool I'm sorry, I apologize, ex-husband in town.
Mothafucka get a Vietnam flashback and come lookin for me.

I don't know why he wanna fuck wit me, I come from a big family of girls, my daddy didn't play; he raised us tough, baby.

He was like "I ain't raising no punk bitches."

And you couldn't go to my daddy wit what he called "sissy shit," you know,

"Daddy, can we go outside and play with Barbie?"

Fuck Barbie! Betta get your ass out there and build me a sofa.

And he taught us to stick together too; you marry one of us, you marry all of us, OK.

And when there's some problems we'll get together baby, cause moms is da dispatcher.

Oh, my lil sista got in trouble, she had to call mama.

"Mama, dis nigga hit me"...ooh mama was cool tho, she was like "don't worry bout it baby." Moms hung up da phone; dial one number; all our phones rang.

"Bertha, Laura, Yula, Ruthie, get on ova to Alice's house; dat nigga don gone crazy."

That's all we needed; we jumped in da car; we rolling, we slappin five ova the seat,

"Here bitch; hit this, shit." We get to da house, screetch up real fast, walk in da door. Da nigga just bout to hit my sista; we go..."Oh no not tonight, mothafucka" (takes off her wig)

Nigga what, nigga who?

Ahh unn, we ain't play that.

Queen #2

Adele

my grandma, I need to pay tribute to her; in fact, she's the reason why I'm still standing here doing comedy. For real she is 'Cause you know I had got discouraged; I said I wasn't gon do it 'cause I had did a show and I gave it my all. I don't 'know if ya'll know but I use ya'll for therapy; I talk to ya'll cause I know y'all can relate to the shit I'm talkin bout, you know? So I talk to y'all and I gave a great show one night, and a lady came up to me one night and she said,

"Adele we loved you, you was funny as shit," she said, "but you have a filthy mouth" and I was all fucked up 'cause I wasn't thinking at the time that was a control issue. When somebody tell you how you should talk, that's a mothafucka that wanna control you, but I wasn't thinking that, see; I was just discouraged that one of my fans thought I had a filthy mouth and I said, "fuck it. I'm through; I'm quittin shit."

My grandmother talk to me, and said, "look you don't quit, bitch, unless you wanna quit; you don't let nobody make you quit."

I say, "but grandma that lady said I had a filthy mouth."

She said, "come here baby; let me tell you something;" she say, "the next time somebody tell you you got a filthy; mouth, you let em know; it ain't what come out your mouth that make it filthy; it's what you put in there."

She said, "then you tell them you wash all the dicks you suck, here?" I say, "yes mam."

Queen #3

Sommore

Now ya'll know a bitch just got out of jail. Ya'll need to act like ya'll happy to see me in this mothafucka. Baby, I'm telling ya'll right now; first they started lockin up football players, then they started lockin up rappers, now they lockin up bitches with good pussy. Baby, they put a bitch in jail. I thought they was playin. They put a bitch in jail for five mothafuckin days. And you know when you in jail, five days feel like 50 days. But I was strong; a bitch was strong. You know what I'm sayin? I tried holdin it together. I felt like Tupac when I went in there, Keep ya head up. Baby, but when the reality that a bitch was in jail set in, I felt like Miss Sophia in the Color Purple, "Lawd, please, help me, Lawd." Woohh I ain't neva seen so many dykes in my life! Baby the dykes was on me. Lawd there was this one dyke, the bitch was aggressive. One dyke wouldn't leave me alone. I said, "bitch bitch leave me 'lone; leave me lone." I figured since I was incarcerated I'd talk like a slave bitch. Leave me lone. "Look I's got a man; leave me lone." That bitch looked at me and said, "eatin ain't cheatin." I said, "bitch we gone be fightin 'cause I ain't dykin."

Queen #4

Mo'Nique

Now, you know what sistahs? I, I gotta share some shit wit ya'll. Now ever since I came out here tonight I have used this one word bout nine-thousan' time and dass "bitch." From the time I came out here I been usin that word "bitch." We give that word so much mother-fuckin power; we are willing to leave our husbands and our boyfriends because he called you a "bitch." It's a motherfuckin word. But if at that *time* if that's what you was representing, dass what the fuck you needed to be called, ya bitch. You just get the motherfuckin point. Sometime, baby, it helps close the sen'ence out. "Shut the fuck up, bitch." You understand me better when I put dat closin on there. And if the word is used at the *right* time, at the *proper* time, oh it's a wonderful word, baby. If it's used at da *right* moment.

All of the comediennes use four "talking that talk" features in the segments of their monologues included above: (1) culturally toned diminutives, (2) bawdy language, (3) reading dialect, and (4) smart talk. I shall focus on the first two due to their greater pertinence.

Culturally toned diminutives (CTDs)

All four women use the CTD "baby," at least once. Mo'Nique uses "sistahs," as well. The following examples occur:

Miss Laura: My daddy didn't play; he raised us tough, *baby*.
Adele: She said, "come here *baby*".
Sommore: *Baby*, I'm telling ya'll right now...
Mo'Nique: Sometime, *baby*, it helps close the sen'ence out.

In the real-time context, *baby* refers to audience members, generically, excluding Adele's usage. In her monologue, Adele uses reportative speech, in which her grandmother calls her *baby*, as a term of endearment. Mo'Nique uses another CTD *sistahs* to introduce content intended for the women in the audience. The word *bitch* is used by all the comediennes, as well, and segues between a CTD and bawdy language.

Although *bitch* has standardly been used in U.S. contexts and within the AASC as a negative referent for women,[9] its current usage has broadened. First, apparently due to the influence of rap music, *bitch* has broadened in its reference to include males. Secondly, *bitch* has broadened semantically, now optionally construed with a positive meaning, which is determined contextually. The monologues mark *bitch* as an element of bawdy language when used in its negative sense and as an extended CTD when used in its positive sense. As with *baby*, all the comediennes use *bitch*, as either a personal or a generic reference:

Miss Laura: "Here bitch; hit this, shit."
Adele: My grandmother talk to me, and said, "look you don't quit, bitch, unless you wanna quit."

Sommore: But I was strong; a bitch was strong.
Mo'Nique: Sometime, baby, it helps close the sen'ence out. "Shut the fuck up, bitch."

Miss Laura uses the term in a generic, positive way. As she delivers the lines, it is not clear who takes on the role of speaker, nor does it matter. Four sisters are riding in a car, headed for Alice's house, intensifying their solidarity by giving each other "five"[10] and sharing a "hit" of marijuana. *Bitch* is not used here as a tool to denigrate anyone. It fills a noun slot and implies acceptability by speaker and receiver(s). Adele also uses *bitch* in its positive sense. Again, she reports her grandmother's teaching, "Look you don't quit, bitch, unless you wanna quit." *Bitch* may be added here for effect; nonetheless, it functions to indicate the referent, non-pejoratively.

Sommore uses the semi-CTD in both senses. She refers to herself through indirect, impersonal speech: "Now ya'll know a bitch just got out of jail.... But I was strong; a bitch was strong." As these examples show, Sommore does not refer to herself negatively, yet may use *bitch* to serve a marked function, noun filler and/or identifier. The context of her monologue "flips the script" for Sommore's usage. Thus, she uses *bitch*, in contrast to a positive self-identity label, as a pejorative referent under conditions that she views as adverse and where she must defend herself: "That bitch looked at me and said, "eatin ain't cheatin." I said, "bitch we gone be fightin 'cause I ain't dykin."

In contradistinction to the previous comediennes, Mo'Nique intends and conveys a negative sense of *bitch* and, significantly, discusses it meta-linguistically. Without any direct mention or referencing of her usage by others (e.g. audience members, producers/directors of the program), she clearly has become cognizant of her language:

> Now, you know what sistahs? I, I gotta share some shit wit ya'll. Now ever since I came out here tonight I have used this one word bout nine-thousan' time and dass "bitch." From the time I came out here I been usin that word "bitch."

Mo'Nique is not a linguist, nor does she need be; she does not discuss all the senses of *bitch*, nor does she need to. She does, however, demonstrate a keen meta-cognizance of language and power.

> We give that word so much motherfuckin power we are willing to leave our husbands and our boyfriends because he called you a "bitch." It's a motherfuckin word.

Here, she seems to hint that women ought not imbue language with such power that they "are willing to leave...husbands and... boyfriends" over it, especially remaining conscious that *bitch* is just a word. The empowering stance that Mo'Nique suggests is admirable, even though she may not have considered that some words used within certain contextualized frames do hurt (e.g. *nigger*).

Mo'Nique ends her monologue, referencing *bitch* in "the Old School"[11] sense. It may be decomposed partially with the semantic features [+ female], [+ negative]. Mo'Nique asserts that sometimes certain women deserve to be called *bitch* if the shoe fits.

> But if at that *time* if that's what you was representing, dass what the fuck you needed to be called, ya bitch. You just get the motherfuckin point....And if the word is used at the *right* time, at the *proper* time, oh it's a wonderful word, baby. If it's used at da *right* moment.

Finally, she seems to suggest two additional functions of the word: to hurl an invective (*Sometime, baby, it helps close the sen'ence out. "Shut the fuck up, bitch." You understand me better when I put dat closin on there*) and to display the power inculcated in its utterance, especially based on its location at the end of a sentence and the prosodic features used in the pronunciation (*"Shut the fuck up, bitch"*). Today, some young people have taken *bitch* to another level, the current usage apparently emanating from the rap scene. As indicated above, it may designate a female or male and the prosodies may be varied to produce *bee-otch*, a more intensified invective.

Bawdy language

Not only do the comediennes use raucous language, but they also use it humorously (judging by audience responses). What makes their language bawdy?

Hudson (2001) examined the written works of African American female writers from the 1880s to 1990s, devoting one chapter to "Bad Language." She describes, among other categories (phonological and grammatical structures, word choice, and expressive behavior), the "bad language" of the characters presented in novels, slave narratives, diaries, and so on. Based on work by Andersson and Trudgill (1992), Hudson defines "bad language" as swearing, with two main subcategories, taboo words and swearwords (functioning as expletives or to name-call and to curse someone). She also discusses the grammatical function of swearwords (which I do not focus on in the Queens' monologues). Among her findings, she reports that *shit* occurred most frequently in different grammatical positions, as an adjective, verb, object, and filler; taboo words were used by a small segment of the women characters; swearwords were strung together in the written works by the women writers of the later time periods; stringing of swearwords occurred rarely with strangers, yet mostly with female friends, younger people, and well-known male friends, primarily during casual and intimate conversations.

The language of the "Queens" is construed as bawdy due to their swearing, consequently their violating a social code of feminine politeness.

Stringing swearwords together

Miss Laura: nigga just bout to hit my sista; we go ... Oh no not tonight, mothafucka
Nigga what, nigga who?
Adele: I said fuck it. I'm through; I'm quittin shit.
Sommore: They put a bitch in jail for five mothafuckin days.
Mo'Nique: "Shut the fuck up, bitch."

Name-calling

Miss Laura: Mothafucka get a Vietnam flashback and come lookin for me.
Adele: that's a mothafucka that wanna control you
Sommore: Ya'll need to act like ya'll happy to see me in this mothafucka. That bitch looked at me
Mo'Nique: dass what the fuck you needed to be called, ya bitch

Use of expletives to express emotion

Miss Laura: "Here bitch; hit this, shit."
Adele: I'm quittin shit.
Sommore: Ø
Mo'Nique: Ø

Use of taboo words

Miss Laura: Fuck Barbie!
Adele: I said fuck it.
You tell them you wash all the dicks you suck, here?
Sommore: now they lockin up bitches with good pussy
Mo'Nique: dass what the fuck you needed to be called

Curses

Miss Laura: Ø
Adele: Ø
Sommore: Ø
Mo'Nique: Ø

The comediennes' language evinces "bawdiness" in its fulfilling the functions of taboo words and swearwords. Although swearwords used to curse someone does not occur at all, nor do expletives to express emotion occur in Sommore and Monique's monologues, the present data set reflects a limited portion of the Queens' entire monologues. It is not unreasonable to expect that the non-represented forms of bawdiness actually occur in the larger data set.

Discussion of AAWL and bawdy language

The linguistic resources presented above are used in public contents by many African American women,[12] creating a different voice/availability of voice for these women in contradistinction to the domain of the female voice in public contexts established in the literature for European American women.

One explanation for a difference in the public voices is that the history of the two groups of women diverges. Coates (1998) and Giddings (1984) note the historical significance of the nineteenth century. The industrial revolution established demarcations of public and private domains and discourse, in general. "A woman's place is in the home" became the accepted slogan with the rise of a new middle class. Many women strove for upper class status through adherence to the "cult of the lady" or the "cult of true womanhood" (Giddings, 1984: 47). This private domain established private discourse within the home as the acceptable norm, where domesticity, piety, purity, and submissiveness became markers of the "cult of the lady." The industrial economy forced men to work in public domains away from farms. Public discourse patterns arose for men, marking the public domains as male dominated. Race measured saliently within this general frame. Middle-class white women and "Puritan girls" were expected to remain at home during the adoption of the "cult of the lady," while poor immigrant women replaced the "Puritan girls" in factory work. Black women were excluded from industrial labor and were relegated to the lowest rung of work, as domestics. Here, Houston Stanback (1982) interjects a difference in communicative styles for Black women. As a result of a tradition of working a double shift, "of historically operating in both the domestic and public spheres", Black women developed particular ways of speaking. "The strength and independence of black American women[13] is reflected in their communication. They are generally self-assertive and outspoken". In fact, they are allowed to use the "full range of black communicative registers".

Community norms for language usage

One of the social ramifications within both Black women's speech community and the broader AASC is the restriction on Black women, expressed in various ways, for example "don't talk like a man," "don't have (such) a filthy mouth," or "don't be a hard mouth" (Houston Stanback, 1982). In the excerpt discussed before, in fact, Adele makes this exact point. Being told that she has a "filthy mouth" was discouraging to Adele, yet her grandmother provided the encouragement that she needed to "stay in the business": "You don't let nobody make you quit." Sommore comments on the same restrictedness: "In the beginning, I used to worry about being too nasty because people criticized me. But I realized I just have to be myself" (Byrd, 2001).

Another critical element that requires notation within the present analysis is the social reality bound into the speech style and linguistic resources available within African American women's speech community. Here, I establish and highlight the point that the manner of speaking (the prosodic features, especially intonation, stress, and length at the microanalytic level) and the linguistic strategies (including "bawdy language" at the macroanalytic or discourse level) available to the four comediennes markedly parallels the manner of speech and linguistic strategies available in Black women's everyday talk.[14] Although comedians, in general, may season their stand-up routines with "bawdy language," there are distinct differences in language usage for the Black comediennes and other comedians, one of which pertains to social reality and the manifestations of that social reality in everyday speech. The comediennes' speech style and strategies go beyond performance only, closely aligning with the everyday speech of many Black women across the U.S. Thus, the first-syllable stress on two-syllable words, the smart talk or bawdy language, is not for performance sakes only, yet they reflect actual usage among members of Black women's speech community.

George Carlin, during a television interview, commented that "comedy is about exaggeration" (November 19, 2004). Of course, exaggeration and performance are elemental in these Black comedienne's routines, yet a critical distinction emerges in the social reality of the routines. There is a subset of African American women within the U.S. who use the same manner of speech and presentation as the queens of comedy.

My coining of "bawdy language," in fact, stems from my observation of its usage by some Black women within my social network: colleagues, family members, associates.[15] Maya Angelou writes of her mother in *I Know Why the Caged Bird Sings*, recording that her mother "cussed freely as she laughed" (176). As well, I have informally polled a few Black undergraduate and graduate students who have reported that they know Black women firsthand who use "bawdy language." They spoke of family members who punctuate their sentences with language that others may find offensive. During a student-sponsored film festival (Spring 2004), I introduced the "Queens of Comedy" video. Mostly Black women, undergraduate and graduate, and one Black male attended the showing. I asked a series of questions pertaining to social reality and the comediennes' routines. All of the students reported that they knew someone who talked as the comediennes, although they [the women respondents] did not talk that way. According to one male informant, the "bawdy" style in everyday speech does not show disrespect. Thus, the illocutionary force and the perlocutionary effect may be the same for some AASC members: to enthrall, entertain, amuse.

Informal assessments of the language used by the "Queens" from AASC insiders, then, indicate a few underlying features of acceptability and usability as constructed by community standards:

1. Subsets of Black women (not a negligible number) throughout the U.S. use bawdy language and speak similarly to the four "Queen" comediennes.
2. The bawdy language is not intended or received offensively.[16] It punctuates, accessorizes sentences/communication.
3. Women are given more limited permissibility rights for bawdy language usage than men, yet the women may use it.
4. Within the same family unit, variability of bawdy language usage occurs among women.
5. Personality, social context, permissibility rules, local/family practices, and self-image/concept influence use of bawdy language.

Conclusions

The wording in Franklin's song title and the juxtaposition of the wording signify meta-meanings intrinsic to this chapter and the socially desirable execution of gender equity/parity for some African American women. "Do Right Woman—Do Right Man" symbolizes parity in its linear structure. The title is "balanced": both sides/parts of the title consist of three words, which are ordered sequentially/grammatically the same. What type of woman/man? The answer is the same. The relevant lyrics inform: "If you want a do right woman, you got to be a do right man." Furthermore, the title suggests that women and men coexist side by side; as some Judeo-Christian bibles present it, Yahweh Elohim took one of Adam's ribs and made woman, conceptualized as a jointedness, a partnership. Parity, then, can exude from a multiplicity of behaviors.

As soul sister Franklin constructed it in song, these comediennes convey in action that it is not a man's world only. Language exists as a resource, available for human communication, modification, play, thus, in a bigger, bolder scheme, not as a marker of limits. Through the use of "bawdy" language, the comediennes display confidence in their linguistic prowess.

Eckert and McConnell-Ginet (2003) state that

> many women [in the African American community] do not shrink from the kind of spirited exchanges that can emerge...exchanges that would intimidate the average "nice" white girl.... We would suggest that girls who are not of African descent might have a lot to learn from their African American sisters about confidence and standing up for themselves.
>
> (142, 143)

Black women's linguistic practices have not been fully documented to date. This chapter illustrates one overlooked practice, yet others also exist. "Bawdy language" serves as one vehicle for establishing and maintaining personal and social identity. The four comediennes and African American sisters throughout the U.S. assert their images and values, in part, through "bawdy language," demonstrating that they know how to "talk that talk."

Afterword

The African American women that I write about are my sisters; they are real in my life and circumstances. Despite media exploitation, stereotypes and disinformation, these women and their language patterns not only hold social reality, they are social reality.

Someone must record and represent their contributions to the languages called Ebonics and U.S. Englishes, even though their language usages are marginalized, especially within hegemonic, Europeanized cultural and/or academic settings.

Notes

1. My conjecture, however, is that many, if not all, of these features occur in the speech of Black women in many parts of the Americas, especially the Caribbean, U.S., and Canada.
2. I contend, for the most part, that African American women reared in dense African American contexts are socialized differently than European American women, thus creating different gendered beings. Overlap in some gendered behavior, however, does exist to an extent due to the unmarked category of "femaleness" in a White, patriarchal society and the acceptance of socially mediated behaviors.
3. Note that African American men have not imitated Black women in serious portrayals.
4. Playing the dozens, today, has been transformed into a broader means of signifying. Formerly known as "yo momma" jokes, playing the dozens has broadened into a game of verbal wit centered on an opponent's family members at large. In order to reflect the broadened focus, the game is currently referred to as "snaps," although many users/players can and do "sound" and signify on each other by using the two-word phrase, "yo momma."
5. Affirmative Action is a policy designed to redress past discrimination within the U.S. Its intent is to increase the representation of people of color (African/Asian/Latino/Native Americans) and women in educational and work settings.
6. Within the AASC, this rhetorical presentation is idealized as, "Did I st-st-stutter?" The locution is conveyed in question form, yet members of the AASC interpret it as a statement. The intended and received meaning within the speech community is "I am not playing/scared/unequivocal in my position. I am as serious as a heart attack."
7. At this juncture in their lives, the majority of the females in this course, first-year students at a predominantly White, mid-western university in the U.S., refer to themselves as "girls," not women, as I have used the word.
8. "Cut-eye and suck teeth" refers to a kinesics act, typically used by Black women, of moving/rolling the eyes from one position to another to convey displeasure; thus, this portion of the kinesics act is called "cutting" the eyes. Concomitant with "cutting" the eyes can be the other portion of the act, literally sucking one's teeth, again to convey displeasure.
9. I have not included *bitch* as a CTD due to its historically negative connotation.
10. "Giving five" is another kinesics act used by interlocutors to show agreement. They execute this act by touching or slapping each others' palms, using a downward motion.

11. "Old School" within the AASC refers to an older, sometimes outdated, way of viewing the world and referencing things in the world due to the time period in which individuals were born.
12. Context, of course, measures critically in decisions to use the linguistic resources. More work on discourse pragmatics within AAWL would make this distinction/usage clearer.
13. Houston Stanback establishes that "the responsible, financially independent woman who assumes a strong role in the family has always been considered the norm, rather than the exception" within Black communities (7).
14. I reiterate that variation indubitably manifests itself within Black women's talk. There is, nonetheless, a segment of Black women throughout the U.S., within the broader speech community of Black women, who use the same strategies in their day-to-day conversations as the four comediennes.
15. One sista friend reports that she has been characterized by others at various times by a variety of descriptors, including "cussing too much" (Personal communication, January 31, 2005).
16. This acceptability/usability standard varies, as can be expected, among community members.

Bibliography

Abrahams, Roger. 1975. 'Negotiating Respect: Patterns of Presentation among Black Women.' *The Journal of American Folklore*. Volume 88, No. 347 (Jan.–Mar.), 58–80.
Alston, William P. 1964. *Philosophy of Language*. Englewood Cliffs, NJ: Prentice-Hall, Inc., pp. 34–36.
Andersson, Lars-Gunnar and Peter Trudgill. 1992. *Bad Language*. NY: Penguin.
'Aretha Franklin.' Wikipedia Encyclopedia. http://en.wikipedia.org/wiki/Aretha_Franklin.
Brown, H. Rap. 1972. 'Street Talk.' In Thomas Kochman, ed., *Rappin' and Stylin' Out*. Urbana: University of Illinois Press, pp. 205–208.
Byrd, Kenya. 2001. 'Gimme Sommore.' *Essence*. (July) www.findarticles.com.
Coates, Jennifer. 1998. 'Women's Talk in the Public Domain.' *Language and Gender: A Reader*. Oxford: Blackwell Publishers, 295–297.
Collins, Patricia Hill. 1991. *Black Feminist Thought: Knowledge, Consciousness, and the Politics of Empowerment*. NY: Routledge.
Crystal, David. 1987. *The Cambridge Encyclopedia of Language*. NY: Cambridge University Press, 15.
Eckert, Penelope and Sally McConnell-Ginet. 2003. *Language and Gender*. NY: Cambridge University Press.
Farley, Christopher John. 1998. 'Aretha Franklin: The Queen of Soul reigns supreme with a heavenly voice and terrestrial passion.' www.time.com/time/time100/artists/profile/franklin.html.
First year student and smart talk. Conversational data collected November 3, 2005.
Folb, Edith A. 1980. *Runnin' Down Some Lines*. Cambridge, MA: Harvard University Press.
Giddings, Paula. 1984. *When and Where I Enter: The Impact of Black Women on Race and Sex in America*. NY: William Morrow and Company, Inc.

Law students and smart talk. Conversational data collected July 5, 2005.

Hayakawa, S. I. 1964. *Language in Thought and Action*. NY: Harcourt, Brace & World.

Holmes, Janet. 1998. 'Women's Talk: The Question of Sociolinguistic Universals.' In Jennifer Coates, ed., *Language and Gender: A Reader*. Malden, MA: Blackwell Publishers, pp. 461–483.

Houston Stanback, Marsha. 1982. 'Language and Black Woman's Place: Toward a Description of Black Women's Communication.' Paper presented to the Speech Communication Association.

Hudson, Barbara Hill. 2001. *African American Female Speech Communities: Varieties of Talk*. Westport, CT: Bergin & Garvey.

Maltz, Daniel N. and Ruth A. Borker. 1998. 'A Cultural Approach to Male-Female Miscommunication.' In Jennifer Coates, ed., *Language and Gender: A Reader*. Malden, MA: Blackwell Publishers, pp. 417–434.

Mitchell-Kernan, Claudia. 1972a. 'Signifying and Marking: Two Afro-American Speech Acts.' In John J. Gumperz and Dell Hymes, eds, *Directions in Sociolinguistics*. NY: Holt, Rinehart & Winston, pp. 161–179.

Mitchell-Kernan, Claudia. 1972b. 'Signifying, loud-talking and marking.' In Thomas Kochman, ed., *Rappin' and Stylin' Out*. Urbana: University of Illinois Press, pp. 315–335.

Morgan, Marcylena. 1996. 'Conversational Signifying: Grammar and Indirectness among African American Women.' In Elinor Ochs, Emmanuel Schegloff, and Sandra Thompson, eds, *Interaction and Grammar*. NY: Cambridge University Press.

Morgan, Marcylena. 2002. *Language, Discourse and Power in African American Culture*. NY: Cambridge University Press.

Nehusi, Kimani K. S. 2001. 'From Medew Netjier to Ebonics.' In Clinton Crawford, ed., *Ebonics and Language Education*. Brooklyn, NY: Sankofa World Publishers.

Rickford, John R. and Rickford E. Angela 1976. 'Cut-Eye and Suck-Teeth.' *Journal of American Folklore*, 89: 294–309.

Rickford, John R. and Russell J. Rickford. 2000. *Spoken Soul: The Story of Black English*. NY: John Wiley & Sons.

Smitherman, Geneva. 1977. *Talkin and Testifyin: The Language of Black America*. Detroit: Wayne State University.

Troutman, Denise. (1996). 'Culturally toned diminutives within the speech community of African American women.' *Journal of Commonwealth and Postcolonial Studies* 4(1): 55–64.

Troutman, Denise. (2001). 'African American women: Talking that talk.' In Sonja L. Lanehart, ed., *Sociocultural and Historical Contexts of African American English*. Philadelphia: John Benjamins Publishing Company, pp. 211–237.

Troutman, Denise. 2004. Presentation on African American Women and Language to English 405 class. Michigan State University. March 24th.

13
Effective Leadership in New Zealand Workplaces: Balancing Gender and Role

Meredith Marra, Stephanie Schnurr and Janet Holmes
School of Linguistics and Applied Language Studies, Victoria University of Wellington

Introduction[1]

'Workplace leadership' is a gendered concept. As a public rather than a private domain, the workplace is typically male-dominated (e.g. Kendall and Tannen, 1997; McConnell-Ginet, 2000), and in most societies, men occupy the most powerful positions in companies and organisations (e.g. Hearn and Parkin, 1988; Sinclair, 1998). Until very recently, the prevailing stereotype of a leader, chief executive officer, and even senior manager has been decidedly male (e.g. Marshall, 1995), and the female voice in these public contexts has often been silenced.

The Wellington Language in the Workplace Project (LWP) has been investigating effective workplace communication in New Zealand organisations for almost a decade. In that time we have seen the rise of women to many positions of public office in the country; in 2001, for example, the New Zealand media was quick to comment on the number of high level posts that had recently been filled by women: the Governor General, the Prime Minister, the Leader of the Opposition, the Solicitor General, and many leading CEOs were women (Marra, 2001; Holmes and Stubbe, 2003a). In 2004, almost all these positions were still held by women, the exception being the Leader of the Opposition.[2] Despite this, many people continue to "think leader, think male".[3]

One of the reasons that this supposed overrepresentation of women is newsworthy, and perhaps also why public perceptions are slow to catch up with social realities is that in many cultures women are associated more closely with the private and the domestic sphere, while men are associated with more public settings. While the distinction has been critiqued, the work of McElhinny (1997) and Philips (2003) indicate that gender expectations in public and private settings continue to provide a legitimate and valuable basis for analysis in many societies. As Philips says, "It simply was and still is true that men dominate public talk, and not just in village level politics, and not just in non-western societies. Even if this talk has been influenced backstage by women, whatever is accomplished, in activities conceptualised as public ideologically, men are talking and women aren't" (2003: 258).

Earlier research undertaken in a range of New Zealand contexts suggests that, holding status constant, males tended to dominate interactions in public settings, including public meetings, classrooms, seminars, conferences, television interviews, and formal management meetings (e.g. Franken, 1983; Holmes, 1992, 1995).[4] In these contexts, men typically talked more than women, asked more questions, interrupted more often, and when they got the floor men were more likely than women to challenge and disagree with the speaker. By contrast, women in a variety of contexts were more likely than men to provide supportive and encouraging feedback, to agree rather than disagree, to look for connections, and add to and build on the contributions of others. These stereotypically female interactional patterns were especially prevalent in less formal interactions and in more private settings, such as the home, and when talking to other women (Meyerhoff, 1986; Holmes, 1992, 1995), while the stereotypically male patterns tended to emerge most obviously in public settings.

Likewise, workplace leadership is stereotypically male-dominated (e.g. Hearn and Parkin, 1988; Maher, 1997; Sinclair, 1998). Crucial aspects of leadership performance are often associated with masculine ways of doing things and hence it has been argued that "the language of leadership often equates with the language of masculinity" (Hearn and Parkin, 1988: 21). In this context, women leaders may be perceived as deviant aberrations from the male norm and therefore face a double bind in terms of professionalism and femininity (Kendall and Tannen, 1997: 92). If a female leader "talks like a manager she is transgressing the boundaries of femininity: if she talks like a woman she no longer represents herself as a manager" (Jones, 2000: 196). For women, "doing leadership" requires a fine balance.[5]

Not surprisingly, early definitions of leadership concentrate on normatively masculine strategies such as directness, authoritativeness and dominance, behaviours largely relating to transactional goals and the accomplishment of tasks (e.g. Hearn and Parkin, 1988; Sinclair, 1998). Current research, however, tends to highlight, as components of a complete leadership "package", more relational or people-oriented goals – goals stereotypically associated with femininity (e.g. Kotter, 2001). Our definition incorporates both these aspects of leadership behaviour, and, as sociolinguists, we focus on how these are expressed through communicative interaction or how leaders construct themselves through their talk. Thus, effective leadership, we contend, can be defined as consistent communicative performance which results in acceptable outcomes for the organisation (transactional/task-oriented goals), **and** maintains harmony within the team or community of practice (relational/people-oriented goal) (Schnurr, fc).

In an extensive review of previous studies investigating gender differences in leadership styles, Eagly and Johnson (1990: 233) found both similarities and differences in the styles typically preferred by men and women leaders. The minor differences they report claim that women tend to be more democratic whereas men are "more likely to use a directive command and control style" (e.g. Robbins *et al.*, 1998: 399). However, the stereotypical norm against which leaders are compared is still a masculine one, that is typically women and men are evaluated differently for the same behaviour. In this comparison, women leaders are often judged as less competent than men by their colleagues and subordinates (e.g. Sinclair, 1998; Baxter, 2003; Schnurr, fc).

Despite the prevalence of this predominately masculine stereotype of leadership at work, our data suggests that in fact effective leaders of both sexes draw on a range of discourse strategies to "do leadership" – strategies which have been associated with both normatively masculine and normatively feminine ways of talking. Our LWP data provides many examples of women leaders effectively managing teams, departments, sections, and even whole organisations. Our objective in this paper is to explore how these women construct themselves as leaders at work, and in particular how they balance the demands of their gender identity with those of their professional identity, especially in the relatively public sphere of formal workplace meetings.

The data

Much of the research on leadership relies on perceptions and self-reported data, as opposed to the kind of authentic data we have collected. To explore leadership styles, and especially the delicate balance between enacting gender and enacting professional role, we use two case studies recorded in authentic workplace settings.

Since 1996, the Wellington Language in the Workplace project has recorded interactions in a wide range of New Zealand workplaces, examining how people communicate in authentic workplace settings. The data on which we base our claims and from which we extract our examples forms part of Victoria University's Language in the Workplace corpus (www.vuw.ac.nz/lals/lwp). Currently, our database includes 20 different workplaces, approximately 450 participants, and more than 2500 interactions. The data on which this paper draws comprises a set of larger meetings that were video-recorded in two organisations. Using video cameras in addition to sensitive audio-recording equipment not only facilitated the identification of the speakers, but also captured important aspects of the participants' non-linguistic behaviours, such as gestures and smiles (see Holmes and Stubbe, 2003b for a detailed account of the methodology).[6]

Our research has consistently adopted an appreciative inquiry approach (e.g. Fry *et al.*, 2002); the volunteers who recorded their interactions were considered worthy models within their organisations for investigation and we have focused on identifying how they earned that status. This means that the evaluation of the participants' communicative skills is not based solely on our assessment of the effectiveness of their communication, but also reflects the opinions of their colleagues and other organisational members. The leaders we discuss were all positively evaluated by the people that matter most – the people they work with.

The leaders

The two focus leaders, Clara and Tricia, come from very different workplaces – a large commercial organisation and the IT section of a large institution. Because communication is context-sensitive, it is important to consider the community of practice (Eckert and McConnell-Ginet, 1992; see also Editor's Introduction) in which each of the leaders operates.

In the light of the discussion on leadership and gender above, one useful way of comparing communities of practice for our purposes is to place them on a gender continuum. As discussed in Holmes and Stubbe (2003a), New Zealanders readily describe workplaces as more or less "feminine" and more or less "masculine" in orientation. Rather than simply referring to the gender composition of the group, however, the gendered labels refer to practices, including communicative practices (consistent with the Community of Practice framework). There are many distinguishing features which have been widely cited as identifiers of male and female styles of interaction (as summarised in Holmes, 2000). The identification of different groups as more feminine or masculine refers to the ways in which these gendered patterns of communication are sustained in the shared practices of each community. For example, a workplace team who display predominantly feminine interactional patterns, such as a collaborative style, an egalitarian philosophy, and who are routinely indirect and supportive of one another might represent the more feminine end of the continuum, whereas a team who are competitive, individualistic, and challenging could be considered to represent the more masculine end of the continuum.

Using such a continuum of communities of practice, we would assign the two leaders along the continuum as indicated in Figure 13.1.

In comparing the different leadership styles of these two leaders, we have focused on their discursive behaviour in more formal meetings. As discussed earlier, researchers have considered the formal meeting as a public context – there is an audience, there are (informal or formal) rules for behaviour, and topics are restricted.[7] Moreover, meetings are obvious sites of power display (e.g. Mumby, 1988), where leaders have certain "rights" to dominate various parts of the interaction.

Within formal meetings, we consider how the two leaders manage meeting openings, decision-making, and humour. Meeting openings are often routinised and ritualistic sequences (e.g. Chan, fc), and are generally associated with the chair and those in authority (e.g. Hanak, 1998; Onyx, 1999). Opening sequences are thus one obvious site for examining how these two women "do leadership". The role of leaders in the decision-making process is another important area for examination. Marra (2003) identified a clear relationship between the decisions that were ratified in a meeting and the status of the participant who proposed the decision. Thus the decision-making style in their meeting is another potential source of insight into the style of the leaders. Humour is a third source of information on leadership style. Humour may function to construct and maintain solidarity within a team (e.g. Clouse and Spurgeon, 1995; Morreall, 1991); hence exploring the way humour is used in the

Figure 13.1 The leaders in their communities of practice (CofPs)

respective communities of practice provides potential insights into the relational or people-oriented goals of leadership.

Clara: Leader in a large commercial organisation

Clara's leadership style is consistent with the relatively masculine orientation of the community of practice in which she operates. She leads a team of approximately fifty people in the New Zealand division of a large multinational corporation. Her team has a sparky, interactional style which is "individualistic" and "competitive", a description consistent with the masculine stereotypes described in the literature (see Holmes and Marra, 2002). Clara, herself, plays up to the role of "Queen", a nickname given to her by her team, and a running joke throughout the meetings we recorded. In line with this caricature of her personality, she often behaves in relatively authoritarian ways, and is prepared to exercise a right of veto when she judges it necessary; but she is equally quick to contribute to team humour when appropriate, and even mimic the British Queen's accent to the amusement of her subordinates (see also Marra and Holmes, fc).

In example 1, Clara chairs the weekly meeting of a project team. Meeting openings have an inherently transactional function; they move the interaction into meeting mode, and this is the task of the chair (e.g. Marra, 1998, 2003; Chan, fc).

Example 1
Clara opens the meeting (with contributions from Renee and Benny).[8]

1	Cla:	I got the # hi I got the system to book the room which meant
2		I I (wasn't quite sure how to) I unbooked fifteen twenty two
3		and booked sixteen oh six ah variety is the spice of life though
4		isn't it ...
5		okay well we might just start without Seth
6		he can come in and can review the minutes from last week
7	Ren:	are you taking the minutes this week
8	Cla:	no I'm just trying to chair the meeting
9		who would like to take minutes this week
10	Ren:	who hasn't taken the minutes yet
11	Ben:	I haven't yet so I will
12	Cla:	thank you //Benny\
13	Ren:	/oh Benny\\ takes beautiful minutes too
14	Ben:	don't tell them they'll want me doing it every week [laughter]

15 Cla: it's a bit of a secret
16   okay shall we kick off and just go round the room um
17   (doing) update the and then when he Seth comes in with the
18   the minutes we can just check on any action items that are
19   outstanding
20   # over to you Marlene

This sequence contains many transactional turns, i.e. utterances in which Clara is attending to her task as meeting chair. She opens the meeting by declaring the official start, providing a verbal headcount of who is present (lines 1–3), finding a minute taker (line 9), setting the agenda for the meeting, i.e. that the discussion will consist of update reports from each participant (lines 16–17), and finally allocating Marlene the first turn (line 20).[9]

However, there is more to this example than just the "nuts and bolts" task of opening the meeting. Clara also attends to relational aspects of leadership, that is people-oriented goals. She first describes the problems she encountered using the electronic room booking system, resulting in her booking room 1606 instead of the normal 1522 (lines 2–3). Although this comment appears to be simply an explanation for why they are having the meeting in an unusual space, it also operates as a way for Clara to minimise the status difference between her and her subordinates, that is she conveys the message that she is not perfect; she does not always get things right. She also joins in when the group teases Benny about his minute-taking skills (line 15), although this humour is kept relatively brief. Both of these sections are, strictly speaking, irrelevant to the task, but they soften what would otherwise be a very direct and overtly authoritarian meeting opening.

Clara's transactional turns also include a number of hedges, *well we might just start* (line 5). She asks for a volunteer to take the minutes rather than nominating a minute taker, and her proposal for the meeting procedure is expressed as a question rather than a statement, *shall we kick off and just go round the room* (line 16). Nevertheless, her management of the meeting opening clearly indicates that she is in charge.

Example 2, a decision-making sequence, provides another illustration of how Clara does leadership. This very short extract concerns the date of the upcoming staff dinner. Marlene (who is in charge of organising the event) proposes some dates for the others to consider.

Example 2
Clara approves Marlene's suggestion, which is then supported by Troy,
Seth, Renee, and Benny.

1	Troy:	have we got a date for that Marlene
2	Mar:	at this stage we're shooting for the twenty seventh which is the
3		friday
4		but if people think we should do it that thursday
5		I've checked for availabilities on the thursday nights
6		which is the twenty sixth and it's available as well
7		I thought probably a friday would be best what do people think
8	Cla:	I think a friday's best
9	Troy:	yeah
10	Mar:	friday?
11	Ren:	//mm\
12	Seth:	/yeah\\
13	Mar:	twenty seventh it is then
14	Ben:	that's march isn't it
15	Mar:	//yep yep twenty seventh of\ march
16	Cla:	/[quietly]: of march yeah:\\

Superficially, this appears to be a very democratic process with several
participants (Troy, Renee, Seth, and Clara) agreeing with the suggestion
made by Marlene that they have the dinner on Friday the twenty
seventh without any obvious opposition. However, a closer inspection
shows that in fact Clara is first to approve the suggestion (line 8), and
then the others agree with her, leading to Marlene's confirmation of the
decision in line 13. An alternative strategy might have been to wait and
hear the opinions of others before making the final decision, but again we
see that Clara takes a pro-active role. We can never know how the others
felt about this proposal, but it is plausible to propose that Clara makes
this decision and the others simply agree with the Queen's decree.

   In contrast to the more task-oriented aspects of meeting management
represented by meeting openings and decisions-making, the third
example from Clara and her team involves humour. Humour is prevalent
in workplace interactions (e.g.; Morreall, 1991; Holmes *et al.*, 2001) and
one of its many functions is to serve relational goals, for example to
build solidarity or "create team" (in Fletcher's (1999) terms), to soften
criticisms and directives. Such relationally oriented behaviours are
stereotypically associated with femininity.

In example 3, the team generates a fantasy scenario which conceptualises their company call centre as a brothel. The team is considering a photo of the call centre which includes an unrepresentatively high number of men. Example 3 is a brief excerpt from the sequence, which is seeded by a witty comment from Clara about high testosterone levels.

Example 3
Clara starts the humour. Rob, Sandy, Seth, Peggy, and Marlene add their own contributions to the humour.

```
1   Cla:   I think that the testosterone level has been overstated in this
2          photo
3          in this picture ... the picture overstates the number of men
4          in the call centre
5   Rob:   oh okay
6   San:   there's one gigolo and one pimp and the rest of them are
7   Cla:   [laughs]: call girls:
8   San:   call girls
9   Peg:   [laughs]
10  Mar:   and you'll need some more //chunky gold jewellery\ .....
11  Cla:   /and maybe a moustache\\
12  Mar:   yeah and a shirt that unbuttons (to the waist) ...
13         [general laughter]
14  Cla:   moving right along
```

Picking up the theme of Clara's comment about testosterone levels (line 1), the team members collaborate in jointly constructing an extended fantasy which wittily develops the image of the organisation's "call" centre, with its telephone-answering "call girls", as a brothel. The amusing sequence clearly serves a valuable function in cementing team relations as well as illustrating team members' ability to generate witty and entertaining verbal interaction. Team members compete to provide the wittiest contributions (lines 5, 8, 10, 12).

This humour, however, also has a transactional function. Clara signals that she is not happy with the photo that has been chosen to represent the call centre for which the section is responsible, and she "gets buy in" from the rest of the team concerning its inappropriateness. At the end of the sequence (line 13), Clara skilfully moves the discussion back to more serious topics with her routine catchphrase *moving right along*.

In sum, Clara is a relatively authoritative leader who keeps discussion brief and to the point, and permits only brief digressions for relational purposes. She sits at the more task-focussed or masculine end of the continuum of gendered leadership styles. Nonetheless, she is popular and well respected within her team, and is always willing to contribute her own pithy comments to the team's humorous discourse. We turn now to a contrasting case, a woman leader with a much more feminine style of interaction.

Tricia: Leader of the IT section in a large institution

Tricia is the director of the IT department of a non-profit organisation in Wellington. She supervises around 100 staff members who deal with the various aspects of IT related issues in the organisation. Most of the services that Tricia's team offers revolve around providing adequate IT support for organisational members. Example 4 is typical of the way in which Tricia opens the regular two-weekly meeting of the IT managers.

Example 4

Fortnightly managers meeting, chaired by Tricia. Most of the other participants, that is Noel, Carol, and Serena, are managers, while Garth is an external HR consultant, and Evelyn is Tricia's Personal Assistant (PA).[10]

1	Tri:	it'll be a quick meeting //[laughs]\
2		we're just waiting for Carol now #
3		do you want to just give her a ring
		[...*several minutes of chat*]
4	Tri:	okay well Tracey's not here and Isabelle's laid up
5		+ so there's only [voc]
6	Noel:	is everything running?
		[...*discussion of recording and the video cameras which been borrowed from a meeting participant*]
7	Tri:	okay so they're not theirs they're yours [laughter]
8	Car:	all right //just checking\
9	Tri:	/no it's\\ not no what we've got here is a little thing that
10		Garth and I put together for training managers
11		and team leaders
12	Car:	good
13	Tri:	um and
14	Car:	[laughs]
15	Tri:	[laughs]: (oh sh-):[laughs]
16	Ser:	what are you laughing //about\
17	Tri:	/priority one\\ planning

```
18  Car:   //[laughs]\
19  Tri:   /that's the one\\ er the reason that we've made it priority one
20          is because we have to start doing budgeting shortly
21          so if we do the planning stuff now
22          and then it can roll into our budgets and get reflected
            [inhales]
23          er so one is planning two is budgeting [tut] um
```

Unlike Clara (see example 1, line 5), Tricia waits until everyone has arrived, and even calls them up to check whether they are coming if necessary (lines 3–4). After two of the missing participants have arrived, Tricia attempts to open the meeting by employing the discourse marker *okay* and providing apologies for those who could not attend the meeting (line 4). After a short pause she seems to intend to start with the meeting proper *so there's only* (line 5) when she gets interrupted by Noel who checks that the recording equipment is running (line 6).[11] This interruption then develops into a sequence of small talk between Noel and Carol who discuss the recording equipment in more detail.

Tricia interrupts their discussion and brings them back to the agenda, *okay so they're not theirs they're yours* (line 7), and signals to them explicitly that she wants to start on the meeting agenda. However, this potentially face threatening expression of power is considerably mitigated by her subsequent laughter (line 7). And Carol's apologetic remark *all right just checking* (line 8) indicates that she has understood Tricia's covert criticism and is willing to comply.

(Lines 9–11) Tricia attempts to open the meeting again by naming the first item on the agenda: training for managers and team leaders. Although she manages to get people's attention and to start discussing the agenda, Tricia still does not succeed in opening the meeting as Carol and Serena start laughing, apparently at the fact that Tricia has made a particular item "priority one". Tricia then proceeds to justify her choice with an explanation, and eventually manages to open the meeting and successfully launch the discussion of the first item on the agenda (line 19).

This example illustrates some characteristic features of Tricia's leadership style. Although she is clearly less authoritarian than Clara, and although she takes considerably longer (as measured in the turns it takes) to open the meeting, she successfully integrates her transactional and relational leadership objectives in a style appropriate to the more relaxed community of practice in which she works. She successfully opens the meeting in a non-threatening and non-authoritarian style, minimising displays of power and emphasising collegiality.

Tricia's decision-making style is similarly democratic.

Example 5(1)
Participants (including, in this extract, Serena and Noel) discuss budgeting issues and whether they are getting new Personal Computers (PCs).

```
1  Ser:   so will desktop support be making recommendations all across
2         all of ITS //machines\ so we don't individually have to do that
3  Tri:   /mm\\ no but I suggest that you actually talk to them
4  Noel:  who's doing it from //inside desktop\
5  Tri:   /[drawls]: er:\\ well I that's a jolly good question
6         um we'll probably talk to Wendy about putting it together
7         or alternatively Trevor a – we might get Trevor to do it
8         for across ITS
9  Ser:   oh okay so he's gonna do desktops
10 Tri:   mm
11 Ser:   none of us here need to worry about servers...
12 Tri:   can you just put an email to Trevor for me
```

This extract gives the impression that it does not take Tricia and her team very long to reach a decision. They apparently agree that a particular IT employee, Trevor, will be responsible for desktop support. Tricia suggests that staff should approach Trevor if they need his help (line 3). Tricia's statement of the decision is characterised by a number of mitigating devices, such as the discourse marker *well*, the modal particle *probably* (line 5), and the modal *might* (line 7). The other managers apparently agree with Tricia's suggestion to *get Trevor to do it for across ITS* (lines 7–8), as indicated by their positive and agreeing responses (lines 9, 11).

However, about six minutes later, Noel and Carol return to the issue of whether they should approach Trevor or whether he is going to talk to them. They ask some clarifying questions regarding Trevor's responsibilities and the procedure of applying for new PCs. After Tricia has answered them, the participants go on to discuss another issue. But about two minutes later Evelyn brings up the issue of how to contact Trevor in order to get new PCs. Tricia again says that people should approach Trevor. Evelyn, the PA who takes the minutes during this meeting then summarises the budgeting process for all participants. But it seems that Noel and Carol are still confused. Tricia provides further clarification and eventually advises them *to go and have a chat to him* [Trevor]. After this comment, the discussion proceeds as follows:

Example 5(2)

13 Noel: but he's [Trevor] gonna come and see
14   he's gonna come and say
15   Noel // + does your area need (. . .) or PCs\ . . .
16   or am I gonna go
17   Trev I need to talk to you we need //something\
18 Car: /if you want\\ anything round here
19   you find the person and go and talk to them
20 Tri: [laughs]
21   [inhales] I will get . . .
22   I will get Trevor to come and to talk to you
            [. . . *some discussion among Carol, Noel and Evelyn on the
            process of asking for new equipment*]
23 Tri: but for ITS Trevor will go and talk to each manager
24 Noel: [quietly]: oh good: +

It is apparent that Noel is still confused about the decision that had apparently been reached earlier, as indicated by his clarifying question (line 13). And although Carol answers his inquiry by outlining the agreed procedure, it seems that Tricia has understood his concerns: she changes her mind and agrees to organise for Trevor to meet with each manager individually (lines 22 and 23). Her laughter (line 20) and the fact that she inhales before she eventually changes her mind (line 21) suggest that she changes her initial decision to accommodate her subordinates' concerns, and to facilitate the process for them. Although Tricia here appears to accommodate to pressure from her subordinates, it is important to note that she achieves her transactional objectives: Trevor will be the one who is responsible for the process, as suggested by her in the early stages of the decision-making (line 7). The issue she accedes to – who should go to whom – is for her a minor issue.

In contrast to Clara's relatively direct and on-record strategies for reaching decisions with members of her team, Tricia's approach is much less explicit. She does not display her power blatantly like Clara; rather, she empowers her subordinates by allowing them to actively participate in the decision-making process, and by taking account of their concerns. In example 5, then, Tricia achieves her transactional objective (i.e. convincing her managers that Trevor is the appropriate person to oversee the desktop replacements), while also taking account of her subordinates' feelings and concerns, thereby "doing" relational aspects of leadership. She puts a great deal of effort into making sure that everyone understands and agrees with the final decision, and her employees clearly contribute to that decision. Her style can be described as more "feminine" and "democratic" than Clara's. Example 6 also illustrates this point.

Example 6
In the future, good performance of employees will be rewarded with morning teas.

```
1 Gar:  morning teas are a good reward...
2 Ser:  oh we'll all look forward to Evelyn putting these in our diary
3       [laughter]
4 Tri:  she's looking forward to it as well
5 Eve:  and I'm loo//king forward to all the acceptances and\
6       I don't care what else you've got in there eh
7 ??:   /( )\\
8       [laughter]
```

This relatively short sequence of conjoint humour is initiated by Serena's teasing and perhaps slightly sarcastic remark (line 2) about morning teas as rewards for good performances. Her comment seems to be directed both at Garth (who came up with this idea) and at Tricia (who agreed to put it in place). Using the inclusive pronouns *we* and *our* Serena indicates that she assumes that the other participants agree with her, and by including them in her humorous critique, she also expresses in-group solidarity and enhances a sense of belonging, thereby creating team. The laughter which follows Serena's remark indicates that the other managers do indeed agree with her opinion about this kind of reward system.

Tricia then skilfully challenges Serena's attack by redirecting the teasing towards her, thereby protecting Evelyn (line 4). Using Serena's words to express a contrary meaning, Tricia dismisses Serena's critical comment and justifies the morning teas. After Tricia's intervention, Evelyn joins the humour by defending herself in an amusing manner, thereby also asserting her status within the group. Her use of the pragmatic particle *eh* at the end of her utterance (line 6) is a positive politeness marker, a frequently used device for signalling group membership in New Zealand (Meyerhoff, 1994).

The role Tricia plays in the construction of this humorous instance is quite typical of her unobtrusive leadership style. As in example 6, when she participates in a humorous sequence, she tends to develop and ratify someone else's humour rather than initiating the humour herself. Thus this relatively passive or reactive role in the use of humour in meetings is consistent with her democratic leadership style, which is also reflected in the ways she opens meetings, and with her role in decision-making as described above.

Discussion

Our research suggests that effective leaders skillfully address both transactional and relational goals (a finding reflected in our definition of effective leadership above). To illustrate how these orientations are successfully integrated in day-to-day workplace talk, we have focused on evidence from the more formal meeting sets of two effective leaders. In particular, typical examples of meeting openings, decision-making and collegial humorous exchanges have been used to illustrate how the leaders orient to both transactional and relational goals in the ways they run formal meetings.

The analysis has also demonstrated that each leader accomplishes these goals differently, adopting an interactional style that is both responsive to and contributes to two contextual conditions: (i) the distinctive communities of practice in which they operate – one more corporate and relatively "masculine", the other more egalitarian and relatively "feminine" with respect to preferred ways of interacting; and (ii) the relatively public nature of the meetings from which the extracts have been taken.

Communities of practice

Operating in a very hierarchical organisation, with relatively masculine ways of interacting as the norm, Clara opened meetings smartly, with no waiting for latecomers, and made non-contentious decisions crisply, without waiting for everyone to contribute a view. However, as discussed above, she also engaged in skilful relational practice in the process, constructing herself as technically incompetent, for instance, and thereby downplaying her status as the boss; joining in with the humour, and mitigating her pre-emptive decision, thus taking some account of others' face needs. Tricia, by contrast, in a more democratic and egalitarian workplace with a more feminine style of interaction, puts greater emphasis on consultation and empowerment. Using a rather different approach, she waited for all participants to arrive before starting the meeting; she negotiated through to a decision that was acceptable to, and reflected the views of, all participants; and she tended to hedge decisions and make suggestions rather than give directives.

The different styles of humour which characterise and construct the different communities of practice in which the leaders operate also illustrate these contrasts. Clara's team is competitive and challenging; when she initiates the humour the team members compete to contribute wittily. In her more democratic community of practice, Tricia tends to take a background role in humorous sequences, supporting, but generally allowing, other team members to develop the humour.

The community of practice also contributes to the expectation of different workplace roles. For example, when Sandy (Clara's male second in command) is the meeting chair, he often constructs Clara as the overarching authority to whom the team are accountable. This frees Clara up to focus on relational goals (and indeed to simultaneously construct a very feminine gender identity). In one such meeting in our data we see her bragging about having been away from work and also interrupting the progress of the meeting opening, behaviour not typically associated with an authoritarian leader. In example 1 where Clara was chairing the meeting, Renee's attempts to subvert the agenda were quickly and firmly resisted by Clara, but in this case Clara's high-spirited and boisterous good humour are received with laughter from the rest of the team.[12] Thus Sandy and Clara here work together to achieve both transactional and relational goals, while simultaneously constructing appropriate leadership roles within their community of practice.

Public/private distinction

To investigate the female voice in public contexts, the data in this paper focuses on a relatively public domain, namely the workplace (compare the much more private domain of the home). Moreover, within the workplace formal meetings tend to exemplify the more public aspects of workplace interaction. The relatively public nature of such meetings was certainly something our participants were aware of, and we identified this as another influence on the ways leaders behaved, and especially as a factor which influenced them differently and which contributed to their contrasting leadership styles.

The potential influence of a more public domain on leadership style is particularly clearly exemplified, however, by the fact that Tricia radically alters her style in less formal one-to-one encounters with her staff. In these more private contexts, where power relations are perhaps more clear-cut, she behaves in a much more authoritative and direct way. In the conversations we recorded with her PA, Evelyn, for example, Tricia is clear and decisive. She displays her power and higher status much more overtly, and is clearly the one directing the conversation. This is very different from her performance in larger, more public meetings, where she constructs herself as a democratic or even *laissez-faire* leader. As Baxter (2003: 130) suggests, formal public meetings are more complex in many ways and "speakers are involved in a constant negotiation of power relations which enables them to prove their worth as effective decision-makers and insight-bringers". In these contexts, it seems that Tricia aims to construct an egalitarian atmosphere, and to play down her status and authority. This is risky behaviour, since, as Baxter notes, a "fair-minded, cooperative and power-sharing approach... may be perceived as a lack of leadership and clear direction according to a discourse of masculinisation" (2003: 173). And this interpretation was certainly expressed by some, especially those who had joined Tricia's community of practice from different and more commercially oriented organisations. In one-to-one interactions, by contrast, authority relations are generally less of an issue, and in these more private contexts, Tricia focuses on getting things done efficiently and decisively (though always with attention to relational considerations). In these contexts, she behaves in ways that satisfy the demands of those who prefer more assertive and authoritative leadership.

Thus the behaviour of these leaders is constrained by both the community of practice and the relative "publicness" of the context within which they operate.[13] If being effective involves skillfully integrating transactional and relational goals, as we argue, then a thorough understanding of how they achieve this delicate balance is complicated further by the need to take account of the different contexts in which they interact and demonstrate this integration. Effective leadership for these women is far from easy.

Conclusion

Effective leadership involves achieving a balance between getting the work done and keeping people happy. Good leaders use language skilfully for these purposes – integrating discourse aimed at task achievement with talk which is oriented to relational goals and maintaining the harmony of the team. In addition, women face the challenge of combining "doing leadership" with "doing gender", while also avoiding negative evaluations, for example that they are too masculine or not authoritative enough. The women leaders we have focussed on in this paper are highly skilled at managing their seemingly contradictory roles. And, as the analysis has demonstrated, although they achieve their organisational goals and manage interpersonal relationships, the community of practice in which each operates clearly influences the way they enact leadership, as does the relative "publicness" of the setting.

It is also worth noting that the distinction between gender identity and professional identity is not always easy to maintain, especially when particular linguistic features are associated with more than one kind of identity. As Cameron and Kulick note, "the same way of speaking signifies both a professional identity and a gendered identity, and in practice these are difficult to separate" (2003: 58). In a recent discussion of the relationship between gender ideologies and power, Philips notes, "an important theme of the writing on women in the workplace has been how much both women and men vary in their deployment of interactional strategies [that] feminists have long argued were gendered in power-laden ways. Gender ideologies have not been in the foreground of this work as such until recently" (2003: 267). Our analyses of workplace discourse contribute to and complexify the picture of the ways in which talk is differently gendered in different contexts, and especially the various ways in which women of different status and playing different roles "do" power and solidarity at work.

LWP transcription conventions

[laughs] : :	Paralinguistic features in square brackets, colons indicate start/finish
+	Pause of up to one second
#	Signals end of "sentence" where it is ambiguous on paper
...//......\...	Simultaneous speech
.../........\\...	
(hello)	Transcriber's best guess at an unclear utterance
?	Rising or question intonation
-	Incomplete or cut-off utterance
......	Section of transcript omitted
??:	Unidentified Male/Female
[voc]	Untranscribable noises
[tut]	Bilabial/alveolar/dental clicks
[*comment*]	Editorial comments italicised in square brackets
turn=	Turn continues
=continues	

All names used in examples are pseudonyms.

Notes

1. We thank those who allowed their workplace interactions to be recorded, and other members of the Language in the Workplace Project team who assisted with collecting and transcribing the data.
2. In a sports programme broadcast in September 2004, the male hosts humorously complained about the "bloke rot" or lack of male power in New Zealand.
3. The tendency to "think leader, think male" is discussed by a number of feminist analysts: e.g. Gunnarsson, 2001; Hearn and Parkin, 1988; Holmes, 2000; Kendall and Tannen, 1997; Sinclair, 1998.
4. Note, however, that an analysis of length of turn in a set of meetings from our corpus indicated that the chair, whether female or male, dominated the talk time (see Holmes, 2000).
5. See also Brewis, 2001; Chase, 1988: 276; Martin Rojo and Esteban, 2003.
6. To avoid unnecessarily confusing transcripts, as a rule of thumb we only signal non-linguistic behaviour where it is relevant to the point being made.
7. In a review of the literature related to meetings, Tracy and Dimock (2004) refer to workplace meetings as private meetings, with wider community meetings, such as School Board meetings, characterised as public meetings. This simply reflects the different scope of their discussion.
8. It may be useful for readers to be aware of the gender of the various speakers from Clara's team: Clara (f), Renee (f), Benny (m), Marlene (f), Troy (m), Seth (m), Rob (m), Sandy (m), Peggy (f).
9. Holmes and Stubbe (2003b: 57–58) discuss the way Clara deals with the obvious challenges from Renee.
10. Again, it may be useful for readers to be aware of the gender of the various speakers from this team: Tricia (f), Noel (m), Carol (f), Serena (f), Evelyn (f), Garth (m).
11. Noel, who also participated in our research, had agreed to be responsible for this.
12. It has been pointed out to us that an alternative interpretation of this example would be that Clara is emphasising her authority by interrupting Sandy. However, differences in the tone of voice used by Clara in this example and Renee in the earlier example have contributed significantly to the interpretation we present here.
13. It should be noted that in neither case are we dealing with extremes on this continuum. Tricia's community of practice is by no means the most "feminine" CofP in our data, and nor is Clara's the most "masculine".

References

Baxter, J. (2003) *Positioning Gender in Discourse: A Feminist Methodology* (Basingstoke: Palgrave Macmillan).
Brewis, J. 'Telling it like it is ? Gender, language and organizational theory'. In R. Westwood and S. Linstead (eds) *The Language of organization* (London: Sage, 2001), pp. 283–309.
Cameron, D. and Kulick, D. (2003) *Language and Sexuality* (Cambridge: Cambridge University Press).
Chan, A. (forthcoming) Small talk in business meetings in Hong Kong and New Zealand. Unpub. PhD Thesis, Victoria University of Wellington.

Chase, S.E. 'Making sense of "the woman who becomes a man".' In A.D. Todd and S. Fisher (eds) *Gender and Discourse: The power of Talk* (Norwood, New Jersey: Ablex, 1998), pp. 275–95.

Clouse, R.W. and Spurgeon, K.L. (1995) Corporate analysis of humor, *Psychology: A Journal of Human Behaviour*, 32 (3–4), pp. 1–24.

Eagly, A. and Johnson, B. (1990) Gender and leadership style: A meta-analysis, *Psychological Bulletin*, 108 (2), pp. 233–256.

Eckert, P. and McConnell-Ginet, S. (1992) Communities of practice: Where language, gender and power all live. In K. Hall, M. Bucholtz and B. Moonwomon (eds), *Locating Power: Proceedings of the Second Berkeley Women and Language Conference* (Berkeley, University of California: Berkeley Women and Language Group), pp. 89–99.

Fletcher, J. (1999) *Disappearing Acts. Gender, Power and Relational Practice at Work* (Cambridge: MIT).

Franken, M. (1983) Interviewers' strategies: How questions are modified. Unpub. Terms paper, Victoria: University of Wellington.

Fry, R., Barrett, F., Seiling, J. and Whitney, D. (eds) (2002) *Appreciative Inquiry and Organizational Transformation: Reports From the Field* (Westport, Conn.: Quorum Books).

Gunnarsson, Britt-Louise (2001) Academic women in the male university field: communicative practices at postgraduate seminars. In Bettina Baron and Helga Kotthoff (eds), *Gender in Interaction* (Amsterdam: John Benjamins), pp. 247–281.

Hanak, I. (1998) Chairing meetings: Turn and topic control in development communication in rural Zanzibar, *Discourse and Society*, 9 (1), pp. 33–56.

Hearn, J. and Parkin, P.W. (1988) Women, men, and leadership: A critical review of assumptions, practices, and change in the industrialized nations. In N. Adler and D. Izraeli (eds), *Women in Management Worldwide* (London: M.E. Sharpe), pp. 17–40.

Holmes, J. (1992) Women's talk in public contexts, *Discourse and Society*, 3 (2), pp. 131–150.

Holmes, J. (1995) *Women, Men and Politeness* (London: Longman).

Holmes, J. (2000) Women at work: Analysing women's talk in New Zealand workplaces, *Australian Review of Applied Linguistics (ARAL)*, 22 (2), pp. 1–17.

Holmes, J. and Marra, M. (2002) Having a laugh at work: How humour contributes to workplace culture, *Journal of Pragmatics*, 34, pp. 1683–1710.

Holmes, J. and Stubbe, M. (2003a) 'Feminine' workplaces: Stereotypes and reality. In J. Holmes and M. Meyerhoff (eds), *Handbook of Language and Gender* (Oxford: Blackwell), pp. 573–599.

Holmes, J. and Stubbe, M. (2003b). *Power and Politeness in the Workplace. A Sociolinguistic Analysis of Talk at Work* (London: Longman).

Holmes, J., Marra, M. and Burns, L. (2001) Women's humour in the workplace: A quantitative analysis, *Australian Journal of Communication*, 28 (1), pp. 83–108.

Jones, D. (2000) Gender trouble in the workplace: 'Language and gender' meets 'feminist organisational communication'. In J. Holmes (ed.), *Gendered Speech in Social Context. Perspectives from Gown and Town* (Wellington: Victoria University Press), pp. 192–210.

Kendall, S. and Tannen, D. (1997) Gender and language in the workplace. In Ruth Wodak (ed.), *Gender and Discourse* (London: Sage), pp. 81–105.

Kotter, J. (2001) What leader really do, *Harvard Business Review. Special Issue on Leadership*, 79 (11), pp. 85–96.

Maher, K. (1997) Gender-related stereotypes of transformational and transactional leadership, *Sex Roles: A Journal of Leadership*, 37 (3–4), pp. 209–226.

Marra, M. (1998) My job's a joke! Humour in the workplace. Unpub. Master's Paper, Victoria University of Wellington.

Marra, M. (2001) Kiwi women and power. Contribution to postgraduate seminar, Linguistics Department, University of California at Berkeley, 10 April 2001.

Marra, M. (2003) Decisions in New Zealand business meetings. Unpub. PhD Thesis, Victoria University of Wellington.

Marra, M. and Holmes, J. (forthcoming). *Queen Clara: Identity Construction and Humour as Components of Effective Leadership*.

Marshall, J. (1995) *Women Managers Moving On. Exploring Career and Life Choices* (London: Routledge).

Martín-Rojo, L. and Esteban, C.G. Discourse at work: when women take on the role of manager. In G. Weiss and R. Wodak (eds), *Critical Discourse Analysis. Theory and Interdisciplinarity* (Basingstoke: Palgrave Macmillan, 2003), pp. 241–71.

McConnell-Ginet, S. (2000) Breaking through the 'glass ceiling': Can linguistic awareness help? In J. Holmes (ed.), *Gendered Speech in Social Context: Perspectives from Gown and Town* (Wellington: Victoria University Press), pp. 259–282.

McElhinny, B. (1997) Ideologies of public and private language in sociolinguistics. In R. Wodak (ed.), *Gender and Discourse* (London: Sage), pp. 106–139.

Meyerhoff, M. (1986) A study of sex differences in New Zealand English. Unpub. MA Thesis, Victoria University of Wellington.

Meyerhoff, M. (1994) Sounds pretty ethnic, eh: A pragmatic particle in New Zealand English, *Language in Society*, 23, pp. 367–388.

Morreall, J. (1991) Humor and work, *Humor: International Journal of Humor Research*, 4 (4), pp. 359–373.

Mumby, D.K. (1988) *Communication and Power in Organizations: Discourse, Ideology, and Domination* (Norwood, NJ: Ablex).

Onyx, J. (1999) Power between women in organizations, *Feminism and Psychology*, 9 (4), pp. 417–421.

Philips, S.U. (2003) The power of gender ideologies in discourse. In J. Holmes and M. Meyerhoff (eds), *Handbook of Language and Gender* (Oxford: Blackwell), pp. 252–276.

Robbins, S., Millett, B., Cacioppe, R. and Waters-March, T. (1998) *Organisational Behaviour: Leading and Managing in Australia and New Zealand* (2nd edn) (Sydney: Prentice Hall).

Schnurr, S. (forthcoming) Leadership, humour and gender. An analysis of workplace discourse. Unpub. PhD Thesis, Victoria University of Wellington.

Sinclair, A. (1998) *Doing Leadership Differently. Gender, Power and Sexuality in a Changing Business Culture* (Melbourne: Melbourne University Press).

Tracy, K. and Dimock, A. (2004) *Meetings: Discursive sites for building and fragmenting community*. Communication Yearbook 28: 127–165.

Victoria University's Language in the Workplace corpus. See www.vuw.ac.nz/lals/lwp for details.

Index